SYMBOLIC INTERACTIONISM AS
AFFECT CONTROL

SUNY Series in the Sociology of Emotions

Theodore D. Kemper, Editor

SYMBOLIC INTERACTIONISM AS AFFECT CONTROL

NEIL J. MacKINNON

STATE UNIVERSITY OF NEW YORK PRESS

Front cover:
MASK, 1989 by Evan Penny
Bronze, 6' high × 5' high 3' × deep
Donald Forster Sculpture Park at Macdonald Steward Art Centre, Guelph, Canada

Published by
State University of New York Press, Albany

For information, address State University of New York Press,
90 State Street, Suite 700, Albany NY 12207

Production by M. R. Mulholland
Marketing by Bernadette La Manna

Library of Congress Cataloging-in-Publication Data

MacKinnon, Neil Joseph, 1944–
    Symbolic interactionism as affect control / Neil J. MacKinnon.
        p.   cm.—(SUNY series in the sociology of emotions)
    Includes bibliographical references and index.
    ISBN 0–7914–2041–8 (cloth : acid-free paper).—ISBN
0–7914–2042–6 (pbk. : acid-free paper)
    1. Social interaction.   2. Affect (Psychology)   3. Social role.
I. Title.   II. Series.
HM291.M23   1994
302—dc20   93–38563
                                                         CIP

10 9 8 7 6 5 4 3 2 1

To my wife
VALERIE

AND MY DAUGHTERS
KARIN, BONNIE, AND CARRIE

CONTENTS

TABLES AND FIGURES

FOREWORD

Affect control theory proposes that humans try to manage experiences so that immediate feelings about people, actions, and settings affirm long term sentiments. The theory's roots penetrate several fields of sociology and psychology, back to the founding of social psychology. However, affect control theory's formulation became possible only in the second half of the twentieth century, after the development of multidimensional measures of affect and after principles of hierarchical control were understood. The theory is distinguished from most other social psychological formulations by its empirical quantification and its systems formulation.

The first brief outlines of the theory appeared two decades ago (Heise 1969; 1970)[1]. Detailed presentations focusing on how role behaviors confirm social identities and on how deviant actions can lead to inferences of deviant identities came later in an article by Heise (1977), and then in his book, *Understanding Events: Affect and the Construction of Social Action* (1979). Subsequent work by researchers affiliated with a U.S. National Institute of Mental Health (NIMH) project refined the theory's empirical base, expanded the theory's scope to the study of attributions and of emotions, and obtained some provisional tests of the theory, as reported in another book, *Analyzing Social Interaction: Progress in Affect Control Theory* (Smith-Lovin and Heise 1988). Recently, researchers including Lynn Smith-Lovin, Neil MacKinnon, Herman Smith, and myself, with students and overseas colleagues, have been deepening the theory's treatment of emotions, conducting new experimental tests, and expanding the theory's empirical base with cross-cultural data.

Neil MacKinnon is exceptionally qualified to author an opus on affect control theory. His graduate work at the University of Illinois focused on role theory and on quantitative research methods, including psychometrics. He used his 1978–79 sabbatical leave from the University of Guelph in Ontario, Canada, to become a year-long Visiting Scholar at the University of North Carolina in Chapel Hill, affiliating himself with the NIMH project on affect control theory. His studies of the theory's mathematical formulation led to suggestions on how to improve the mathematical presentation of affect control theory, and I have incorporated his suggestions in subsequent expositions. After his sabbatical, MacKinnon obtained support from the Social Science and Humanities Research Council of Canada and fielded his own empirical project, a replication of all the work done on affect control in the U.S., along with some new inquiries into relations between affect and the normative frequency of actions. The Canada project, conducted from 1981 to

1987, surveyed thousands of sentiments and affective reactions from thousands of Canadian respondents.

MacKinnon began this book as a report on his empirical research in Canada. However, not wanting to discuss technicalities without preliminary conceptual clarifications, MacKinnon initiated his writing with a thoughtful, scholarly examination of affect control theory. T. David Kemper, the editor of this series of books, and I read drafts of MacKinnon's early chapters and encouraged his presentation of affect control within a general social psychology framework. MacKinnon's methodical exposition of affect control theory's social psychological significance eventually grew into a book-length manuscript, and on seeing his lucid presentation, I advised against discussing any statistical, mathematical, or computerization issues so that the completed book would appeal to a general social science audience. Thus MacKinnon relinquished his report on the Canada project, using the Canadian dictionaries of sentiments and the Canadian equations describing affective processes only to construct substantive examples in this book. A systematic report of his empirical work will come in later publications.

MacKinnon's book offers a number of theoretical advances. It includes the first propositional formulation of affect control theory, a conceptual survey that allows a reader to see easily the scope and logic of the theory. The book traces roots of the theory in more depth than any prior source, establishing linkages to social psychological issues that before were only tacit, even to researchers working on the theory. The book accurately interprets the theory's complex quantitative model and empirical materials without resorting to mathematical or statistical discourse, and thereby it offers the theory's insights to anyone with general interests in social psychology.

Chapter 1 starts by outlining affect control theory's social psychological environs in symbolic interactionism and the sociology of emotions, while drawing forth conceptual elements that are used in affect control theory, such as linguistic framing of experience, generalized affective responses, self–correcting control, and the act as the fundamental unit of thought and social process. Chapter 2 presents the propositional formulation of affect control theory, mentioned above. Chapters 3 and 4 link affect control theory to classic concerns in psychology and sociology and interpret affect control theory as an approach to motivation that explicitly allows for sociocultural organization of individual energies. Chapters 5 and 6 focus on how affect control theory allows us to understand norms and roles as products of culturally defined, individually adopted social identities. Chapter 7 discusses the affect control model of emotions, which allows for interpreting emotions as reflections of social structure, social process, expectations of others, and individual states. Chapter 8 deals with breakdowns in the control of social experience that lead to changes in conceptions of interactants. The final chapter sketches new directions of research on affect control that currently are being explored.

I encouraged MacKinnon to focus on conceptual issues in this book, but I do want to emphasize that affect control theory involves more than a conceptual formulation. Any presentation of the theory also implicitly involves the theory's empirical base, its mathematization, and its computerization.

The *empirical* aspect consists of extensive measurements of culturally determined sentiments in a population and of statistically derived equations describing how people in that population respond affectively to events. Through its empirical aspect, the theory is grounded in observable sociocultural phenomena. A discussion of the theory's empirical aspect is provided in Smith-Lovin's chapters in the Smith-Lovin and Heise book (1988).

The theory's *mathematical* aspect is a formulation based on the empirical affective response equations and on propositions from the conceptual formulation of the theory. Affect control theory's mathematical aspect gives it exceptional logical coherence for a social theory and allows new extensions of the theory to be derived in a disciplined way even though the theory's view of social process is intricate and complex. Most of the mathematical aspect is presented in the first chapter of the Smith-Lovin and Heise book. A more up-to-date presentation, "Affect Control Theory's Mathematical Model, with a List of Testable Hypotheses: A Working Paper for ACT Researchers" (Department of Sociology, Indiana University, Bloomington, IN 47405:1992), is available from me personally.

The *computerization* aspect of affect control theory consists of software that allows an analyst to define social situations and see what those definitions imply with regard to interactants' behaviors, emotions, and emergent views of each other. The computerization aspect amounts to a facility for thought experiments in affect control theory, incorporating large empirical databases and complicated mathematical analyses. The computer program INTERACT 1 is available commercially (Heise and Lewis 1988a); INTERACT 2 is available from me personally.

Each aspect of affect control theory—its conceptual formulation, its empirical grounding, its mathematical formulation, and its computer implementation—provides a course for introducing the theory, and each such presentation constitutes an invitation to explore the other aspects in order to understand the theory in its entirety.

Theories assemble selected portions of our experience into logical and understandable patterns, and simultaneously they fashion realities that we experience. Affect control theory focuses on the many feelings we have in social interaction and shows that these feelings are predictably related to one another and to sociocultural framings of interpersonal encounters. On appreciating the logical coherence of feelings and their sociocultural concomitants, one experiences a new world where human capacity for refined feeling is as important as human reasoning, where sentiments, feelings, and emotions are core constituents of social life rather than antisocial disruptions, where the notion of affective self-control permits coherent understanding of disparate phenomena, like the dynamics of achievement and of failure, or the unfolding of morality and of evil.

Our civilization, built on reason, is riddled with problems deriving from human passions. As we move into the twenty-first century with sudden hope of foregoing nuclear annihilation, it seems crucially important to discern a social reality in which human affect is ubiquitous, comprehensible, and manageable so that we can make our civilization more livable. Affect control theory offers knowledge about such a reality, and you can begin studying that reality immediately. You have a definitive source on affect control theory in your hands.

David R. Heise
Bloomington, Indiana

PREFACE

Affect control theory applies principles and insights derived from balance and consistency theories in psychological social psychology, modern systems theory, linguistics, attitude measurement, and mathematical modeling to symbolic interactionism in sociological social psychology. Although it is a continuation of symbolic interactionism, affect control theory is not simply an *extension*—an application of a rather complete explanation of a limited region of inquiry to adjoining regions. Instead, it represents an instance of what Kaplan (1964, 305) calls theory growth by *intension*, whereby a partial explanation of a general area of inquiry is made more complete and adequate. Whereas theory growth by extension can be likened to the process of completing a jigsaw puzzle, Kaplan suggests, growth by intension answers to the metaphor of increasingly illuminating a darkened room.

However, while this book emphasizes the features of affect control theory that advance symbolic interactionist theory and research, I wish to stress the indebtedness of the theory to earlier interactionist theories, especially, but not exclusively, those that fall under the rubric of identity theory. Personally, I am more interested in contributing to an integrative social psychology than in being an apologist for a particular theory or, worse still, a protagonist in any of the paradigmatic squabbles that inhibit the advancement of social psychology. Indeed, it is the integrative power of affect control theory, in conjunction with its empirical base and mathematical formalization, that enkindled my interest in the theory and that has sustained my research and writing for well over ten years.

I began researching this book and drafted some ideas during 1985 and 1986 as a Fellow of the Social Science and Humanities Research Council of Canada, shortly after the completion of an extensive, SSHRCC-funded study in affect control theory (MacKinnon 1985). Work on the book was interrupted for nearly two years by a second SSHRCC-funded study that extended the Canadian database to traits, status characteristics, and emotions and estimated equations for reidentification and emotion processes (MacKinnon 1988), and by related writing projects along the way. I began seriously writing this book about four years ago, devoting my summer research semesters almost exclusively to the project. As the book evolved from an anticipated research monograph on my affect control research to a conceptual/theoretical piece, I soon discovered the greater time and effort demanded by the latter kind of enterprise.

In addition to my gratitude to the SSHRCC for its generous support of my research in affect control theory, I am indebted to a number of individuals for their input and encouragement. Patrick Mates, a research officer of SSHRCC, must be acknowledged for all his assistance. Ken Menzies commented on early drafts of Chapters 1, 2, and 4; Stanley Barrett, an early draft of Chapter 4. Jay Jackson provided a critical assessment of an early draft of Chapter 1 that profoundly influenced the direction taken by this book as a whole, although he can not be held accountable for its deficits. David Kemper provided invaluable editorial commentary and advice on Chapters 1, 2, 4, and 7. David Heise read and made important editorial and substantive input to all nine chapters. John O'Brien also reviewed the entire manuscript and offered invaluable suggestions, most of which were incorporated in the final product.

I wish to thank David Kemper, the editor of this series, and Rosalie Robinson, editor of SUNY Press, and Christine Worden, her successor, for patiently moving this book along to completion. I am grateful to Stanley Barrett for his colleagueship and encouragement throughout this writing project, and for the frequent use of his Northern Ontario retreat in Temagami where much of this book was written or revised. I wish to thank David Heise for graciously offering to write a preface for this book, and without whose encouragement and infectious enthusiasm this project would never have been initiated or completed. Finally, I am grateful to my wife for her assistance and encouragement, and for the many sacrifices she endured during the writing of this book.

Ursula McMurray and Leo Keating were valuable research associates during the course of the SSHRCC research projects preceding this book. Valerie MacKinnon skillfully typed the manuscript and Carolyn Walker provided much appreciated assistance in its final stages of preparation.

For those who provided academic or personal assistance at critical junctures in the past, I wish to thank Stan Barrett, Ken Duncan, David Heise, Jay Jackson, Lynn Smith-Lovin, Walter Schmidt, Gene F. Summers, and Everett K. Wilson. Finally, I am grateful to the Department of Sociology at the University of North Carolina for granting me the opportunity to explore affect control theory.

ACKNOWLEDGMENTS

Quotations from David R. Heise. *Understanding Events: Affect and the Construction of Social Action.* Copyright © 1979 by Cambridge University Press. Reprinted with the permission of Cambridge University Press.

Quotations from *Review of Personality and Social Psychology,* Vol. 5, edited by Philip Shaver. Copyright © 1984 by Sage Publications, Inc.. Reprinted with the permission of the Publisher.

Quotations from *Analyzing Social Interaction: Advances in Affect Control Theory,* edited by Lynn Smith-Lovin and David R. Heise. Copyright © 1988 by Gordon and Breach Science Publishers, Inc.. Reprinted with the permission of the publisher.

Quotations from Randall Collins. "On the Microfoundations of Macrosociology." *American Journal of Sociology* 86:984–1014. Copyright © 1981 by the University of Chicago Press. Reprinted with the permission of the University of Chicago Press.

Quotations from George Herbert Mead. *Mind, Self, and Society,* edited with an introduction by Charles W. Morris. Copyright © 1934 by the University of Chicago Press. Reprinted with the Permission of the University of Chicago Press.

Quotations from *Social Psychology: Sociological Perspectives,* edited by Morris Rosenberg and Ralph H. Turner, New York: Basic Books. Copyright © 1981 by the American Sociological Association. Reprinted with the Permission of the American Sociological Association.

Quotations from Nelson Foote. "Identification as the Basis for a Theory of Motivation." *American Sociological Review* 16:14–21. Copyright © 1951 by the American Sociological Association. Reprinted with the permission of the American Sociological Association.

Quotations from David R. Heise. "Effects of Emotion Displays on Social Identification." *Social Psychology Quarterly* 52:10–21. Copyright © 1989 by the American Sociological Association. Reprinted with the permission of the American Sociological Association.

1

INTRODUCTION

We would never guess from reading George Herbert Mead that emotion plays a significant role in the social psychology of the person or in social life.[1] Mead effectively banished affect to the biological substratum of human consciousness, restricting its role in social psychology to the emotional overtones of impulses in the incipient stage of the act. For Mead, 'mind', and by implication, 'self' and 'society', are essentially cognitive phenomena grounded in social behavior.

Indeed, Mead and the symbolic interactionist tradition he inspired in sociological social psychology have been widely admonished for their neglect of emotion (Gerth and Mills 1964; Meltzer 1972; Collins 1986), although there have been exceptions to or qualifications of this criticism (see Baldwin 1985, Denzin 1985, 223; Scheff 1983, 334; Stryker 1981, 28; Stryker and Statham 1985, 354–5).[2] Whatever the relative merits of these divergent interpretations of Mead, a reawakened interest in emotion in the sociology of the late 1970s and early 1980s sent symbolic interactionists scrambling to pin down Mead's position on the role of emotions in social life (Denzin 1985; Franks 1985; Scheff 1985b). If a social theory of emotions could be found in Mead, symbolic interactionists could expand their theoretical scope to encompass affect without publicly renouncing his cognitivist legacy.

While the neglect of emotion is a widely acknowledged criticism of Mead, the reason why he ignored affect is not generally well known. Mead's cognitive conceptualizations of mind, self, and society grew out of his attempt to develop a social psychology that was immune to the dangers of solipsism, one that could deal with mind and consciousness without disintegrating into a theory of general psychology.[3] To realize his ambition, Mead searched for a universal, objective principle that transcends the subjectivity of individual consciousness. He found this principle in the significant symbols that constitute a society's language. Through the social psychology he established on the bedrock of language, Mead hoped to escape "the trail of the epistemological serpent" (Mead 1924–5/1964, 268) that bedeviled the attempts of his contemporaries to construct a genuine *social* psychology.[4]

What made language universal and objective for Mead is the *symmetry of response* that significant symbols allegedly evoke in people sharing the same language. For example, shouting "fire!" in a crowded theatre creates the behavioral disposition to flee in both the person announcing the danger and those hearing it. At the same time, significant symbols create similar objects of consciousness in symbol users and recipients. These social cognitions are the basis of human intersubjectivity.

Now, to the extent that what individuals say in social interaction is understandable to both themselves and to others, social objectivity exists. The individual transcends mere subjective experience when, through communication, he or she finds that others experience the same world (Morris 1934, xxviii–xxix). The intersubjectivity created by language makes Mead's provocative theory of mind as a social process and a product conceptually possible. It also provides a conceptual basis for the mutual orientation and coordination that is the essence of the *social act* (Mead 1934, 7n.), the unit of analysis in his social psychology.

Unfortunately, Mead viewed the intersubjectivity created by language as strictly cognitive in nature, making it difficult for later symbolic interactionists to develop a social psychology of emotions within his conceptual framework. Despite his occasional flirtation with emotions, he maintained that the natural function of language is the arousal of the same cognitions in self and others, rather than the elicitation of common affective response. While acknowledging the capacity of language to evoke emotions, he insisted that emotional communication does not necessarily evoke the symmetry of response that is the essence of cognitive communication. For example, one person's expression of anger might instigate fear, rather than anger, in another person. Therefore, to grant emotions the conceptual status of social phenomena would seriously weaken his attempt to build a social psychology upon the universal and objective foundation of language. As a result, Mead assigned affect a peripheral role in his social psychology.

Despite this shortcoming, Mead's theory that language is the basis for a social psychology of mind, self, and society remains his greatest contribution. It seems strange, then, that symbolic interactionists traditionally have paid lip service to the role of language in social psychology—exceptions to this generalization, including Denzin's (1972) study of names and pronouns in childhood socialization and his later work (1987) on semiotics and symbolic interactionism, notwithstanding. It remained for the ethnomethodologists, as Collins (1986) observes, to open up the field of sociolinguistics. However, like Mead's treatment of language, theirs has been too cognitive to be of much utility in the development of a social psychology of emotions.

Paradoxically, considering Mead's denial of the social significance of affective communication, symbolic interactionists began to appreciate the importance of language only when they seriously turned their attention to emotions in the late 1970s. Among their contributions to the social psychology of emotions, they identified the role that culturally influenced cognitive labels play in identifying present emotional experiences and evoking memories of past ones (Shott 1979). Gordon

(1981, 583) articulated this notion at a conceptual level, pointing out that naming a sentiment "reifies [it] in the learner's understanding . . . [making] an otherwise transient impulse or gesture socially significant and memorable." However, despite the widespread recognition by interactionists and other theorists in recent years that language plays an important role in eliciting emotional experience, virtually nothing has been done to operationalize this understanding and derive its empirical consequences.

For example, symbolic interactionists have failed to generalize the affective significance of language beyond its obvious function of providing a "vocabulary of emotions" (Gordon 1981). Surely, the affective significance of language applies to all linguistic stimuli, not just those identifying and designating emotional experience. The word, "mother," for example, is not merely a kinship designation in a cognitive sense, but also, and perhaps more significantly, a social identity evoking feelings of warmth, goodness, and quiet determination. In contrast, the word, "bully," elicits feelings of negative affective tone and greater liveliness. Similarly, words designating interpersonal acts and social settings convey affective overtones. Consider the feelings generated by "assault" as compared to "hug"; "cemetery," as compared to "party." In short, the names with which we designate all kinds of social stimuli evoke affective associations such that language functions as a linguistic warehouse, so to speak, for storing affective meaning. By this account, affect is more pervasive in social life than the experience of specific emotions, and symbolic interaction involves the processing not only of cognitive information about objects and events, but also, and perhaps even more fundamentally, their affective associations.

There is, then, a need for an interactionist social psychology that deals explicitly and more extensively than in the past with the affective component of language and its role in social interaction. As Collins (1986, 1349) stated emphatically, "the time is ripening for a theoretical upheaval . . . as we have to come to grips with the grounding of language not only in cognitive aspects of social interaction but in what may turn out to be its emotional interactional substrate."

Besides failing to operationalize symbolic interactionism in terms of language, interactionists have generally ignored Mead's other great contribution to social psychology—his conceptualization of mind as a process of cybernetic feedback and control and, by implication, human behavior as "constructed in a succession of self-correcting adjustments" (Shibutani 1968, 331). For Mead, the physiological capacity for reflexiveness that "is the essential condition . . . for the development of mind" (1934, 134) means that "the thing we are going to do is playing back on what we are doing now" (1934, 71). Although the concept of cybernetic control articulated in modern systems theory (Buckley 1967, 1968) and perceptual control systems theory (Powers 1973) was clearly anticipated by Mead and by Dewey (1896), it is strangely absent in the work of symbolic interactionists who laid claim to Mead's intellectual legacy.[5]

Moreover, the concept of control has found no place at all in interactionist treatments of emotion (cf. Heise 1979, 36–7). Instead, interactionists have generally dealt with emotions as dependent variables—culturally influenced cognitive constructions and expressions of ephemeral affective states—and have paid notably less attention to the consequences of emotions in social life (cf. Stryker 1987). This one-sided emphasis on the "primacy of cognition" in emotional experience is simply not conducive to cybernetic thinking (Scheff 1985a).

What is needed, therefore, along with a greater application of Mead's emphasis on language, is an interactionist social psychology that incorporates and operationalizes his conceptualization of mind as a process of cybernetic feedback and control and behavior as an anticipatory, self-adjustive process.

These preliminary considerations bring us to the theory that is the focus of this book.

Affect Control Theory

Affect control theory (Heise 1979; Smith-Lovin and Heise 1988) proposes that people construct social events to confirm the affective meaning of their situated identities and those of other actors; and when events occur that strain these sentiments, people initiate restorative actions and cognitive revisions to bring affectively disturbing events back into line with established sentiments. The formalization of the theory comprises a set of elegant mathematical models representing the interpretation and construction of social action (Heise 1979, 1988, 1992), along with a powerful interactive microcomputer program, INTERACT, for simulating these processes (Heise 1978; Heise and Lewis 1988a).

Although a contribution to the social psychology of emotions, per se, was not anticipated in the early statements of the theory (Heise 1978, 1979), it soon became evident that affect control theory could make substantial contributions to this emerging field. This was quickly verified through the collection of data on the affective meaning of emotion terms and the refinement and expansion of the original theory to accommodate emotions (Averett 1981; Averett and Heise 1988; Smith-Lovin 1990). More recently, the theory has brought under its purview the external expression of emotion and its role in the dynamics of labeling and attribution processes (Heise 1989a).

Much effort has been expended in the last decade on the theoretical development and empirical refinement of affect control theory and identifying its connections with other theories in social psychology (Smith-Lovin and Heise 1988). Nonetheless, the theory has yet to be formally codified in deductive form, nor have its linkages with other social psychological theories been systematically detailed and brought together in a single publication. Moreover, the metatheoretical assumptions of the theory have never been carefully examined.

This book is devoted to a formal exposition of affect control theory, an examination of its fundamental assumptions, and a systematic comparison of the theory with other theories in social psychology. In particular, this book, as its title suggests, focuses on the symbolic interactionist tradition in sociological social psychology inspired by the seminal work of George Herbert Mead (1934). While the affinity of affect control theory with symbolic interactionism has been acknowledged (Heise 1979; Stryker 1981, n.49; Stryker and Statham 1985, 356–7), the structural resemblance of the two theories has never been closely examined, nor has the relation of affect control theory to Mead's original social psychology been explored.

In this regard, affect control theory addresses the shortcomings of Mead and symbolic interactionism identified in the introduction to this chapter. While much of this book is devoted to evidencing this claim, an anticipatory sketch is in order here. First, congruent with Mead's emphasis on language as the basis for a social psychology that is irreducible to principles of general psychology, affect control theory conceptualizes and operationalizes social interaction in terms of its symbolic representation in language—the semantics of interactional components, such as identities and interpersonal acts, and their combination in syntactically ordered events. At the same time, by rejecting Mead's rather gratuitous assumptions about the affective significance of language, affect control theory expands the scope of his theory so that it can serve as the basis for a social psychology of emotion. Specifically, affect control theory embraces Mead's premise that language creates shared objects of consciousness, but supposes, in turn, that all social cognitions evoke affective associations. It is at the level of the affective associations evoked by cognitions that affect control theory is formulated.

Second, in contrast to the efforts of symbolic interactionists in the last fifteen years to extend Mead's social psychology beyond cognition, affect control theory does not consider affect to be coextensive with those specific, intense, and ephemeral affective states we call *emotions*. Instead, it views affect as a more general and pervasive component of human consciousness that subsumes the emotions as a special case.

Third, because the principle of control is a defining feature of the theory, affect control theory maintains Mead's model of mind as a socially engendered, internal linguistic process of cybernetic feedback and control, and his conceptualization of social interaction as a process of mutually adjusted response. However, the theory applies the principle of control to affective, rather than cognitive, processing.

Because affect control theory is framed and operationalized in terms of language and linguistic theory, it is essential that I state in the first chapter of this book what the theory assumes about language and what it does not.[6] A discussion of two closely interrelated points should accomplish this. The first concerns nonverbal and other kinds of language systems; the second, the relation between language and culture.

Language systems are, of course, not all verbal in form. Human language, broadly conceived, also includes such nonverbal forms as intonation or inflection, tone, and volume of speech; gestures; and body language.

> A social world in which people communicate with one another only through language would be colorless and flat—like a place where people could exchange only typed messages with others they could not see. It is what we "say" to one another by physical appearance, expressions, gestures, tone of voice, and the way we arrange ourselves in space that add rich dimensions to human social life. We not only send "linguistic [verbal] messages" to one another but we also exchange information about our internal states (what "mood" we are in), about our relationships to one another (are we hostile or friendly?), and about the way our linguistic messages or acts are to be interpreted (are we joking, serious, playing, or fighting?). Such nonlinguistic communication is the very fabric of social life. (Keesing 1976, 166).

Nonverbal communication systems not only augment and complement verbal linguistic ones, they may parallel them (Hall 1966). Because they have their own grammars, syntaxes, and other rules of meaning and organization, they may even equate to verbal language systems, as might be the case with verdant grammars of social behavior (Gregory 1985). However, compared to verbal linguistic systems, we know relatively little about the structure of such systems. Bateson's (1972) analysis suggests that our relative lack of knowledge about nonverbal language may stem from the fact that what it codes and communicates—the operations ("algorithms") and subject matter (relationships between self and others and between self and environment)—lie in the realm of the unconscious, inaccessible and defying description in verbal terms: "It is not only that the conscious mind has poor access to this material, but also the fact that when such access is achieved, e.g., in dreams, art, poetry . . . and the like, there is still a formidable problem of translation" (1972, 139).

While formalized in verbal linguistic terms, it must be emphasized that affect control theory recognizes the importance of nonverbal forms of communication in social interaction. The theory employs verbal language because it shares with Mead the assumption that it is the primary symbolic system through which social cognitions are represented, accessed, processed, and communicated (see Proposition 2, next chapter); because verbal linguistic systems have been well investigated; and because verbal language is amenable to quantitative, attitudinal measurement on universal dimensions of response employing the semantic differential (see Proposition 4, next chapter). At the same time, there is nothing inherent in the theory that would proscribe the application of affect control principles to other kinds of symbolic systems, or to attitudinal data collected with nonverbal instruments such as the *projective differential scale*, a nonverbal projective imaging measure paralleling and revealing at least the evaluation and potency dimensions of the semantic differential (see Raynolds, Sakamoto, and Raynolds 1986).

In fact, affect control theory invokes the operation of nonverbal forms of communication in its modeling of reidentification processes, where it presumes that the external expression of emotion influences the labeling and trait attribution of social interactants (see Propositions 20 and 24 next chapter). Finally, if the semantic differential captures the affective overtones of cognitions, as Osgood (1969) contends, semantic differential responses to verbal stimuli may reflect the relationships of "the heart or . . . unconscious" (Bateson 1972, 139) coded in nonverbal linguistic systems (primary process in Freudian terms). Indeed, the predictive power of affect control theory may very well stem from this possible connection between verbal and nonverbal linguistic systems.

The classic statement of the influence of language upon culture can be found in what has become known as the "Whorfian" or "Sapir-Whorfian hypothesis"—essentially, the idea that through language, people break up their culture for purposes of communication. Words are categories of reality, and their grammatical organization, an organization of reality. By implication, "language is not merely part of the culture, but . . . also a reflection of the total culture . . . a reflection, more importantly perhaps, of the organization of that total culture" (Bohannan 1963, 42).

Widely misunderstood and misapplied, the Safir-Whorfian hypothesis is best understood as an expression and partial explanation of cultural uniqueness and diversity. Transformational linguistics and the search for linguistic and cultural universals has for some time rendered the Sapir-Whorfian hypothesis outdated and intellectually unfashionable (see Keesing 1976, 159–163).

In any case, affect control theorists, like anthropologists and sociologists concerned with culture, recognize that language and culture are not coextensive. That is, while language is part of culture, and while the principles of organization underlying language may parallel the principles of organization found in culture, language is not equal to culture by any stretch of the imagination. Therefore, while affect control theory purports to deal with culture, it makes no pretense that it is definitive of culture. The theory measures and models the influence upon psychological processing and social interaction of cultural sentiments embedded in language—no more, no less.

Plan of this Book

The rest of this chapter reviews the rediscovery of emotion by psychologists and sociologists in the late 1970s and argues that if the study of emotion is to develop into a unified field of inquiry, social psychology must adopt a conceptual framework that transcends the parochialism of its parent disciplines. These discussions provide a context for evaluating the contributions of affect control theory to an integrative social psychology and to the social psychology of emotion.

The next two chapters are devoted exclusively to affect control theory. Chapter 2 presents a concise propositional statement of the theory, from its metatheoretical assumptions about language, cognition, and affect to the basic premises of affect control theory proper and their application to event recognition, event construction, emotions, and reidentification processes. Chapter 3 expounds the fundamental assumptions the theory makes about cognition, affect, and human motivation. A discussion of the primacy of cognition versus affect debate in psychological social psychology provides the context for discussing the relation between cognition and affect as viewed by affect control theory. A discussion of human motivation, from instinct to incentive theories, sets the stage for introducing the affect control theory of motivation based upon language, identification, and control.

Revisiting the thesis with which this introductory chapter began, Chapter 4 details how Mead's social behavioristic theory of language, the foundation upon which he built his social psychology, led him to conceptualize 'mind,' 'self,' and 'society' as exclusively cognitive phenomena. Drawing a point by point comparison with Mead, this chapter shows how affect control theory retains the essential features of his social psychology, while vitalizing its affectively and motivationally lifeless constructs.

Chapters 5 and 6 apply affect control theory to the analysis of social interaction. Chapter 5 establishes the affinity of affect control theory with identity theory, an application of the general symbolic interactionist framework to role analysis (McCall and Simmons 1966/1978; Stryker 1968, 1980, 1981). The chapter includes detailed comparisons between affect control theory and Burke's model of role-identity processes (Burke 1980; Burke and Tully 1977) and situated identity theory (Alexander and Wiley 1981).

Against this theoretical background, Chapter 6 presents affect control theory simulations of social interaction in both institutionalized and novel settings, the respective foci of the *structure* and *process* schools of symbolic interactionism which grew out of one-sided exaggerations of Mead's ideas (Meltzer and Petras 1972). The chapter concludes with a discussion of how roles are learned and later accessed in memory, comparing the account of these processes provided by affect control theory to the social learning model of Heiss (1981) and the associative addressing model of Wallace (1983).

Chapter 7 presents the affect control theory of emotions. The chapter begins with a discussion of the positivist versus constructionist debate in the social psychology of emotions. Following the introduction of the emotions model of the theory, simulations illustrate the manifold ways in which emotions function in social interaction. The chapter concludes with a discussion of how affect control theory helps to reconcile the positivist and constructionist positions by integrating important features from both sides of this conceptual and theoretical divide.

Chapter 8 addresses the reidentification processes set in motion when events fail to confirm the situated identities of interactants. Part I of this chapter opens with a discussion of the synthesis of attribution theory and symbolic interactionism achieved by Stryker and Gottlieb (1981) that makes it conceptually possible for affect control theory to incorporate both trait attribution and labeling processes within a single reidentification model. The established reidentification model of the theory is described and illustrated with simulations of labeling and attribution processes. Part I concludes by showing how affect control theory contributes to the further integration of attribution theory and symbolic interactionism. Part II deals with the revised reidentification model which, by incorporating the effect of emotion displays upon reidentification outcomes, connects attribution and labeling theory with the social psychology of emotions. The revised model is described and illustrated with a systematic analysis.

The final chapter of this book discusses connections between affect control theory and social psychological theories that lie outside the symbolic interactionist tradition. It evaluates the theory as sociological explanation and as integrative social psychology, and presents a critical assessment of the theory, along with a prospectus for future research and application.

The examples of affect control theory predictions that appear in this book are based on models and cultural data from a large–scale Canadian replication (MacKinnon 1985, 1988) of the U.S. study conducted by Heise and associates (Smith–Lovin and Heise 1988). In this regard, cross–cultural comparisons are drawn in a number of places throughout the book.

The Rediscovery of Affect

Affect registers our reactions to objects and events around us and our successes and failures in dealing with them; it accompanies our anticipation of future events and our memory of past ones; and it marks the establishment and dissolution of our most intimate and intense social relationships. Affect is the dynamic principle of human motivation, mobilizing action in the search for functional or gratifying experiences and the avoidance of dysfunctional or displeasing ones. Affect is also an important basis of human intersubjectivity: people infer how others are thinking and feeling by observing their emotional reactions to events, and control the revelation of their own thoughts and feelings by monitoring their external expression.

In view of the potency and pervasiveness of affect in everyday psychological experience and social life, why have psychologists and sociologists neglected its study for almost fifty years? There had been a serious concern with emotion around the turn of the century in the theoretical work of psychologists like James

(1890), Dewey (1894, 1895), and McDougall (1908), and sociologists like Cooley (1902/1956 and Durkheim (1912/1954). There was significant empirical work as well, which reached its peak around 1930 (Scheff 1984a). During the next four or five decades, however, the study of affect fell into a state of somnolence, interrupted only occasionally by isolated attempts to reawaken interest in the area (Gerth and Mills 1964; Tomkins 1962; Shibutani 1961).

The moribund state into which the study of emotion slipped during this period was part of a more general neglect of the subjective life of the person by psychologists and sociologists alike. In psychology, the study of both cognition and emotion was eclipsed by behaviorism. Adopting the "from Missouri" attitude of a misplaced emphasis on observable data, the study of the subjective component of human behavior was sacrificed upon the alter of a supposed objective science. In sociology, the paradigmatic hegemony of functionalism and other macro sociological theories from the late 1940s to the early 1960s neglected the construct of the individual person in favor of more abstract concepts like 'role', 'status', and 'social system' (Dahrendorf 1958; Freidrichs 1970; Lockwood, 1956; Wrong 1961). When the individual was finally brought back into the picture, sociologists turned in large numbers to theories that imported the behavioristic perspective from psychology—*exchange theory* (Homans 1958, 1961, 1964) and *social behaviorism* (Burgess and Bushell 1969). The impact of behaviorism upon sociological social psychology was so extensive, in fact, that Friedrichs (1974) contemplated whether eventually it would become the prevailing paradigm in sociology.

The rehabilitation of the subjective as a proper object of scientific inquiry occurred in psychology through cognitive, rather than affective, theory and research. Cognition might have been considered a more scientifically respectable topic of research than affect, which often is conceptualized as a departure from rationality, as in psychodynamic personality theory and neoclassical economics (Etzioni 1988). As the respectability of the subjective became firmly reestablished with the ascendancy of the cognitive paradigm in the psychology of the 1970s (Roseman 1984; Shaver 1984), the intellectual climate was ripe for the rediscovery of emotion. If the 1970s belonged to cognition, it was clear by the early 1980s that "the next decade or so belongs to affect" (Tomkins 1981, 314). By the mid-1980s, the subsequent explosion in theory and research was such that the editor of an entire volume of the 1984 *Review of Personality and Social Psychology* devoted to emotions could boast that "emotion is back, and with a vengeance" (Shaver 1984, 7).

In sociology, an interest in the subjective experience of the individual was kept alive during the heyday of macro theory, and against the later threat of behaviorism, by interpretive sociologies like action theory, symbolic interactionism, ethnomethodology, and phenomenological sociology. These micro theories share an emphasis on cognition and a concomitant neglect of affect. Eventually, however, a growing dissatisfaction with these cognitively biased theories set the stage for the rediscovery of emotion in sociology (Collins 1986). At the same time, the handful of sociologists who had become interested in emotion discovered a niche that could accommodate their efforts. This was made available by the failure of psychologists to seriously attend to the role of social interaction in the production of emotions. Capitalizing upon this neglect, Kemper's groundbreaking book, *A Social Interactional Theory of Emotions*, began with the observation that "there are many theories of emotion, but none is sociological . . . an effort to explain emotions as a product of social interaction is long overdue" (1978, 1).

Kemper's book was followed in short order by a striking number of sociological contributions to the study of emotion. Shott (1979) laid the groundwork for a symbolic interactionist theory of emotion by extending Mead's conceptualization of cognitive role-taking to "empathic role-taking," and by showing how emotions enter into socialization and social control processes. Hochschild (1975, 1979, 1983) analyzed the "emotion work" people engage in because of cultural norms ("feeling rules") governing emotions and their expression. Collins (1975, 1981) showed how Durkheimian social solidarity is built up from the everyday, shared affective experiences he terms "interactional ritual chains." Scheff (1979, 1984b) developed a theory of "emotional catharsis" based upon psychoanalytic theory. And, Denzin (1980, 1984, 1985), combining elements of symbolic interactionism and phenomenological thought, proposed a theory of emotions as "lived experiences" that has the self as referent and that locates people in the world of social interaction. Closer to home, Heise (1978) published a modest introduction to affect control theory, followed by a major theoretical statement in 1979. While these works were not all inspired by the same theoretical traditions, they had in common an emphasis on social interaction as the wellspring of emotion.

By the early 1980s, interest and output by sociologists had developed to the point that comprehensive review articles were required to take account of the progress to date, to assess the degree to which the extant sociological literature contained latent or inchoate theories of emotion, and to delineate the issues and controversies that had already begun to crystallize in the field (Gordon 1981; Scheff 1983). By the middle of the decade, Collins (1986) was able to describe the study of emotions as one of the most important developments in the sociology of the 1980s. And, by the end of the decade, a separate section on emotions had been firmly established in the American Sociological Association.

However, the study of emotion in psychology and in sociology grew side by side in the late 1970s and early 1980s with minimum communication and exchange of theoretical orientations and research accomplishments. Their independent development reflected differences in their substantive concerns—one dealing with emotion in terms of its relation to cognition, motivation, and individual behavior; the other, in terms of its relation to social structure, culture, and social interaction.

This divergence has proved unfortunate because the issues considered important by each discipline have not been of exclusive interest and relevance. For example, constructionist theories in sociology stress the role of cognitive interpretation in emotional experience, albeit they have done little with this idea; and cognitive theories in psychology emphasize the importance of the situation of social interaction, although they did not move beyond exhortation until the mid-1980s (de Rivera 1984; Kelley 1984). For these reasons, I have reviewed the study of emotion in psychology and sociology as separate developments, categorizing works as falling in one area or the other solely on the basis of the discipline affiliation of their authors.

However, there has been a growing convergence of interest and orientation in recent years, enhanced by the publication of sociologists' work in psychology journals and handbooks and of psychologists' writings in sociology outlets. As might be expected, this has taken place largely in the area of social psychology.

The Social Psychology of Emotion

Like the study of emotions itself, social psychology developed independently in psychology and sociology (House 1977; Stryker 1977; Rosenberg and Turner 1981; Jackson 1988). Psychological social psychologists have been more likely to study the effects of experimentally manipulated social factors on individual attitudes and behavior; sociological social psychologists, the effects of naturally occurring patterns of social and cultural structure on social attitudes and interaction. The psychological approach has paid much greater attention to the study of *intra*individual processes, like cognition and motivation, than to the social factors presumed to affect them. The sociological approach has attended to *inter*individual processes like social interaction, the establishment of intersubjective beliefs and attitudes, and the situation of social interaction within which these processes occur.

In a classic definition, Gordon Allport (1968) defined social psychology as "an attempt to understand and explain how the thought, feeling, and behavior of individuals are influenced by the actual, imagined, or implied presence of others." Allport's definition of social psychology is one-sided, however, because it ignores the reciprocal effects of individual personality and behavior on social and cultural structure. Moreover, because it fails to acknowledge the inherently social nature of individual personality, it renders social psychology a simple extension of general psychology. Despite these shortcomings, Allport's definition identified a promising point of rapprochement between the two social psychologies—the effect of the situation of social interaction on the individual's thoughts, feelings, and behavior.

Employing this theoretical commonality as a criterion, the study of emotion in psychology until recently has not constituted a social psychology of emotions at all. In fact, from the turn of the century to the 1980s, the psychology of emotion had largely employed a physiological perspective (see Kemper 1978; Roseman 1984). This includes the classic work of James (1884, 1890), Lange (1885), and Cannon (1929), as well as more recent efforts that continue to emphasize the physiological determinants and concomitants of emotional experience. The role of cognition in emotional experience was not introduced into the picture until the 1960s (Arnold 1960; Schachter and Singer 1962; Schacter 1964), and the role of interpersonal relations much later still (de Rivera 1984; Kelley 1984). Yet, the growing interest in the 1980s in "close relationships, the crucible in which powerful emotions are formed" led Shaver to "wager . . . that the emerging psychology of emotion will necessarily be a *social* psychology" (1984, 7, 10).

In contrast to its treatment in psychology, the study of emotion in sociology has been a social psychology from the outset. For example, Kemper based his pioneering analysis on the premise that "most human emotions result from outcomes of interaction in social relationships" (1978, vii). And, as observed above, symbolic interactionists and those of other theoretical persuasions who contributed to the development of a sociology of emotions share an emphasis on the dynamics of social interaction as the genesis of emotions.

However, if social psychology is to serve as the arena for the study of emotion as a unified field of inquiry, the intersection between its psychological and sociological variants must become much more expansive and profound than a common concern with social interaction. While building upon this point of consensus, the field must develop an autonomous and distinctive conceptual framework that transcends the restrictions of its parent disciplines. A recent historical analysis of social psychology by Jackson (1988) suggests that, indeed, this has been gradually taking place.

According to Jackson, a unified conceptual framework became more or less crystallized in the social psychology of the 1980s, promising to integrate the field not only across disciplines, but within psychology itself where the history of social psychology has been a particularly stormy one. The new "integrative orientation" delineated by Jackson comprises the following components: (1) a movement towards employing the social act rather than the individual as the unit of analysis;[7] (2) a growing appreciation of the person as an active, reflexive, and social organism; (3) an expanding psychological modality that includes cognition, emotion, motivation, and behavior as inextricably interrelated components; (4) the conceptualization of self as a process of constructing and confirming situated identities in social acts, a mutual process of self-presentation and impression management; (5) a conceptualization of reference processes as interactive (reciprocal), reflexive (involving internal as well as external significant others), and situated (situationally specific to social acts); (6) a conceptualization of normative processes as an attempt by participants in a social act "to coordinate action by taking each others' meanings into account in constructing their behavior" (1988, 125); and (7) a conceptualization of social behavior as occurring within unitary bounded periods of time, beginning with the construction of situated identities for mutual acceptance and confirmation and terminating with a discontinuity of the social process, often accompanied by a change in spatial location. An important metatheoretical implication of this integrative orientation, meaning thus becomes a social construction, rather than the personal cognitive property of individual actors.

A social psychology embracing this integrative orientation will attend to both the intraindividual and interindividual aspects of emotional experience. The sociologically trained social psychologist will not hesitate to trespass upon the territory preempted by psychologists, nor will the psychologically trained researcher balk at violating the turf previously staked out by sociologists. An integrated social psychology of emotion will approach affect as inextricably bound up with the cognitive, motivational, and behavioral components of the psychological modality of the person. It will deal with emotions as outcomes of social acts that have implications for the situated identities of participants, as governed by socially situated reference and normative processes, and as sustaining the social life of the person and the group. To a large extent, the production of such a social psychology is the aspiration of this book.

I will revisit this integrative orientation in the final chapter of this book, where I assess affect control theory in terms of its potential contributions to an integrated social psychology and to the study of emotion as a unified field of inquiry.

Summary

I began the *tour d'horizon* of this book by discussing the reason for Mead's reluctance to grant emotion an important role in his social psychology. I then argued that symbolic interactionism must pay greater attention to Mead's emphasis on language and control, while extending his cognitive social psychology to include the affective life of the person. Following a concise summary of the rediscovery of affect in the psychology and sociology of the late 1970s and early 1980s, I suggested that the social psychology of emotion as a unified field of inquiry is predicated upon the development of an integrated social psychology, one that rises above the conceptual limitations of its parent disciplines. In this regard, I introduced a recently proposed integrative orientation in social psychology and briefly considered its implications for the social psychology of emotion.

The following two chapters introduce affect control theory and examine its assumptions about cognition, affect, and human motivation.

2

AFFECT CONTROL THEORY

This chapter expands the preliminary statement of affect control presented in Chapter 1 into a formal propositional exposition of the theory.[1] In the interest of accessibility, I omit discussion of the mathematical formalization of the theory, which has been adequately presented elsewhere (Heise 1979, 1988, 1992) and which I summarize at strategic points in later chapters. For the same reason, I sidestep a discussion of INTERACT, the computer program which contains the mathematical models of the theory and cultural data and by which simulations of social interaction reported in this book are generated. This has been presented in an eloquent and user-friendly fashion by Heise and Lewis (1988a). Nor do I discuss the historical development of affect control theory, which is provided in MacKinnon and Heise (1993). Finally, to avoid compromising the expository nature of this presentation, I make minimum reference to the social psychological literature that deals with issues relevant to affect control theory. The remaining chapters in this book attend to this task.

In the formal presentation of the theory that follows, I present seven sets of propositions. The first set, comprising four propositions relating to symbols, language, and affective meaning, covers the basic assumptions of the theory. The second set consists of two propositions that specify an auxiliary cognitive theory. The third set comprises the three basic principles of affect control theory proper—affective reaction, affect control, and reconstruction. The fourth set consists of four propositions that apply these principles to event interpretation, while the fifth set of four propositions applies these principles to event production. The sixth set contains three propositions pertaining to emotions; and the final set, four propositions dealing with reidentification (labeling and trait attribution) processes.

Symbols, Language, and Affective Meaning

1. Social interaction is conducted in terms of the social cognitions of interactants.

This proposition aligns affect control theory with the social psychology of George Herbert Mead, symbolic interactionism, and other interpretive theories in sociological social psychology, as well as with cognitive theories in psychological social psychology. Like these traditions, and in contrast to radical behaviorism, affect control theory dares to peer inside the black box of "minded behavior" that intervenes between external stimuli and overt behavioral response. From this perspective, people do not react; they act. Behavior is not released; it is constructed. People are not simply constrained by an environment of external stimuli; through interpretation, the environment is radically transformed so that it takes on a decidedly subjective character.

All this is made possible by the human capacity to employ symbols. People transform external stimuli into objects of consciousness or cognitions by invoking the social classifications provided by significant symbols. People manage their interaction with others through cognizing or recognizing themselves, others, objects, settings, and ongoing behavior, and combining these creatively into a definition of the situation that mobilizes and directs their action. Mead's great contribution was to show that these concepts, and the significant symbols or language that embody them, are profoundly social, so that social interaction in its covert phase can be characterized as symbolic interaction.

While profoundly social, concepts and definitions of situations are expected to vary among individuals because people have different interests, priorities, biographies, and socialization experiences. It is beyond the scope of affect control theory to predict the initial definitions of situations (the identities assembled and the relevant setting); but when provided by the researcher, affect control models generate predictions for all subsequent situational definitions precipitated by the unfolding of events. Hypothetically, affect control theory could consider incorporating cultural variables having initial definitions of the situation embedded in them.

Affect control theory recognizes that social interaction is influenced by factors other than the social cognitions of actors. The material constraints of physical distance and barriers set limits on who can assemble with whom; and the availability of physical resources—like medical equipment, religious artifacts, and other props—constrains the actions that can be constructed at any given time and place. Thus, affect control theory acknowledges the importance of social ecology studies in illuminating the material constraints on symbolic interaction. In addition, the theory recognizes, as behaviorists have shown, that the contingencies among events arising out of the dynamics of ongoing interaction profoundly affect cognition and other psychological processes.

2. Language is the primary symbolic system through which cognitions are represented, accessed, processed, and communicated.

Affect control theory assumes that social cognitions are embodied in language. Affect control research involves the collection of attitudinal data on words designating the constitutents of social events—such as social identities, personality traits and status characteristics, and interpersonal acts. Also, the modeling of cognitive processes in affect control theory is heavily influenced by linguistic theory; that is, events are structured in terms of case grammar, and additional grammars are invoked to explain the cognitive constraints that occur within and between events. Affect control theory's emphasis on language is consistent with Mead's conceptualization of mind as an internal symbolic process in which language mediates sensation and reflective thought.

However, as emphasized in Chapter 1, affect control theorists recognize the operation of nonverbal languages in human thought and social interaction, and, anticipating a point made in Chapter 4, the inadequacy of Mead's model of 'mind' to circumscribe the entire spectrum of human consciousness.

Additionally, as discussed in Chapter 3, the theory recognizes that cognitive processing often, if not normally, occurs below the conscious level of symbolically mediated thought. That is, the theory supposes that social cognitions are initially learned through language; but, once established, they become elements of a preconscious or preconceptual system that functions rather automatically without the intervention of a great deal of highly conscious, symbolically mediated thought. Nonetheless, the theory supposes that affect control principles are operative whether cognitions occur at the lower level of consciousness, where things are more felt than recognized, or at the higher level of conscious awareness and reflective thought.

3. All social cognitions evoke affective associations.

This proposition connects the cognitive tradition of Mead and symbolic interactionism with affect control theory. Affect control theory supposes that all cognitions evoke quantitatively measurable affective associations which vary in intensity and direction along several qualitatively distinct dimensions (specified in Proposition 4). The various constituents of social events—such as social identities and interpersonal acts—become comparable in this affective space, engaging a mode of psychological process that integrates these different kinds of cognitions, and which is general across different individuals.

While the qualitative richness of social cognitions presents a classification problem that is infinite in scope and beyond the capacity of any researcher, their affective meaning represents a more tractable research problem. Through the affective associations evoked by cognitions, we get a quantitative handle on the dynamics of social life.

While situation definitions and other cognitive processes are the framework for social interaction, social dynamics are largely governed by an affective system relating to values, motives, emotions, etc. Classifications of places, people, objects and behaviors get transformed into a domain of feelings where things lose their qualitative uniqueness, become comparable to one another, and begin obeying quantitative principles. This is analogous to observing that Sun, Earth, Mars, Saturn, etc., are identifiable by their unique characteristics, but the dynamics of the solar system are governed by the distances, masses, and velocities of these bodies and the operation of physical laws (Heise 1988, 6).

4. Affective associations can be indexed to a large degree on universal dimensions of response.

In measuring the affective associations evoked by cognitions, affect control theory capitalizes on the work of Charles Osgood and associates (Osgood, Suci, and Tannenbaum 1957; Osgood 1969; Snider and Osgood 1969; Osgood, May, and Miron 1975), who demonstrated that the *evaluation, potency* and *activity* (EPA) dimensions of the semantic differential are universal dimensions of meaning.

The EPA dimensions have been related to patterns of neurological activity (see Heise 1988, 6), as well as to three dimensions of social life. Evaluation and potency correspond, respectively, to the sociological dimensions of status and power (Kemper 1978; Kemper and Collins 1990); the activity or liveliness dimension to the subjective counterpart of social expressivity (Parsons and Shils 1951), the emotional energies of social interactants (Collins 1990), or some task–related dimension of meaning (Kemper and Collins 1990). While universal dimensions of affective meaning, the EPA measurements for particular stimuli are expected, of course, to vary both across individuals and cultures.

In affect control research, the evaluation dimension has been measured by employing "good-bad" and "nice-awful" as the prototypical bipolar adjectives of the semantic differential; the potency dimension, "big-little" and "powerful-powerless"; and the activity dimension, "fast-slow," "young-old," and "noisy-quiet." All three dimensions are measured by a scale ranging from –4.0 through 0 to +4.0, where 0 is adverbally anchored by "neutral"; –1 (+1), "slightly"; –2 (+2), "quite"; –3 (+3), "extremely"; and –4 (+4), "infinitely." In affect control research, this "assumed" metric is rescaled for each dimension using the method of successive intervals to obtain an approximately interval metric (Diederich, Messick, and Tucker 1957).

All kinds of concepts are measured on semantic-differential scales in affect control research. For example, the average EPA rating for the social identity, "professor," is 1.47, 1.36, –.55 for a sample of Canadian male university students; for "student," it is 1.18, .20, 1.86. Thus, for this particular culture, a professor is rated on average as between slightly and quite good, slightly powerful, and edging towards slightly slow, old, and quiet. In contrast, a student is rated on average as slightly good, neither powerless nor powerful, and quite lively. As an example of an interpersonal act, "to assault someone" is rated as extremely bad (–3.01), slightly powerful (1.21) and quite active (2.03); "to hug someone," quite good (2.32), quite powerful (1.87), but not too lively (–.21). Traits and status characteristics, emotions, and social settings also are measured on semantic differential scales in affect control research.

Cognitive Constraints

Affect control theory supposes that both the cognitive and affective systems of the individual operate in constructing events, or, more specifically, that affective processes operate within a cognitive framework.

5. Events are constructed in the framework of a definition of the situation that establishes the identities of participants.

Before social interaction can proceed meaningfully from one event to another, each interactant must settle upon a single, plausible interpretation of what is occurring—specifically, the identities of participants and the institutional context within which they are assembled. "A definition of the situation identifies the setting and the relevant persons and objects that are present, so it presents the actors and objects that can be combined into recognition of events in that situation (Heise 1979, 9)." Defining the situation is an essential part of establishing the cognitive framework within which affective processes operate.

Defining a situation involves complex perceptual processing in which various conceptual schemes (Sowa 1984) are raised and entertained, and categorization devices (Sacks 1972) employed. The definition of the situation also entails inferences about social institutional context, knowledge on the part of the observer of ritual or scripted behavior, and negotiation with other observers present at the scene (Heise 1979, 3–8; 1988, 2–4).

In its earlier formulations, affect control theory treated each person in a situation as attempting to actualize a single social identity. As discussed in Chapter 5, current research allows for the complication that each individual possesses a hierarchy of identities, more than one of which might be invoked in a given situation.

6. Grammatical structures of various kinds constrain event construction.

Affect control theory supposes that the cognition of social events is organized in terms of case grammar, consisting minimally of an actor (A) performing an act (B) on some object–person (O)—e.g., "The mother abandoned the child." As affect control theory developed, the case-grammar approach was extended to settings (S) yielding ABOS events (Smith-Lovin 1988b)—e.g., "The mother abandoned the child at the picnic"—and to trait, mood, and status modifiers of social identities—e.g., "The angry mother . . . " (Averett 1981; Averett and Heise 1988). In addition, some preliminary work has explored the effect of frequency modifiers ("never" to "always") on interpersonal acts in event sentences (MacKinnon 1985; Keating 1985). It is likely that the case-grammar approach will be extended further as the theory progresses. For instance, it would be interesting to study how possessives are psychologically processed, as in events like, "The mother abandoned the neighbour's child."

According to Proposition 5, the definition of the situation enables two of the case slots (A and O) in ABO events to be filled from the available social identities at the scene. The selection of a concept to fill the behavior slot (B) is constrained by the actor and object-persons provided by the definition of the situation, if one supposes the operation of projection rules (Katz 1972). According to this grammatical principle from semantic theory, social identities generally have characteristic acts associated with them. Doctors, for example, are expected to "counsel" and "medicate"; patients, "listen" and "obey."

> A given type of actor and a given type of object can be sensibly combined only with certain acts. Thus projection rules allow people to reject some interpretations of an event, reducing the alternative ways in which the event can be defined (Heise 1979, 11).

As discussed in Chapter 5, this notion is important in identity theory, which views social identities as having implications for action. Like defining situations, applying projection rules involves the inference of institutional context.

In addition to the definition of the situation and the application of projection rules, the construction of events is further structured by situationally-specific grammars of action. Action grammars imply that the event constructions possible at each point in the ongoing process of interaction are constrained by logical and causal thinking about what has already happened and what is expected to happen next. In short, the selection of the act (B) that completes the process of recognizing ABO events is the outcome of complex cognitive processing (Heise 1979, 8–13; 1987, 5).

Affective Response and Control

7. The Affective Reaction Principle: People react affectively to every social event.

The first major premise of affect control theory proper is that "events cause people to respond affectively" (Heise 1979, viii). Proposition 7 expands the general idea contained in Propositions 1 and 3 by incorporating the research-based understanding that events generate new affective meanings for the actor and object-persons, interpersonal acts, and social settings of preceding events. These event-generated feelings may differ from earlier ones either in intensity, direction, or both.

Consider an initial event, "The mother scolds the child." According to affect control theory, the affective reaction to this event depends on the affective meanings for the social identities (mother and child) and the act (to scold some-one) prior to their combination in the specified event. These culturally established affective meanings are called *fundamental sentiments* in affect control theory. The event-generated feelings are called *transient impressions* or *feelings* because subsequent events may quickly undo them—either restoring them closer to fundamental sentiments or causing them to be deflected even further away.

Different configurations of social identities and acts produce different transient impressions. For example, "a mother scolding a child" generates transient feelings that are negative for both mother and child; but, "a mother hugging a child" produces transient feelings that are positive. An observer of the event from the same culture is expected to react with feelings similar to those experienced by participants.

The *impression formation* equations of affect control theory model the process by which fundamental sentiments for social identities and interpersonal acts combine during event cognition to generate transient feelings for these event components. I do not discuss these equations here so as not to disrupt the expository nature of this presentation. (A clear discussion can be found in Smith-Lovin 1988a.) Instead, I examine a few predictions to illustrate the psychological processes they purportedly model.

As discussed under Proposition 4, the affective meaning of concepts is measured by the evaluation, potency, and activity dimensions of the semantic differential, the scale values for which generally range from +3.00 to –3.00 in affect control research. In a sample of Canadian female university students, the fundamental EPA profile for mother is 2.7, 1.6, 1.0, indicating that, on average, mothers are considered extremely good, quite powerful, and slightly active in the population sampled. The transient EPA profile for mother generated by the impression formation equations for the event, "mother scolds child," is –1.4, 0.9, 1.0. Thus, the equations predict that a mother scolding a child (without known justification) would become negatively evaluated and viewed as somewhat less powerful, but that the transient impression of her liveliness would remain unchanged.

The affective meaning of object-persons also undergoes revision as a consequence of the event. The fundamental EPA profile of 1.7, –1.1, 2.5 indicates that a child is generally considered quite good, slightly powerless, and extremely active. The transient impression –0.4, –0.5, –0.6 generated by the impression formation equations for object-persons predicts that, by virtue of being scolded, a child would appear bad, a bit less powerless, and dramatically less active.

Behavior also becomes affectively colored by the context of events. The impression formation equations predict that the act of scolding (with a fundamental EPA profile of –0.4, 1.7, 0.7) becomes even more negatively evaluated when performed on a good object-person, like a child, declines slightly in potency, but does not appreciably change in terms of activity.

Finally, events transform the affective meaning of settings in which they occur. For example, Smith-Lovin (1988b, 91), who developed impression formation equations incorporating event settings, found that "places are viewed as more pleasant when they have been the scene of conciliatory, inquisitive acts like Appease, Consult, Contemplate, Josh, and Serve," but that "settings which have been defiled by violent aggressive interactions are viewed retrospectively as unpleasant places or gatherings."

8. The Affect Control Principle: People try to experience events that confirm fundamental sentiments.

As noted above, fundamental sentiments in affect control theory refer to the affective associations evoked by concepts prior to their combination in social events and are operationalized as the average EPA profile of concepts measured outside the context of events. Fundamental sentiments are considered culturally established and stable in the sense that virtually the same EPA profile for a concept is obtained by repeated sampling from the same population. Sampling from different populations, of course, is expected to yield different results.

In affect control theory, fundamental sentiments serve as the affective point of reference for assessing the transient impressions produced by social events. This leads us to the second major premise of affect control theory proper—the principle of affect control:

> People . . . act to maintain established feelings and when an event occurs that strains these feelings the individuals anticipate and implement new events to restore normal impressions. Events cause people to respond affectively. In turn, people expect and construct new events that will cause established sentiments to be confirmed (Heise 1979, viii).

According to the affect control principle, people construct events so that the transient feelings they generate are as close as possible to fundamental sentiments. The discrepancy between fundamental sentiments and transient impressions in affect control theory is called *deflection.* Deflection is operationalized as the sum of the squared differences between transient impressions and fundamental sentiments, computed across all dimensions of affective response (EPA) and across all components (ABO) of social events.[2] In operational terms, the principle of affect control proposes that people construct social events in order to minimize affective deflection. Conceptually, they do so in order to experience a knowable, meaningful social existence.

Affect control theory views the affect control principle as pervasive in social life. As discussed in the next chapter, the confirmation of meaning through minimizing deflection is the basic motivational principle in affect control theory, mobilizing and directing the identity-confirming actions of self and the reidentification of self and others in the wake of disruptive events.

While the affective reaction principle (Proposition 7) pertains to the effect of cognition on affect; the *affect control* principle pertains to the return effect of affect on cognition. Taken together, these two propositions define a cybernetic process of affective reaction and control, describing the effect of past events on present affective states and the interpretive and constructive work required to maintain or restore affective balance.

The *impression management* equations embodying the principle of affect control are mathematically derived from the empirically-grounded impression formation equations modeling the affective reaction to events. The impression management equations are not discussed here because, again, this would prove distracting to the expository presentation of the theory attempted in this chapter. (A clear and comprehensive statement of these equations can be found in Heise 1988.)

9. The Reconstruction Principle: Inexorably large deflections instigate changes in the sentiments which are being used to appraise the meaning of events such that the new sentiments are confirmed optimally by recent events.

Proposition 9 proposes that if people cannot confirm fundamental sentiments through action, they change the sentiments they are trying to confirm by redefining the situation that produced them. In cybernetic terms, when the lower-order feedback provided by action fails to maintain consistency between fundamental and transient sentiments, higher-order feedback kicks in to reduce the inexorably large deflections produced by disturbing events (Heise 1979, 3). Most often, sentiment change is effected by reidentifying event participants.

Thus, there are two ways in which the affective deflection produced by disturbing events can be reduced—by the construction of restorative acts (Proposition 8) or by the cognitive revision of what has been recognized as having taken place (Proposition 9). The first is covered by the cluster of propositions dealing with event production (Propositions 14–17), the second, by the set dealing with cognitive revisions (Propositions 21–24). This latter group of propositions applies the reconstruction principle to the reidentification of event participants via labeling and trait attribution processes.

The reconstruction principle raises two issues. The first involves the problem of identifying the components of an event most amenable to reconceptualization. Given the framework of ABO events, one possibility for reducing deflection is to reconceptualize the behavior (B) that has occurred, leaving intact the situated identities of the participants (A and O). For example, a mother may not have *abandoned* her child but had been simply *teasing* him or her; or, a bully may not have *helped* a boy but had been *manipulating* him. According to Proposition 6, the revision of behavior is limited by such grammatic structures as *projection rules*, which define some acts as implausible for the given configuration of identities and institutional context.

Many acts may not be subject to revision at all because of their unequivocal nature. An observer of a killing, for example, would be hard-pressed to cognitively revise the act of killing. As suggested by attribution theory, the overwhelming salience of behavior in the perception of social events implies that observed acts should be resistant to reconceptualization. The reduction of affective deflection through behavior thus is generally effected by the anticipation or implementation of restorative acts, rather than through reconceptualization of those that have occurred.

Because of their resistance to reconceptualization, a redefinition of context may provide justification for the act. Perhaps the actor killed in self-defense. Alternatively, specification of setting may accomplish the same thing. Perhaps the act of killing occurred on a battlefield (Heise 1988, 12–13).

In view of these considerations, affect control theory supposes that the components of events most amenable to reconceptualization are the social identities of participants. Culture provides a large repertoire of identities, as well as an extensive vocabulary of traits and other identity modifiers with which to reidentify people acting out of character vis-à-vis their situated identities. Moreover, in contrast to the observability, salience, and finality of behavior, social identities are more latent and tentative, hence more amenable to cognitive revision. In many situations people have to make inferences based on behavioral and other observable cues as to what identities others are announcing or claiming.

The second issue raised by the reconstruction principle concerns predicting when people will resort to reconceptualization and sentiment change, rather than action, in order to minimize affective deflection. According to the proposition at hand, affect control theory supposes that reconceptualization is instigated by events that produce inexorably large deflections—those that cannot be easily undone by restorative action. This supposition squares with the psychological literature suggesting that unexpected or high deflection events stimulate trait inferences about actors. On the other hand, the sociological literature suggests that people are reluctant to revise their initial definitions of the situation, even when events fail to confirm current sentiments. At some point, however, as disconfirming events pile up and deflection grows cumulatively large, it appears likely that inexorably large deflections will eventually instigate cognitive revisions, producing a change in current sentiments. The present state of affect control theory does not afford greater precision than this.

Event Assessment

10. Events are recognized within the framework of a defined situation.

11. Grammatical structures constrain event recognition.

Propositions 5 and 6 specify the cognitive constraints that influence event construction in general. Propositions 10 and 11 simply tailor these two propositions to the specific case of event recognition.

12. The likelihood of event interpretations is inversely related to the affective disturbances they produce.

This proposition is a corollary of the affect control principle (Proposition 8), which asserts that people try to experience events that confirm fundamental sentiments. Applied to event recognition, people should select low deflection events for interpretation:

> Given a set of different events to recognize or several possible interpretations of one event, the recognition that achieves maximal restoration (or minimal disturbance) of fundamental affects would be the one finally selected (Heise 1979, 13).

In this way, affective dynamics intrude into the later stages of event recognition, so that what we perceive in the social world is profoundly affected by what we feel. Event recognition is a product not only of cognitive processing but also of affective preferences.

For example, most people in our culture would judge mean, nasty acts as uncharacteristic of mothers, particularly if directed toward good and vulnerable object-persons like children. Thus, if a mother is perceived to be possibly threatening her child, an alternative act might be selected for perception in the final stages of event recognition—perhaps that she is only teasing, playing with, or bluffing the child. The event, "mother threatening child," is avoided, not because it is a cognitively implausible act, but because it disconfirms our cultural sentiments for mother and child.

While it is a corollary of the affect control principle (Proposition 8), Proposition 12 invokes the affective reaction principle (Proposition 7) as well; that is, it implies that a person has reacted affectively in a provisional manner to each of a number of possible events before selecting a low deflection one for recognition.

13. The perceived likelihood of events is inversely related to the affective disturbances they produce.

Like Proposition 12, Proposition 13 is derived directly from the affect control principle (Proposition 8), along with some auxiliary assumptions. According to the traditional sociological perspective, socially structured and established ways of acting are a reflection of cultural sentiments. Thus, events producing large affective deflections should be rare relative to low deflection events; and, to the extent that people are cognizant of this rarity, they should judge low deflection events as more likely than high deflection ones. Put another way, when low deflection, routine events occur, people will believe that the world is unfolding as it should.

Findings reported by Heise and MacKinnon (1988) support the proposition that the perceived likelihood of events varies inversely with the affective deflection they produce. Yet, affective deflections were shown to account for only about one–third of the variance in perceived likelihood in the major U.S. study (Heise and MacKinnon 1988), and the Canadian study (MacKinnon 1985) replicated this finding. Further analysis revealed that while events producing large deflections were, indeed, perceived as unlikely, many events producing little affective deflection were perceived as unlikely for apparently cognitive reasons.

When analysis was restricted to events with actors having standard institutional identities (e.g., family or legal identities), unlikely low deflection events were eliminated and high levels of predictability obtained. At the same time, analysis of events with institutionally vague identities (e.g., child, hero, as well as mildly deviant identities like smart aleck, loafer) produced especially low levels of predictability.

In explaining these results, Heise and MacKinnon reasoned that:

> Institutionally clear identities provide a definite cognitive context and automatically instigate affective processes that govern likelihood assessment (Fazio, 1985). However, identities that are vague may call for cognitive work along the lines of the cognitive availability model [see Kahneman, Slovic, and Tversky 1982] (1988, 149).

According to this line of reasoning, event descriptions involving institutionally vague identities demand so much cognitive work on the part of subjects that these events appear to be unlikely or farfetched at the outset. Hence, their perceived likelihood is independent of the affective deflections they produce.

Earlier statements of the theory supposed a much tighter connection between affective deflection, the perceived likelihood of events, and the actual probability of events occurring:

> Because expected events are those seen as "certain or probable" in the near future, the operation of minimizing deflections would seem to correspond to maximizing likelihoods, and a relation between deflections and the perceived likelihood of an event is implied if the theory is correct (Heise 1979, 67).

However, as suggested by the empirical analysis just discussed, the linkage between deflection and perceived likelihood is looser than originally thought. Apparently, some events producing little deflection are perceived as rare simply because there is no institutional support for their occurrence. Conversely, other events producing a lot of deflection might be considered likely because they are institutionally required, they are the only possibilities in certain situations, or because others are known to have a different definition of the situation or different sentiments.

Therefore, the property of events which deflection predicts may not be their objective probability, but rather their singularity. Events producing high levels of deflection appear as singular, unique, extraordinary; and when they occur, they are experienced as exceptional and unusual happenings.

Event Production

Like symbolic interactionism, affect control theory supposes that people construct, rather than simply react to, events—whether as observers in event recognition or as actors in event production. The preceding set of propositions dealt with event recognition. The present set covers event production.

14. A person develops actions by employing situational identities of self and other as actor and object.

15. Actions are produced within the constraints of relevant grammars.

According to Propositions 5 and 6, the construction of events is cognitively constrained by definitions of the situation and various kinds of grammatical structures. Propositions 10 and 11 apply these propositions to event recognition; Propositions 14 and 15, to event production.

The construction of an event involves filling in the slots of an ABO grammatical structure. Consider the situation where a professor has a neighbor's child as a student. For the professor as actor (A), the choice is simply the self in one of its situated identities (e.g., professor, neighbor); the selection of object-person (O), the student in one of his or her situated identities (e.g., student, neighbor). The possibility of either person adopting multiple identities in a situation complicates matters. (Perhaps the student announces both identities—student and neighbor.) And in groups larger than dyads, the choice of object-person becomes more problematic (e.g., How should a professor treat a neighbor's child in a triad including another student?). In any case, the theory assumes that the selection of identities for actor and object-person are circumscribed by cognitive grammars, and that within these boundaries, identity selections for actor and object positions of an ABO event are made so as to minimize affective disturbance.

Having settled upon the identities for the self (A) and other (O), the selection of a behavior (B) is constrained by the characteristic acts associated with social identities, applying the grammatical principle of projection rules to event production (e.g., The characteristic acts associated with the identity of professor are different and more limited than those for neighbor.). As implied by a situational theory of action, the choice of behavior also is constrained by logical and causal thinking about previous events in a sequence of interaction and those perceived as necessary to achieve a target event (e.g., a successful lecture).

16. The likelihood that a person will engage in one feasible behavior rather
than another is inversely related to the affective disturbances which the behaviors produce.

According to Propositions 14 and 15, cognitive constraints limit the selection of behavior to a set of "free variates," to use another linguistic metaphor.
However, because innumerable acts are usually conceivable for a given frame of
actor and object persons, this set might still be unmanageably large, and considering each possibility would tax the cognitive system beyond its capacity. Thus,
Heise (1979, 71) reasoned "that there must be a proactive system for choosing acts
that will reduce affective deflections within a given actor-object frame, just as there
is a reactive system determining affective responses to completed events."

Proposition 16, which covers the proactive system postulated by Heise,
proposes that after cognitive processes have narrowed the choice of behavior to a
smaller set, affective processes kick in to narrow the choice to a single option.
The theory predicts that a person responsible for the production of a new event
will select and implement an act that minimizes the deflection of transient or
outcome impressions from fundamental sentiments. Therefore, Proposition 16
is a corollary of the principle of affect control (Proposition 8). Because this principle is the explanatory core of the theory, the validity of Proposition 16 is predicated upon the validity of affect control theory itself, along with that of a few
additional, simplifying assumptions made for heuristic reasons (Heise 1979,
85–86).

As in event recognition, both affect control and affective reaction processes
are operative in event production. The theory implies that people have reacted affectively to a number of response options before selecting a low deflection event
for implementation.

The proactive system governing event production applies both to situations
where a sequence of events has already occurred and to those in which there has
been no recent history of interaction. In the latter case, there are no transient impressions built up from past events, and so retrievals of deflection-minimizing acts
are made on the basis of the fundamental sentiments of identities provided by the
definition of the situation.

For example, in an initial encounter between a male juvenile and a female
clerk, the Canadian equations and data predict that a clerk would expect a juvenile to "humor," "ask," "pay for," and "answer" her, while she might "explain,"
"consult," "consider," and "appease" the juvenile. These are acts which, according to predictions, would validate each person's situated identity in a first round
of interaction.

In the case where a history of interaction has preceded the production of a
new event, the transient sentiments built up by past events must be taken into account. In this instance, the logic of event production is as follows:

Fundamental sentiments reflect each person's situational status, power, and expressivity. The impacts of recent events are contained in transient feelings about each person. At any instant, the next event is an opportunity to transform current transient feelings into new transient feelings that verify fundamental sentiments and the social structure that they represent (Heise 1988, 14).

In a sequence of events, event production thus entails the selection of an act that confirms the sentiments for participants in the last event as much as possible within the constraints of the given actor-object frame (Heise 1979, 20–22, 71–72). If the preceding event has been disruptive, the process becomes one of generating restorative action.

For example, the disruptive event, "juvenile cheats clerk," generates a sizeable deflection, instigating the construction of positive restorative action. The optimal acts generated by the Canadian equations and data for the perpetrator of the deviant act would have the juvenile "answer" and "pay for." These compensatory acts would help to restore affective balance, as would those generated for the victim—"accommodate," "inform," and "caution."

At one time, it appeared plausible that restorative acts might be selected according to their capacity for reducing current deflections. However, Wiggins and Heise (1988, 156) found that the likelihood of restorative acts is governed simply by how much deflection they produce, not by how much improvement they offer. While current deflections do not determine the likelihood of subsequent events, they profoundly influence their character. If a person has been mortified, then subsequent events will accumulate to restore some of his or her lost status and power, while less pretentious responses will be built up when flattery has made a person's feelings too positive. An experimental study by Wiggins and Heise (1988) supported these predictions about the character of restorative response. Experience with simulation analyses indicates that a long sequence of subsequent events often is necessary to restore feelings to normal.

Now, the idea that an actor constructs events so as to minimize deflection does not mean that he or she behaves in order to confirm self-conceptualizations only, but rather his or her overall meaning system. This includes the meaning of the identity-situated self, to be sure, but also the meaning of the inferred identities of others and the behavior selected. Events, rather than the individuals creating them, are the units of analysis in affect control theory. The event unit of analysis recognizes the importance of the identity claims of others in social interaction and the integrity of the social act as a process in which people take into account each other's inferred meanings and definitions. Analyses of affect control equations for predicting behavior suggest that confirmation of sentiments for all three components of an ABO event are about equally important (Heise 1985).

By implication, events that confirm the sentiments of one person may be disconfirming for another if he or she has different sentiments or a different definition of the situation. Thus, situations may arise wherein participants unwittingly undermine each other's efforts to maintain meaning, perhaps generating large and unstable increases in deflection that make a sequence of events appear increasingly singular and incredible to both participants. According to the reconstruction principle (Proposition 9), participants may try to reconstruct each other's identity in such cases through attributions of dispositional traits or the imputation of appropriate labels. These specific reidentification processes are dealt with by Propositions 21–24.

17. In the course of validating social identities, people engage in role appropriate acts.

Identities are subjectively viewed social positions—those with which people identify and appropriate as self–conceptualizations. Therefore, in the process of confirming identities, people theoretically should be enacting social roles. Many of the social identities in the databases of affect control research correspond to conventional social roles from standard institutional contexts (e.g., doctor and patient, mother and child). Optimal acts for the self as actor can be considered role *intentions;* those generated for the other as actor, role *expectations.* Heise (1978, 1979) provided many examples of self-other dyads, illustrating how the affective system generates institutionally-scripted behavior corresponding to social roles. Chapter 6 of this book provides additional examples.

Simulations reveal that identity-confirming acts generated by the impression management equations often include the functional activities of social roles. For example, a (male) doctor expects a (female) patient to "consult" him and after she does so, he might "assist" and "rehabilitate" her, and she expects him to "rehabilitate" or "cure" her. To take a second example, a "boyfriend" might "kiss," "court," "massage," "enjoy," or "bed" a "girl," and he expects her to "dance with," "adore," "applaud," "enjoy," or "invite" him (predictions from the Canadian equations and data).

Affect control theory successfully generates institutionally-scripted behavior for deviant roles as well, simulating role interaction of deviant types with victims, cops, and judges. According to simulations from the Canadian study, for instance, a thief might "disconcert," "fool," "confuse," or "bait" a victim, while a victim might "watch," "implore," "obey," or "submit to" a thief; and a cop might "face," "engage," or "release" a suspect.

Besides generating actions for institutionally-scripted roles, the affective system allows people to improvise in novel circumstances—where scripted responses are unknown, for example, or where events occur that disconfirm situated identities and roles. It has been found that such disruptive or identity-disconfirming events evoke positive or negative sanctioning activities, depending on the circumstances. Examples of such role creativity are also presented in Chapter 6.

According to a classic definition, a social role consists of cultural expectations for behavior or attributes for incumbents of social positions in a society's social structure (Gross, Mason, and McEachern 1958). Affect control theory supposes that the evaluation and potency of social identities (viewed as internalized social positions) are directly translatable into status (prestige) and power, respectively, two basic dimensions of social structure (Kemper 1978; Kemper and Collins 1990). For example, the following EPA profiles for family roles are provided by male Ontario undergraduates: father (2.5, 2.6, –0.6), mother (2.5, 1.0, –0.1), son (1.1, 0.4, 1.2), and daughter (2.0, –0.2, 1.3). These profiles indicate that in an average Ontario middle–class family, father and mother have equally high status, commanding considerable voluntary compliance in family interaction. A daughter also has high status, while a son has considerably less status than other family members. The order of family roles from high to low on the power dimension is father, mother, son, and daughter. Thus, fathers can demand a great deal of involuntary compliance from other family members. As powerful subordinates of fathers, mothers also command considerable involuntary compliance, while children are relatively powerless in family situations—daughters more so than sons.

Emotions

18. The Emotion Principle: An interactant's emotion following an event reflects the outcome of the event and also the identity that the person is maintaining. Specifically, the emotion is a function of the transient impression of the interactant that was created by the event; and the discrepancy between this transient impression and the fundamental sentiment associated with the interactant's situated identity.

Affect control theory accepts the common understanding that emotions are episodic, situationally instigated, ephemeral affective experiences with physiological and cognitive components. In addition, the theory proposes a functional theory of emotions, conceptualizing emotions as cognitive signals, rich in affective meaning, that inform people how they are doing in establishing and validating situated identities in social interaction.

The emotions equations are mathematically derived from empirically-based amalgamation equations describing how modifiers combine with identities (Averett 1981; Averett and Heise 1988). The model reveals that emotions are a function of two factors: the transient impression of a person created by an event; and the discrepancy between this transient impression and the fundamental sentiment attached to a person's situated identity.

Each person in a situation really evokes two affective associations: a fundamental sentiment associated with the person's identity, and a current transient feeling built up from observed events at the scene. We register both at once by recognizing emotions. An emotion qualifies an identity in a way that describes where the transient impression of a person is relative to the fundamental sentiment for the person's identity (Heise 1988, 9).

The first factor corresponds to our common sense notions about emotions. Events that leave us in a positively evaluated state produce positive emotions; those that move us to a negatively evaluated state result in negative emotions. Events that produce transient feelings of activation produce lively emotions, and so on.

The second factor suggests that emotions have a relativistic aspect. That is, people do not generally experience highly positive emotions when events leave them in a positively evaluated state if that transient state is less positive than might be expected by virtue of their current identities (Heise 1988, 10). To paraphrase Smith-Lovin (1990, 245), if people are operating from situated identities of highly positive evaluation, the nice things that happen to them are simply what they expect. If, on the other hand, their identities are of relatively lower status, the positive acts of others directed toward them produce emotions bordering on elation. The deflection factor detects such dramatic shifts from fundamental levels of status, or power and activity, produced by events.

Simulations with the emotions model of affect control theory generate a theoretical EPA profile describing the feelings of participants experiencing specific events. Then, modifiers fitting this ideal profile are retrieved from the emotions database. For example, it is predicted that a mother who scolds her child should feel "irate" or "mad," and that the child being scolded should feel "uneasy" and "remorseful" (Canadian model and data). Additional examples are provided in Chapter 7.

19. People tend to maintain emotions that are characteristic of their salient identities.

Proposition 19 follows from Proposition 16 on the construction of identity-confirming action and Proposition 18 on emotions, with the additional understanding that salient identities are those that are invoked across many situations. When people are successful in maintaining impressions of themselves that are consistent with their salient identities, the deflection factor in the emotions model is eliminated, and the emotions people experience become a function solely of the impressions they create through their conduct. In this case, the outcome impressions produced by identity-confirming conduct match the sentiments for their identities, so the emotions people experience are consistent with their identity sentiments. Hence, the confirmation of positive identities should result in the experience of positive emotions; the validation of negative identities, negative emotions.

For example, a mugger should feel "angry," "furious," and "anxious" when events confirm his identity; a victim, "sorry," "apprehensive," and "disgusted"; and a boyfriend, "in love," "delighted," "happy," and "elated" (predictions from the Canadian model and data). In this way, the character of a person's emotions can be said to be profoundly influenced by the nature of his or her salient identities (Smith–Lovin 1990), so that we might speak of the *characteristic emotions* of social identities.

A person is not always successful in experiencing the emotions characteristic of a salient identity because emotions are buffeted by the identities of other participants and their actions. As discussed in Chapter 7, the identity-confirming emotions one person is trying to experience will be pulled in the direction of the characteristic emotions of another person with a different identity. Moreover, whether a person experiences the characteristic emotions of a salient identity depends upon whether the actions of other participants are identity-confirming. For example, a boyfriend who is ignored by a girl is predicted to feel "apprehensive," "irked," "dissatisfied," and "uneasy," rather than "in love" or "delighted." (Predictions from the Canadian equations and data).

20. Emotion displays facilitate intersubjective sharing of definitions of situations and of the operative social structures that are implied by definitions of the situation.

The above propositions and related discussions suggest that emotions are a person's subjective experience of a salient identity in the context of recent events. Emotions, however, are both subjectively experienced and externally manifested. By moving the emotional reaction to events out of the private field of subjective experience into the social arena of observable behavior, emotion displays reveal to others how a person is experiencing his or her identity. And, provided that there is some consensus about what events have occurred, emotion displays allow others to infer the identities and sentiments a person is trying to maintain in the situation.

> Definitions of a situation determine identities, and emotions arise as events do and do not confirm conventional levels of status, power, and expressivity—the EPA profile—for each person's situational identity. The emotions function as subjective and interpersonal signals concerning how the process of social confirmation is going (Averett and Heise 1988, 123).

Thus, emotion displays are an essential mechanism for establishing intersubjectivity in social interaction.

Emotion displays also reflect the social structural context of events. As Hochschild (1983) observes, the "emotion–management" or "emotion-work" required of people varies with their social structural position in the occupational and stratification hierarchies of a society. In this regard, inauthentic expressions of emotion may be coerced from subordinates in order to meet the status and deference demands of powerful others.

Cognitive Revisions

According to Proposition 13, the perceived likelihood of events is inversely related to affective deflection. This connection between affective deflection and perceived likelihood continues after an event has been recognized. High deflection events continue to appear unlikely, even if they have been perceived and cognitively registered. "In such cases, the mind accepts the event perceptually, but the event has to be revised mentally so that it makes more sense (Heise 1988, 12)."

The Reconstruction Principle (Proposition 9) holds that people resort to reconceptualization when they cannot confirm their fundamental sentiments through restorative action. For reasons discussed earlier, the identities of participants are more amenable to cognitive revision than their actions. So, rather than trying to reconceptualize an inconceivable act, people tend to change its affective meaning and perceived likelihood by redefining the situated identities of the people involved in it.

Two types of reidentification processes are modeled in affect control theory: *labeling,* the imputation of new social identities to replace those disconfirmed by recent events; and *dispositional inferences,* the attribution of explanatory traits. In either case, the intended effect is to render the disturbing event more credible by reidentifying the people implicated in it. Sociologists have generally focused on labeling, and psychologists on dispositional inferences, in explaining how people get reidentified in social interaction. The following three propositions deal with these two modes of reconceptualizing events. A fourth proposition deals with the effect of emotion displays on reidentification outcomes.

21. Social labelings render past events more credible by assigning interactants new identities that are confirmed by the past events.

Labeling processes can be applied either to the actor or object-person of an event. In actor reidentifications, the behavior (B) and object-identity (O) of an ABO event are givens, and the objective is to render the event more credible by redefining the actor (A) in a way that minimizes affective deflection. This is equivalent to asking, "Who would perform such a behavior on that object-person?" In the reidentification of object-persons, the actor (A) and behavior (B) are known quantities and the objective becomes the reidentification of the object-person (O). Depending upon the relative salience of the actor and object–person in an event, this is equivalent to asking, "What kind of person would a specified actor treat like that?" or, "What kind of person expects or seeks to be treated in that fashion by a specified actor?"

Whether an actor or object-person is to be reidentified, the given part of an event (BO or AB) implies the appropriate sentiments for the person being labeled (A or O), and these sentiments are generated by employing a variation of the impression management equations described in the discussion of Proposition 4. The predicted sentiments guide selection of an explanatory social identity that is situationally appropriate and that grammatically fits the event.

If the unusual event involves a socially stigmatized behavior, then the new identity selected for an actor is likely to be a stigmatized one as well—a "label" in the terminology of labeling theory. For example, consider the event, "The juvenile cheats the clerk." Simulations reveal that this event would be rendered more credible by reidentifying the actor as a "pusher," "mugger," or "evildoer" (predictions from the Canadian study). Alternatively, redefining the clerk as a "grouch," "miser," or "stuffed shirt" would, according to predictions, accomplish the same thing. The assignment of a stigmatized identity to the object-person in a deviant event accords with the devaluation of the victim literature.

Traditional labeling theory in sociology has focused upon the imputation of negative identities. From the perspective of affect control theory, however, the labeling process is the same whether or not social identities are stigmatized. For instance, a man who uplifts another man might be labeled a "pal" (a prediction from the Canadian study). Affect control theory supposes that the same process underlies the attribution of both stigmatized and socially esteemed identities, providing a more general model than that of traditional labeling theory in sociology (Heise 1979, 130–1).

22. Dispositional inferences render past events more credible by assigning interactants modified identities that are maximally confirmed by the past events.

A less dramatic form of reidentification than the substitution of entirely new identities for current ones is provided by *dispositional inferences*—modifying identities with explanatory personality traits (e.g., "aggressive"), status characteristics ("rich"), affective moods ("depressed"), or moral judgments ("evil"). Instead of redefining a juvenile as a "pusher" or "mugger" in the above labeling example, a similar reduction in affective disturbance can be accomplished by an appropriate dispositional inference. Affect control analysis based on the Canadian study suggests that a "ruthless," "manipulative," "mean," or "greedy" juvenile might cheat a clerk. Alternatively, the event can be rendered equally credible by redefining the victim as a "betrayed" clerk.

The modeling of dispositional inferences has the same starting point as the modeling of labeling processes: a sentiment (an EPA profile) for the person being reidentified is derived so as to minimize affective disturbance for the event in question. However, the inferred sentiment does not serve as a theoretical profile for the selection of a dispositional inference; instead, it defines a result that has to be achieved by modifying the person's current identity. In the case of actor reidentification, this is equivalent to asking, "What kind of person would treat a specified object-person in this way?" In the case of object-person reidentification, the question becomes, "What kind of person would a specified actor treat like that?" or, "What kind of person would expect or seek to be treated in that fashion by a specified actor?"—depending upon the relative salience of the actor and object-person.

The attribution equations of affect control theory are mathematically derived from the empirically-based *amalgamation equations* of the theory (Averett and Heise 1988). The amalgamation equations define the outcome impression produced when a person modifier is combined with a social identity, as in "a manipulative juvenile." In the derived attribution equations, the outcome impression corresponds to the inferred sentiment that would minimize affective deflection for the event in question, the social identity is the one which an actor (or object-person) already has, and the equations are solved to define the EPA profile for an appropriate modifier.

The attribution equations in affect control theory are identical to those used to predict emotions (see Proposition 18). Applied to emotions, however, emotion modifiers are selected to describe the relation between an identity and the transient impression created by an event, rather than to specify how a person's traits and other characteristics transform the sentiment attached to an identity into a different fundamental sentiment confirmed by a person's actions.

23. Dispositional inferences are a more likely form of reidentification than assignment of new identities through labeling processes.

Heider (1958) described lay people as "naive psychologists" trying to make sense of their interpersonal environment by attributing explanatory traits to other people. Reidentifying people through *dispositional inferences,* rather than labeling, has the cognitive advantage of keeping the original definition of the situation relatively intact (Heise 1988, 14), while trying to explain the unexpected or deviant conduct of individual actors. Therefore, attributions are probably a more common form of reidentification than labeling. Consider the earlier example, "juvenile cheats clerk." Reidentifying the actor via the inference of a dispositional trait ("manipulative" or "greedy"), rather than through the requisition of an entirely new identity ("pusher" or "mugger"), has much less cognitive impact on the original definition of the situation.

As labeling theorists have argued, casting a person into a new identity (say, "addict," "delinquent," or "alcoholic") may require a complex sequence of confrontation and negotiation with the person, along with the involvement of therapeutic and other social control agencies. In addition, its accomplishment may have undesirable implications for the identities of other people—for example, the self–imposed reidentifications of self experienced by parents when they participate in the attribution of stigmatized identities to their children. Moreover, in contrast to labeling, a dispositional inference does not have to be validated through an extended social process and can be employed tacitly to understand those whose actions belie their imputed identities.

These considerations beg the question of why labeling processes are ever invoked. One possibility is that reidentification through dispositional inferences can extend only so far. For example, no modifier can be attached to "friend" to account for an act of betrayal; only through labeling the friend a "traitor" can an event be generated confirming the actor's identity. Social labeling also is easily accomplished by people whose political or social power shields them from accountability. Members of the Canadian Parliament, for example, engage in name-calling with relative impunity because they cannot be sued for libel for anything said while the house is in session (within limits established by parliamentary rules; e.g., "liar" is proscribed).

24. Observers forego reassessments of an actor's character after disconfirming events if the person's emotion displays are appropriate to the person's conduct.

According to Proposition 20, emotion displays provide a basis for intersubjectivity by revealing the effects of recent events on each person's situated identity. The proposition at hand deals with the effects of emotion displays on the reidentification of participants.

Because the original reidentification model in affect control theory did not employ information on emotion displays, it assumed implicitly that a reidentified person invariably feels the emotion arising from identity confirming or disconfirming events. A more powerful model would take emotion displays into account as a basis for making inferences about the actual emotions a person is experiencing as a consequence of events. Consider the actor as the person to be reidentified. The question no longer is, "What kind of person would perform such an act on that object-person?" but rather, "What kind of person would engage in such conduct and feel the way this person feels?" (Heise 1989a). To extend an earlier example, "Who would cheat a clerk and feel *happy* about it?" In this case, both the actor's behavior and inferred emotions must be taken into account.

Suppose a person whose situated identity is of high status perpetrates an identity-disconfirming act that generates an unfavorable impression—say, a professor embarrassing a student by an unwittingly devastating remark in front of a class. By the emotion principle, the professor should experience an appropriately negative emotion like "ashamed" or "sorry." Now, if the professor displays such an appropriate emotion, there is no reason for observers to suppose that he or she is invoking an identity other than professor. Thus, the disruptive event cannot be affectively resolved and rendered more credible by simply assigning the person a new identity (a "cynic" perhaps). Instead, observers must address the disruptive event in some other way—through creating their own sanctioning acts, for example, or waiting upon a restorative act by the professor (say, "apologizing"), or by reidentifying another person in the event (deciding that, after all, the student is an "ass" deserving such a put-down.)

The properties of the revised reidentification model that accommodate emotion displays reveal, in fact, that the expression of appropriate emotions leads to status enhancement, while inappropriate emotion displays result in further stigmatization (Heise 1989a). The revised model also covers the effect of emotion displays on reidentification of object-persons. For example, a victim is expected to display negative emotions and risks being stigmatized for failing to do so. In addition to labeling, the revised model considers the effect of emotion displays on dispositional inferences made about known identities. Employing our earlier example for an actor reidentification, the problem becomes "What *kind* of juvenile would cheat a clerk and feel *happy* about it?"

A systematic analysis of the effects of emotion displays on reidentification outcomes is provided in Chapter 8.

Summary

The set of twenty-four propositions presented here covers the fundamental assumptions of affect control theory with respect to symbols, language, and affective meaning; its basic principles of affective reaction, affect control, and reconstruction; and the application of these assumptions and principles to event recognition, production, and reconceptualization, and to the instigation, expression, and function of emotions.[3] For the convenience of the reader, I have assembled the complete set of propositions at the end of this chapter.

In order to keep the presentation of the theory in this chapter as manageable as possible, I have limited my discussion of its fundamental assumptions to what is absolutely necessary. However, an elliptical treatment of the theory's suppositions about such complex issues as the relation between cognition and affect and the nature of human motivation is unsatisfactory. With a concise delineation of the theory in hand, the next chapter addresses these issues in more detail.

Symbols, Language, and Affective Meaning

1. Social interaction is conducted in terms of the social cognitions of interactants.
2. Language is the primary symbolic system through which cognitions are represented, accessed, processed, and communicated.
3. All social cognitions evoke affective associations.
4. Affective associations can be indexed to a large degree on universal dimensions of response.

Cognitive Constraints

5. Events are constructed in the framework of a definition of the situation that establishes the identities of participants.
6. Grammatical structures of various kinds constrain event construction.

Affective Response and Control

7. *The Affective Reaction Principle:* People react affectively to every social event.
8. *The Affect Control Principle:* People try to experience events that confirm fundamental sentiments.
9. *The Reconstruction Principle:* Inexorably large deflections instigate changes in the sentiments that are being used to appraise the meaning of events such that the new sentiments are confirmed optimally by recent events.

Event Assessment

10. Events are recognized within the framework of a defined situation.
11. Grammatical structures constrain event recognition.
12. The likelihood of event interpretations is inversely related to the affective disturbances they produce.
13. The perceived likelihood of events is inversely related to the affective disturbances they produce.

Event Production

14. A person develops actions by employing situational identities of self and other as actor and object.
15. Actions are produced within the constraints of relevant grammars.
16. The likelihood that a person will engage in one feasible behavior rather than another is inversely related to the affective disturbances which the behaviors produce.
17. In the course of validating social identities, people engage in role-appropriate acts.

Emotions

18. *The Emotion Principle:* An interactant's emotion following an event reflects the outcome of the event and also the identity that the person is maintaining. Specifically, the emotion is a function of the transient impression of the interactant that was created by the event; and the discrepancy between this transient impression and the fundamental sentiment associated with the interactant's situated identity.
19. People tend to maintain emotions that are characteristic of their salient identities.
20. Emotion displays facilitate intersubjective sharing of definitions of situations and of the operative social structures that are implied by definitions of the situation.

Cognitive Revisions

21. Social labelings render past events more credible by assigning interactants new identities that are confirmed by the past events.
22. Dispositional inferences render past events more credible by assigning interactants modified identities that are maximally confirmed by the past events.
23. Dispositional inferences are a more likely form of reidentification than assignment of new identities through labeling processes.
24. Observers forego reassessments of an actor's character after disconfirming events if the person's emotion displays are appropriate to the person's conduct.

3

COGNITION, AFFECT, AND MOTIVATION

The introduction of affect into the cognitive social psychology of Mead and traditional symbolic interactionism begs the question of what assumptions affect control theory makes about the relation between cognition and affect and about human motivation. With a comprehensive statement of the theory in hand, I will now address these issues.

Cognition and Affect

To add substance and focus to this discussion, I will first review the "primacy of cognition versus affect" debate, as the issue became known in cognitive social psychology. I will then discuss cognition and affect as *modes* and as *phases* of human consciousness; that is, as structure and process, respectively. An evaluation of the primacy issue on each front will frame my discussion of the assumptions affect control theory makes about the relationship between cognition and affect.

The Primacy of Cognition Versus Affect Debate

Commenting on the rediscovery of affect in the sociology of the 1980s, Collins (1986, 1349) observed that "the relationship between emotion and cognitions is not going to turn out to be a simple one." While his prospectus is probably correct, the issue (as I am certain Collins recognizes) has been around a long time.

For instance, contrary to the common assumption that cognitive awareness precedes emotional experience, the James–Lange theory of emotions (Lange and James 1922/1967) proposed that what we feel as emotion is simply our perception of the behavioral response and physiological arousal (e.g., trembling, crying, sweating, a pounding heart) that has already occurred in response to the perception of external stimuli (e.g., a threatening situation). This counterintuitive theory is encapsulated in the oft-quoted passage, "we feel sorry because we cry . . . afraid because we tremble" (James 1884/1922, 13). An important implication of the James-Lange theory of emotions—a rigid distinction between cognition and emotion (Solomon 1984)—will be addressed in the ensuing discussion.

The critique of Walter Cannon (1929) was hailed as a successful refutation of the James-Lange theory of emotions, and effectively snuffed out the issue for the next five decades. Among his specific criticisms, Cannon observed that the bodily responses are not rapid enough to account for our immediate perception of emotional experience.

However, the issue was rekindled in the 1980s by Zajonc, whose provocatively entitled 1980 article, "Preferences Need No Inferences," precipitated the primacy of cognition versus affect debate. On the basis of experimental evidence, which suggested that subjects could make affective preferences among stimuli presented below the threshold of cognitive awareness, Zajonc concluded that:

> affect and cognition are separate and partially independent systems and although they ordinarily function conjointly, affect . . . [can] be generated without a prior cognitive process. It could, therefore, at times precede cognition in a behavioral chain (1984, 117).

Representing the cognitive position, Lazarus (1982, 1984) countered that:

> cognitive activity is a necessary precondition for emotion because to experience an emotion, people must comprehend—whether in the form of a primitive evaluative perception or a highly differentiated symbolic process—that their well-being is implicated in a transaction for better or worse. A creature that is oblivious to the significance of what is happening for its well-being does not react with an emotion (1984, 120).

Zajonc (1984, 121) argued that Lazarus's broad definition of cognition blurs the distinction between cognition and sensation. As a result, the proposition that cognitive appraisal is a precondition for emotion is true by fiat and, like all tautologies, cannot be falsified. Drawing a much sharper distinction between cognition and sensation, Zajonc proposed that the latter is relatively fixed and untransformed by mental processes, while the former involves some degree of mental work—operations that transform pure sensory input into a subjectively available form or reactivate it from memory.

Employing a similar tactic, Lazarus (1984) argued that Zajonc's position is predicated upon a rather undemanding definition of emotion, one that includes reflex reactions, sensory preferences, and aesthetic reactions; and while these phenomena are often accompanied by emotional experiences, they may in some instances be nothing more than "cold cognitions."

As formulated by Zajonc and Lazarus, the primacy debate has no resolution. By casting his definitional net wide in the case of emotion, while drawing it close in the case of cognition, Zajonc is able to capture research findings suggesting that some emotional experience is independent of cognitive appraisal. By a similar procedure in the case of cognition, Lazarus is able to maintain that cognitive appraisal is a necessary precondition for all emotional experience. Until this conceptual problem is resolved, the primacy issue will remain an unsolved problem in the social psychology of emotions. However, Zajonc's (1984, 118) observation that it "cannot be fully resolved until we have a full understanding of consciousness" suggests a way out of this conceptual impasse.

Cognition and Affect as Modes of Consciousness

Plato distinguished among three components of the human 'spirit'—*cognition, affect,* and *conation*—and since at least the time of Kant, the three categories of consciousness have generally been recognized as 'knowing,' 'feeling,' and 'willing.' These have appeared in psychology as traditional textbook categorizations of psychological states and in sociology as the "orientations" of the actor to the situation of action (Parsons and Shils 1951; Wallace 1983).[1]

As implied by the preceding discussion, the primacy of cognition versus affect debate originated in large part from reifying these traditional categories of consciousness. However, while analytically distinguishable, cognition, affect, and conation are not completely separable and independent components of human consciousness. Charles Peirce clearly recognized this point. Although over a century old, his analysis of consciousness provides a useful viewpoint from which to examine the relation between cognition and affect.

Rejecting the traditional categorization of consciousness, Peirce proposed that consciousness is simply a continuum of cognitive awareness in which 'knowing' is inextricably bound up with elements of 'feeling' and 'willing':

> . . . every phenomenon of our mental life is more or less like cognition. Every emotion, every burst of passion, every exercise of will, is like cognition. But modifications of consciousness which are alike have some element in common. Cognition, therefore, has nothing distinctive and cannot be regarded as a fundamental faculty (Peirce 1956, 94).

On the one hand, every emotion implicates a cognition in the sense that "whenever a man feels, he is thinking of *something* . . . passions . . . only come to consciousness through tinging the *objects of thought*" (1956, 238). The reason emotions appear to us "more as affections of self than other cognitions" (1956, 238) is that they occur when a person is confronted with cognitively perplexing situations that disrupt the flow of consciousness:

> The emotions . . . arise when our attention is strongly drawn to complex and inconceivable circumstances. Fear arises when we cannot predict our fate; joy, in the case of certain undescribable and peculiarly complex sensations. . . . The indescribable, the ineffable, the incomprehensible com-

monly excite emotion; but nothing is so chilling as a scientific explanation (Peirce 1956, 238).

Viewed this way, an "emotion is always a simple predicate [an assertation such as "I am afraid"] substituted by an operation of the mind for a highly complicated predicate ["I don't know what's going to happen"]"(1956, 238).

Just as every emotion implicates an underlying cognition, every cognition evokes a feeling, however slight. For example, feelings of low intensity occur when we recognize the meaning of a sign: "[T]he first proper significant effect of a sign is a feeling produced by it . . . which we come to interpret as evidence that we comprehend the proper effect of the sign" (Peirce 1931, 1935, 1958, Vol.5, 476). Peirce called these feelings of recognition "emotional interpretants" (emotional meanings), which mediate any further effects of a sign on an interpreter. These include "energetic interpretants" (motivational meanings) and "logical interpretants" (the meanings of intellectual concepts) (Almeder 1980, 29–30).

In short, Peirce viewed consciousness as a continuum of cognitive awareness and thought in which affect is implicated at every point. Affect runs the gamut from those mild feelings associated with the recognition of symbols and other signs to those more intense feelings we call emotions that "pop up" when cognitive complexities block the flow of consciousness. Feelings and emotions implicate cognition; and every cognition is accompanied by affect, if only those mild feelings resulting from the recognition of signs. Thus, for Peirce, cognition is not a separate component of consciousness, but rather its essence; and, at the same time, all cognitions evoke some level of affective arousal.

Having rejected the traditional categorization of consciousness into cognition, affect, and conation, Peirce derived what he considered to be its true, exhaustive categories from a phenomenological analysis of perceptual experience. He referred to these, in his own inimitable fashion, as "Firstness," "Secondness," and "Thirdness."

Firstness refers to the simple and unanalyzable quality of immediate perception, that which is experienced but not as yet conceptualized: "[F]eeling, the consciousness which can be included with an instant of time, passive consciousness of quality, without recognition or quality." Secondness occurs in our experience of action and reaction—interruption, shock, intrusion, compulsion, vividness: "[C]onsciousness of an interruption into the field of consciousness, sense of resistance, of an external fact, of another something." Thirdness includes mediation, generality, habit or law, and continuity, and accounts for our sense of the intelligibility and meaningfulness of our experience: "[S]ynthetic consciousness, binding time together, sense of learning, thought." For Peirce, these three categories are "congenital tendencies of the mind" comprehending all of mental experience; and, while he acknowledged that they are analytically separable, he maintained that they cannot be experienced in isolation from one another (Peirce 1956, 93–97; Almeder 1980, 123–4).

Peirce's analysis of consciousness provides conceptual insight into the primacy issue. The kind of affective sensations Zajonc deals with, those more felt than recognized, fall under Peirce's category of Firstness, as do the "primitive evaluative perceptions" alluded to by Lazarus. Cognitive appraisals in which a person becomes cognizant of an "interruption" or "intrusion" of external events lie in Secondness. More fully developed cognitive appraisals, those involving "a highly differentiated symbolic process" (Lazarus 1984, 124) of conscious, deliberate, and rational thought, lie in Thirdness.[2]

In light of Peirce's analysis of consciousness, Zajonc's mistake lies in his restriction of cognition to the highly symbolic level of consciousness Peirce calls Thirdness.[3] As Epstein (1984, 76) puts it, "cognitively oriented students of emotion would not deny that affect occurs in the absence of conscious cognition. They believe, however, that subconscious cognitive processes normally mediate emotions."

Despite the insights provided by Peirce's analysis, I am not proposing that we replace the traditional categorization of consciousness with his phenomenological categories of Firstness, Secondness, and Thirdness. I believe that the distinction between cognition and affect is an analytically useful one, particularly at the extremes of "cold" cognitions (where affective arousal is of low intensity) and "hot" cognitions (where arousal is most pronounced); or, alternatively, at the extremes of affective experience largely unmediated by cognition and that conjoined with a high level of cognitive awareness and appraisal. The principal lesson to be taken from Peirce's analysis of consciousness, as I see it, is that we should dispense with the *rigid* distinction between cognition and affect that spawned the primacy debate in the first place and which has no resolution when cast in these terms. The issue can be resolved, I will now argue, only by stepping outside the conceptual boundaries of the primacy debate and recognizing the inextricability and complementarity of cognition and affect, rather than arguing over their relative primacy.

The idea that cognition and affect are not completely separable components of consciousness which, for convenience, we might call the *principle of inextricability*, finds support in Duffy's (1934) argument that the "distinction between 'emotion' and other patterns of reaction [like cognitive states] is one of degree rather than of kind" (1934, 197), that "emotion does not represent a unique state . . . merely one end of a continuum" (1934, 187).[4] The inseparability of cognition and affect in consciousness is wonderfully captured in Collins' statement that "we feel the emotions . . . in the various ideas with which we think" (1990, 34).

Ortony, Clore, and Foss's (1987) analysis of the "referential structure of the affective lexicon" also supports this idea. While invoking the traditional categories of cognition, affect, and conation, they acknowledged "that Mental conditions always have a significant Cognitive component or a significant Affective component, and sometimes both" (1987, 351). This led them to differentiate between terms that have affect as their predominant referential focus (e.g., "broken–hearted," "thrilled") from other words that have both significant affective and cognitive components (e.g., "confident," "uninterested"). In an empirical test of their conceptual work, Clore, Ortony, and Foss (1987, 760) found that people find it difficult to distinguish pure affective states like "angry" and "afraid" from intense cognitive ones like "astonished" and "bewildered." This may occur, they concluded, because cognitive states appear more emotional as they become more intense or, alternatively, because intense cognitive states are more likely to evoke emotions.

The idea that cognition and affect are inextricable components of human consciousness can also be identified in Scheff's (1979, 1984b) analysis of emotion from the symbolic interactionist conceptualization of the self. Scheff proposed that the conscious awareness of feeling depends upon the relative dominance of the self as subject (Mead's "I") and the self as object (Mead's "me"). Drawing upon the metaphor of dramatic criticism, he describes the dominance of the observer role ("me") as an "overdistanced" state; the dominance of the participant role ("I") as an "underdistanced" state; and an equal balance between the two as a state of "aesthetic distance." In overdistanced states, according to Scheff, there is a relative lack of feeling; in underdistanced states, a relative preponderance of feeling; and in a state of aesthetic distance, a relative balance between feeling and cognition.

Finally, the inextricability of cognition and affect is a conceptual cornerstone of cognitive/constructionist theories of emotions (see Chapter 7). Representing an extreme statement of this position, Solomon (1984) rejects outright the distinction between cognition and affect embodied in the James-Lange theory of emotions (Lange and James 1922/1967). For Solomon, an emotion is not just the perception of a physiological sensation in reaction to the perception of an external stimulus, "it is essentially an interpretation, a view of its cause (more accurately, its 'object') and (logically) consequent forms of behavior" (1984, 249). That an emotion "also has biological backing and includes sensation," he argues, "is inessential to understanding the emotion" (1984, 249). Viewed this way, affect and cognition are not simply inextricable; they become, as Franks (1989, 97) observes, "fused."

In line with Solomon's fusion of cognition and affect, Franks (1989) describes emotions—more correctly, sentiments—as "thought emotions" (1989, 98), the cognitive appraisal of the personal relevancy of situations, a kind of thinking that answers to its own particular grammar, cultural metaphors, and normative rules. When we deal with the experience of emotion, Franks argues, we should focus not on physiological sensations but rather on "feelings"—qualitative experiences that lie on a continuum between physiological arousal (sensations) and personally distanced, cold cognitions. Thus defined, feelings are emotional experiences distinct from sensations and responsive to the kind of social and cultural influences described above. Franks' view of cognition "as a continuum from distanced, impersonal, 'cold' inputs to very personal engrossment and 'hot' involvement" (1989, 99) resonates with my own conceptualization of conciousness as a continuum of cognitive awareness implicating affect in different levels of intensity.

Now, while the principle of inextricability refines our understanding of the relation between cognition and affect, it does not completely resolve the issue. The fact remains that much of our psychological experience appears to be either predominantly cognitive or predominantly affective in nature: "cold" and "hot" cognitions experienced, to an appreciable extent, as qualitatively distinct psychological states. How, then, do we reconcile these seemingly contradictory aspects of human consciousness and comprehend the relation between them? The answer lies in the *principle of complementarity.*

Independently discovered by the psychologist William James (1890) and by the physicist Niels Bohr (1927), the principle of complementarity proposes that what appear to be mutually exclusive phenomena are manifestations of some other underlying unified phenomenon, and that both are necessary to understand it. A discussion of complementarity applied in part to the issue at hand, the relation between cognition and affect, can be found in Stephenson's twin articles (1986a, 1986b)[5], which I now summarize.

James applied complementarity to bring together under a single principle the *transitive* and *substantive* parts of thought—employing the metaphor of a bird in flight, the "flights" and "perchings" (1890, 243) of "the stream of thought, of consciousness, of subjective life" (1890, 239). The substantive part of a thought is conveyed by the semantic denotations and syntactic connections of the printed or written statement; the transitive, by the inflections and affective overtones of the person speaking it. The empirical referent of the former is normative fact; that of the latter, the idiosyncratic meanings and feelings of the speaker, "the whole gamut of human emotion, of skepticism, wonderment, and every other sentiment" (Stephenson 1986a, 523). While empirically separable (albeit, if only by introspection) and mutually exclusive, the transitive and substantive are essential components of any thought: "The one precludes the other. Yet they are part of the same sentence, the same individual whole for a person, whoever spoke it (Stephenson 1986a, 523)." And, since both are necessary to understand human thought or consciousness, Stephenson argues, the principle of complementarity must be invoked in psychology, just as it has been in quantum physics.

Bohr (1950) himself extended the principle of complementarity from its application to the conflicting images of subatomic phenomena implied by quantum and classical physics—the wave-particle duality, for example—to human psychology. In view of the duality of thought and sentiment, the cognitive and affective aspects of human consciousness, he recognized the necessity of invoking the principle of complementarity to accommodate the two.

To bring the preceding discussion to a close, there are two principles which, in my view, describe the relation between cognition and affect as modes of consciousness: (1) the principle of inextricability, the supposition that cognition and affect are never completely separable components of consciousness, but rather a matter of relative preponderance; and (2) the principle of complementarity, the supposition that at the extremes of "cold" and "hot" cognitions, where cognition and affect appear to be opposing and mutually exclusive aspects of psychological experience and where the distinction becomes an analytically meaningful and empirically useful one, cognition and affect can be treated as complementary manifestations of that single, unified phenomenal process we call 'mind' or 'consciousness.' Thus, while Franks clearly argues for the inextricability of cognition and affect, his description of the two "as different sides of the same process" (1989, 97) appears to invoke, at the same time, the principle of complementarity.

Yet, it might seem that the principles of inextricability and complementarity are inherently contradictory, that the validity of one would logically exclude the other. To the extent that the principle of complementarity has stemmed from the rigid distinction between cognition and affect implied by the James–Lange theory of emotions, then one might consider whether the principle is essential to account for the relation between cognition and affect once their inextricability in human consciousness is recognized. However, if one treats inextricability as an ontological principle and complementarity as an epistemological/methodological one, the contradiction largely vaporizes. And, while this resolution will undoubtedly prove less than satisfactory to some readers, especially those of the cognitive/constructionist position with which I identify in some respects (see Chapter 7), it is nonetheless a heuristic one that has enabled this researcher to make conceptual sense of affect control theory and get on with his research.

The principles of inextricability and complementarity are core assumptions of affect control theory, albeit implicit and unstated until now.

The inextricability principle is implied by the theory's assumption of a necessary, operative interface between cognition and affect, exemplified by its general propositions that all cognitions evoke affective associations and that affective reaction and processing, in turn, engenders new cognitions—conceptualizations of events for recognition or production and reconceptualization of those that have already occurred.

As for the principle of complementarity, the theory's recognition of two systems of meaning—denotative (cognitive or conceptual) and connotative (affective)—parallels James' distinction between substantive and transitive thought; and, like James, affect control theory recognizes these seemingly contradictory systems of meaning as complementary and essential components of psychological experience. Conceptually,

> the translation back and forth from the abstract quantitative domain of affect to the concrete qualitative domain of cognitive experience is possible because, so to speak, constellations of remembered identities and acts exist in

affective space, and each serves as a possible entrance to the affectual domain or as an exit back to the conceptual realm (Heise 1979, 94).

While affect control theory and research is framed in terms of linguistically mediated thought, the theory assumes that affect control principles are operative whether or not cognitions are symbolically represented and conscious. In fact, the theory accepts that affect-evoking cognitions, whether verbally coded and accessible or not, normally lie at a preconscious, prereflective level (see discussion on verbal and non–verbal language systems in Chapter 1).

This additional assumption finds support in the cognitive social psychology literature. Epstein (1984, 65), for example, proposed that "everyone develops a personal theory of reality . . . a preconscious conceptual system that automatically structures a person's experience and directs his or her behavior" and that "once a conceptual system is formed, preconscious cognitions are the major sources of emotion." To the extent that personal theories of reality embodied in preconcious conceptual systems are viewed as culturally influenced and encoded in language, this idea resonates with the ethnological concept of "world view" in culture studies.

Combining ideas from behaviorism with the associative network theory of emotions (Leventhal 1980), Thoits (1984) suggests how preconscious conceptual systems become established in early socialization. Associations among four components of conscious emotional experience (situational cues, physiological changes, expressive gestures, and feeling labels), she argues, "are learned and repeatedly reinforced through the indicative use of language" (1984, 223); and that once established, these associative reactions occur with minimal cognitive mediation. At the same time, she maintains that "only through language . . . do we consciously know what we feel and, implicitly, why" (1984, 223. Emphasis removed.).[6]

In his comparison of Mead and modern behaviorism, Baldwin (1985) provides a similar account of how language acquires the capacity to elicit affective response. When a child learns to associate words with the same objects, experiences, and events that others do, words become significant symbols, and conscious awareness occurs. At the same time, words become conditioned stimuli associated with the unconditioned stimuli of "emotional reflexes," so that eventually they become capable of eliciting emotions on their own accord. Learning the verbal designation of objects and experiences, and hence their emotional associations, Baldwin argues, is further strengthened and modified by mechanisms of reinforcement and social learning.

Cognition and Affect as Phases of Consciousness

While the primacy debate was fueled by a conceptually rigid distinction between cognition and affect as *modes* of human consciousness viewed as structure, it also drew sustenance from misconceptions about cognition and affect as *phases* of consciousness conceived as process. Assuming for the sake of argument that cognition and affect are at least partially independent modes of consciousness, the question of causal primacy makes sense only from the viewpoint of an outdated, unidirectional causal model.

On the other hand, the primacy issue becomes a moot point if one supposes a reciprocal relationship, especially a cybernetic one, between cognition and affect. Widely suggested in the literature (Candland 1977; Epstein 1984; Gordon 1981; Lewis and Rosenblum 1978; Scheff 1985a), this idea has been nicely articulated by Mook (1987, 449):

> As to which comes first, and what causes what, there probably is no single answer for all cases. After all, none of these mental events occurs instantaneously and then stops. A process is set in motion that may bounce information back and forth between "cold" thought and "hot" emotion in a dazzlingly complex trajectory. There is no reason to think that the process has only one starting point, or follows only one sequence each time.

Toward the end of the primacy debate, Lazarus himself conceded this point.

> Although I maintain that cognition (of meaning) is a necessary precondition for emotion, this does not imply that emotions, once elicited, do not affect cognitions. Emotions appear to be powerful influences on how we think and interpret events. They are the result of cognition but in turn affect cognition. The causal linkages one perceives among emotion, motivation, and cognition depend, in part, on where in an ongoing behavior sequence one arbitrarily stops the action (Lazarus 1984, 126. Emphasis removed.)

Now, according to affect control theory, three principles govern the relation between cognitive and affective processing—the affective reaction, affect control, and reconstruction principles delineated in the preceding chapter. Taken together, these describe a cybernetic process of lower- and higher-order feedback wherein past cognitions evoke affective reaction and current affective states influence subsequent cognitions. In fact, affect control theory is an extension of Power's (1973) hierarchical control theory of perception to the affective dynamics of psychological processing (Heise 1979, 2).

Motivation

As stated in Chapter 2, affect control theory supposes that the confirmation of meaning through the minimization of affective deflection is the basic motivational principle in human social behavior. In this section, I establish a theoretical basis for this supposition. By showing that identity–confirmation is a derivative of this general motivational principle, I connect the affect control theory of motivation to the interactionist concept of the self. But, first, in order to lay a conceptual foundation for this discussion, I track the concept of motivation from dispositional and incentive theories in psychology to theories in sociology based upon language, identification, and control.

The Concept of Motivation

The question of human motivation has preoccupied psychologists for decades, and philosophers for centuries before them. Stemming from the same Latin verb, *emovere* (to move), motivation and emotion are closely related constructs. This is evident in theories which propose that emotion be treated as a "dynamic" or motivational principle of behavior (Leeper 1948; Webb 1948), rather than a phenomenological category of psychological experience. On the other hand, alleging the conceptual ambiguity and uncertain empirical referents of the two constructs, others have proposed that both concepts be replaced with conceptually clearer, more fundamental, and empirically verifiable dimensions of behavior (Duffy 1941, 1948; Bolles 1967).

Motivation appeared in the psychology of the late nineteenth and early twentieth centuries in the form of "instinct," an innate pattern of behavior, which remained a popular motivational concept until about 1920 when it was replaced by "drive," an unpleasant or aversive internal state activated by conditions of deprivation. Drive remained the dominant motivational construct in psychology until about 1950, when it became largely replaced by the concept of "incentive"—an external event, object, condition, or stimulus in the environment of an organism inducing a state of arousal that energizes response (Cofer 1972).

Incentive theories of motivation propose that organisms tend to approach positive incentives (e.g., food) and to avoid negative ones (painful objects or events). In addition, learned associations between situational stimuli and gratifying or painful objects and events acquire incentive value through secondary reinforcement, becoming capable of evoking approach and avoidance response on their own accord. Because incentive theories of motivation imply goal-oriented behavior, they describe human motivation more accurately than theories invoking predispositional constructs like instincts or drives (Cofer 1972, 92).

An early incentive theory of motivation proposed by McClelland and his associates (1953) suggested that the anticipation of outcomes along the hedonic dimension of pleasantness/unpleasantness sets off affective reactions that provide the energy for mobilizing behavior. Anticipation can be evoked either by internal cues (deprivation) or external ones (situational stimuli). Cues acquire their capacity for evoking affective reaction through their earlier association with a full-blown affective experience. While cues function to direct behavior through their association with affective experience, according to McClelland, the affective reaction or arousal itself is the essence of motivation.[7] Cofer and Appley (1964) attempted a generalization of incentive theories of motivation like that of McClelland and associates.[8]

Of the two functions generally attributed to motivation in the psychological literature—the "energization" of response through affective arousal and response selection or direction (Cofer 1972, 34, 150), incentive theories restrict the function of motivation to the first. However, this becomes tantamount to treating motivation as if it were coextensive with affect, thereby rendering one or the other construct conceptually redundant. Moreover, because human motivation, as commonly understood, implies more than randomly directed response, we would have to search for additional constructs to explain the direction of motivated behavior. And, "accounting for the course of events . . . explaining the direction taken by an individual's activities" is, after all, the major problem facing social psychologists (Shibutani 1968, 330). While the affective mode of consciousness explains the energization of response, the cognitive and conative modes must be invoked to account for its direction.[9]

A more comprehensive theory of human motivation that takes into account the full range of human consciousness, and hence both the energization and direction of behavior, can be found in *action theory* (Parsons and Shils 1951). When Parsons and Shils (1951, 59n) state that "it is through the cathexis of objects that energy or motivation, in the technical sense, enters the system of the orientation of action," they are, in effect, proposing an incentive theory of motivation. However, their treatment of the "motivational orientation" of the actor—"those aspects of the actor's orientation to his situation which are related to actual or potential gratification or deprivation of the actor's need-dispositions"—invokes all three modes of human consciousness (1951, 58–59). Besides the cathectic, or affective attachment to objects (1951, 10n.), they include the cognitive ("the various processes by which an actor sees an object in relation to his system of need-dispositions") and the evaluative or conative ("the processes by which an actor organizes his cognitive and cathectic orientations into intelligent plans"). Notwithstanding its outdated, predispositional concept of "need-dispositions" (Parsons and Shils 1951, 9–10), action theory provides a more adequate conceptualization of human motivation than incentive theories in psychology and moves us closer to one that is consistent with symbolic interactionism and affect control theory.

Despite its merits, the motivational theory contained in action theory has a major deficit in that it fails to explicate the role of language in motivated behavior. Yet, it is only through the symbolic representation made possible by language that human organisms are able to relate to incentives as objects of reflective consciousness, to assess alternative means for realizing goal objects, and to anticipate outcomes of actions in terms of their instrumental value.[10] Moreover, it is only through the names with which people designate themselves—the social identities they have appropriated as self-conceptualizations—that goal objects become personally meaningful.

In a brief article published the same year as Parsons and Shils' action theory, Foote (1951) laid the foundation for a theory of motivation based upon language and identification. His conceptualization of motivated behavior as "distinguished by its prospective reference to ends in view, by being more or less subject to conscious control through choice among alternative ends and means" (1951, 15) coincides with action theory. At the same time, judging by his scathing attack on predispositional theories of motivation, I am certain that Foote would have rejected outright Parsons and Shils' construct of "need–dispositions." Besides being "oblivious to the function of language in motivated behavior" (1951, 21), Foote argues, dispositional theories are inherently tautological because predispositions must be inferred from the behavior which they are drawn upon to explain.

According to Foote, the defining feature of human motivation, ignored by predispositional and incentive theories and given short shrift by action theory, is the "symbolic structuring" of motivated behavior.

> If the regularities in human behavior are organized responses to situations which have been classified more or less in common by the actors in them, then names motivate behavior. It is by analysis of the function of language, and especially of names ascribed to categories of people, that we can dispense with predispositions and yet maintain a theory of motivation subject to empirical testing (1951, 18).

Foote identified two ways in which language functions in human motivation.

First, by naming our "ends-in-view," language provides us with the capacity for remembering and conceptualizing previously experienced gratifications as values. "In place of predisposition, therefore, it is necessary and sufficient to put memory . . . by virtue of which we can call up the present images of past consummations of acts" (1951, 20). The reference to prior experience does not constitute tautological reasoning, Foote insists, because "the operation of values is advisory, not executive" (1951, 19). That is, because a person must consider even the most habitual act to be situationally appropriate before it is implemented, the final determination of an act is made in the immediate context of the situation, not prior to it.

Second, by designating social identities, Foote asserts, language enables people to locate themselves in and identify with organized social activity. A person must know who he or she is in order to ascertain his or her role in a situation and behave with any degree of motivation: "A rose by any other name may smell as sweet, but a person by another name will act according to that other name" (1951, 17). Identification, the "appropriation of and commitment to a particular identity or series of identities . . . is the key which unlocks the physiological resources of the human organism, [and] releases the energy . . . to perform the indicated act" (1951, 17–19). By the same token, cognitive uncertainty or confusion about one's situated identity takes the meaning out of one's action and inhibits the mobilization of response. Without identification, organized social activity, as epitomized in Mead's concept of the "game," would remain "a sort of empty bottle of behavior and formal roles, without motive or incentive save for the undifferentiated physiological necessity to dispense energy and kill time" (1951, 16).

Bringing together the two ways in which language functions in human motivation, Foote argues that our named "ends-in-view" would have little if any incentive value if human organisms lacked the capacity for naming or identifying self because "value only exists or occurs relative to particular identities—at least value as experienced by organisms which do not live in the mere present . . . devoid of self and unaware of impending death" (1951, 20–21).

In contrast to incentive theories in psychology, Foote's identity theory of motivation encompasses both the energization and direction of response.

> In a sentence, we take motivation to refer to the degree to which a human being, as a participant in the ongoing social process in which he necessarily finds himself, defines a problematic situation as calling for performance of a particular act, with more or less anticipated consummations and consequences, and thereby his organism releases the energy appropriate to performing it (1951, 15).

The definition of the situation thus precedes the energization of response and provides direction to human behavior.[11]

While Foote's emphasis on language and identification anticipates the affect control theory of motivation discussed in the next section, it lacks one essential ingredient: an explicit statement of control. For this, we must turn to Mead. While Mead may have little to offer with respect to the energization of social behavior, due to his neglect of affect, he certainly had a lot to say concerning its *direction* (Shibutani 1968, 331). For Mead, behavior is given direction as an organism successively adjusts to constantly changing circumstances in pursuit of a goal. The central mechanism controlling this succession of self-adjusted responses is negative feedback, through which the results of one's current actions and self-images inform subsequent behavior. (Mead's cybernetic model of human behavior is elaborated in the following chapter.)

Affect Control Theory and Motivation

In the preceding section, I argued that an adequate theory of human motivation must: (1) address both the energization or mobilization of behavioral response and its selection or direction; (2) invoke, by implication, all three modes of human consciousness (cognition, conation, and affect); and (3) incorporate features of motivated behavior that are distinctively, though not exclusively, human—language, identification, and control. In this section, I show how the motivational theory contained in affect control theory meets these conditions.

With respect to the first function of motivation, the energization of response, affect control theory proposes that affective deflection—the discrepancy between fundamental sentiments and the transient feelings produced by events—provides the energy for mobilizing response, where response is defined broadly to encompass both overt and covert behavior. As to the second function of motivation, response selection, or direction, the theory proposes that events are selected for recognition or implementation in inverse proportion to the amount of deflection they produce or, equivalently, according to their capacity for confirming a person's fundamental sentiments for his or her situated identity and those of other interactants.

What is the "incentive" in this theory of motivation? At the most general level, affect control theory supposes, like Mead and symbolic interactionists, that people try to experience an orderly, knowable world as much as possible within the vagaries and vicissitudes of everyday existence. In vernacular terms, people "get off on" confirming meanings, and affect control theory accepts that the confirmation of both "cold" and "hot" cognitions, cognitive problem-solving as well as sentiment–confirming activity, can be motivating and rewarding.

However, because deflection signals the maintenance or disruption of the social symbolic system of meaning guiding a person's participation in social interaction, minimizing deflection becomes an important condition for experiencing an orderly, knowable social existence; hence, it is an important incentive in human motivation. Thus, over and above their instrumental value in obtaining valued ends, the confirmation of cognitive meaning and the solution of cognitively perplexing problems can constitute cathected goals or incentives in their own right.

Principles of discrepancy like deflection operate on both the input and output side of motivated behavior. Applied to disconfirmed expectations on the stimulus side, discrepancy "offers both the motivation and reward for trying to make sense of the world: interest in discrepancy as motive, and resolution of the discrepancy—recognition—as reward" (Mook 1987, 435). Applied to intentions or actions on the response side of motivated behavior, disruption motivates modifications of familiar, routine actions and mastery of the novel situation, which is its own reward (Mook 1987, 439–441, after Mandler 1984. See also n.2, Chapter 2 of this book.).

The incentive of minimizing deflection becomes evident when through role-taking a person imaginatively acts out what another person might do next, or tries to make sense out of what has already transpired by reidentifying an actor whose actions belie a claimed or imputed identity. When a person is not only an observer but a participant in an event, however, the incentive of minimizing deflection takes on a decidedly personal tone because it involves confirming his or her identity-situated self. Hence, identity-confirmation is an important instance of the general incentive of minimizing deflection.

The idea that "identities are important motivators of human action" (Stryker 1968, 563) is an important theme in symbolic interactionism (Stryker 1968, 1980; Burke 1980; Hewitt 1990). Like minimizing deflection in general, the incentive of identity-confirmation both energizes and directs response. "To say that each [person] is motivated by an identity is to say that of the large set of responses each could make to the situation, a subset pertaining to the identity is selected and activated (Hewitt 1990, 134)." Affect control theory combines this symbolic interactionist/identity theory view of motivation with the concept of control.

> As soon as a person finds that an event with the self as actor is the one that will best confirm sentiments in the circumstances, the act has begun psychologically, and behavioral implementation follows as a matter of course unless interrupted. The anticipation establishes reference signals, which the organism begins realizing perceptually through action. (Heise 1979, 22–23).

Because individual acts must be aligned with those of other interactants in order to sustain a social act, however, the link between energization and response is far from automatic. A person may not be able to act at all in certain situations because to do so might disrupt or terminate a social act. Or, the translation of arousal into action might become short–circuited or neutralized by a sequential act of another person, thereby revising each participant's current definition of the situation. Definitions of the situation are fragile cognitions that change rapidly with the unfolding of a social act, as each event operates on current deflections, generating new conceptualizations and energizing new events. As emphasized by Mead, a social act consists of a succession of adjustments by each participant to ever-changing circumstances.

And, just as the overall context and unfolding of a social act inhibits the translation of energy into action, it also constrains what acts are selected for implementation. An actor does not simply gauge each conceptualized event in terms of its potential for confirming fundamental sentiments, mindless of the history and future of a social act in which countless events often are embedded. Rather, the overall context of a social act is a powerful constraint limiting the construction of events that would optimally confirm the meaning of self and other. As a consequence, an actor might implement a less than optimum action if nothing else is possible under the circumstances.

Accepting that the confirmation of meaning through the minimization of affective deflection is the general incentive in the affect control theory of motivation, with identity–confirmation as an important instance, can we say anything further about the nature of this incentive? Is affective deflection to be considered an unpleasant or noxious state of arousal and its minimization an internal "drive," like Festinger's (1958) description of cognitive dissonance? Is deflection of a general, unspecified nature dependent upon cognitive interpretation for its meaning, as Cofer (1972, 152) suggests of human motives in general, or is it differentiated along physiological lines? To what extent are people cognitively aware of deflection and their attempts to contain it as they conduct their everyday social lives? Finally, what is the relation of this incentive to other human motives identified in the psychological and sociological literature—the purported need for affiliation, social approval, power, status, stimulation, achievement, and social solidarity? I begin addressing this litany of questions with a few observations concerning the nature of deflection as incentive and its relation to cognitive dissonance.

At first blush, affective deflection appears to be very similar to Festinger's (1957) concept of cognitive dissonance, an internal drive instigating dissonance-reducing cognitive and behavioral response (Festinger 1958). However, affect control theory is premised on the idea that, through the symbolic designation of social objects and events made possible by language, social interaction becomes symbolic interaction conducted in a field of intersubjectivity. And, though psychologically experienced by individual people, it is in this social field that the production and resolution of affective deflection takes place. The difference between cognitive dissonance theory and affect control theory is captured in the distinction between the cognitive and social symbolic traditions in social psychology (Jackson 1988, 95–96, after Moscovici 1972).

To illustrate this distinction, consider identity–confirmation activity. Situated identities are not simply properties of individual actors, nor are they exclusively located in an external social environment (Alexander and Wiley 1981). Rather, they define the *relation* between people at any particular time and place, and it is the unique assemblage of relevant identities in a situation which constitutes each person's identity (Foote 1951, 18). As a process of identity-formation and validation, situated activity is also anchored outside the self and is defined by the psychological presence of others and their presumed monitoring (Alexander and Wiley 1981). Thus, identity-confirmation, and minimizing affective deflection in general, takes place in this field of intersubjectivity where situated identities are located and where situated activity takes place. Applied to motivation, this is quite a different conceptualization than the reconciliation of conflicting cognitions in the minds of individual actors.

While deflection is generated and resolved in a field of intersubjectivity, it is at the same time psychologically experienced by individual interactants. How, then, should we conceptualize deflection at this level? While affective deflection, like cognitive dissonance, refers to a disruption or imbalance that instigates cognitive and behavioral response, there are important differences between the two motivational constructs. First, dissonance refers to inconsistent cognitions; deflection, to inconsistent affective states. Second, dissonance designates inconsistency between two sets of present cognitions; deflection, between fundamental and transient affective states. Third, dissonance implies an unpleasant psychological state; deflection refers to either pleasant or unpleasant affective experiences. The former occurs, for instance, when an act of one person enhances the status of another beyond what might reasonably be expected on the basis of his or her current identity (Smith-Lovin 1990). Finally, and perhaps most important, affect control theory conjoins the tension-reduction approach to motivation with a cybernetic one (Shibutani 1968, 333); it is the theory's emphasis on feedback and control that distinguishes it from other tension-reduction theories of motivation.

Moving beyond cognitive dissonance theory, affect control theory proposes that events induce a state of affective arousal that is defined by deflection. Perhaps the best way to think of deflection (and perhaps dissonance as well) is in terms of its engendering a general motivational state consisting of an interaction between incentive and physiological stimulation, something like Bindra's (1969) notion of a "central motive state."[12]

Assuming this description is correct, we might query further whether the physiological component of this general motivational state is undifferentiated or specific. In this regard, there is some suggestive evidence that the goodness, powerfulness, and liveliness dimensions of affective meaning have correlates in neurological activity (see Heise 1988, 7). And, with respect to the question concerning the conscious awareness of deflection and the psychological processes set in motion to contain it, the discussion earlier in this chapter concerning the cognitive awareness of affective experience applies here. That is, deflection and affect control processes can occur either above or below the threshold of conscious awareness and symbolically mediated thought.

Finally, I turn to the relation between the incentive of minimizing deflection and other human motives identified in the psychological and sociological literature. Again, this discussion will be made clearer if we deal with deflection–minimizing activity in terms of identity-confirmation. To the extent that the satiation or realization of other supposed human motives depends on social interaction, they may be translated into identity-confirmation terms. For example, the purported need for status may reflect the fact that the validation of positive social identities is dependent upon the positive social appraisals and acts of others; the supposed need for power, that powerful acts by self and acquiescent acts by others are required to validate powerful identities; and the alleged human need for stimulation or arousal, that social identities have to be validated on the activity dimension as well.

One of the most genuinely sociological, explicit statements of motivation—Collins' (1989) "interactional ritual/social solidarity" theory, a Durkheimian reformulation of Mead's utilitarian treatment of sociability—can be reconceptualized in identity-confirmation terms. The following discussion anticipates and complements my comparison of Collins' theory of interactional ritual chains and affect control theory in Chapter 9.

Describing Mead's sociability as "the most central human goal," with implications for both thinking and social interaction, Collins proposes that social solidarity, "the pleasure of belonging to a group, is the most important of human motivations" (1989, 14), and is autonomous from the practical, utilitarian motives of pragmatist theory. People come away from successful interactional rituals with "symbols which are highly charged with a sense of social participation" (1989,19) and with emotional energies; and "since humans enjoy these solidarity feelings, the presence of symbols in their minds motivates them towards social situations in which they can recharge the symbols with further emotional experience" (1989, 19–20).

To the extent that the "cultural capital" (1989, 20) of charged symbols and emotional energies acquired in previous interactional rituals pertains to a person's identities and roles in these collective rituals, one might suggest that an important reason people find social interaction and solidarity intrinsically gratifying and motivating is its personal relevancy for confirming their salient identities. Among other things, this identity-confirmation translation of Collins' theory successfully addresses Thoits' criticism (discussed in the following section) that formal deductive theories of emotions like Collins' theory of interactional rituals and affect control theory ignore the role of self in motivation.

In this regard, the need for self-actualization—"the desire . . . to become everything that one is capable of becoming" (Maslow 1954, 92), which occupies the apex of Maslow's hierarchy of human motives—might be recast in identity-confirmation terms as the desire to assimilate identities that have become the objects of personal aspiration. In short, the human motivation to confirm salient identities might underlie many of the putative motives in the psychological and sociological literature, so that an identity theory of motivation may indeed turn out to have broad generality.[13]

However, it is at the very point of embarking on a course of theoretical generalization that one should pull back hardest on the reins of enthusiasm. Human motivation is an extremely complex phenomenon, implicating at various levels of concreteness—biological, psychological, social-psychological, and cultural—the manifold characteristics that make us distinctively human. No single theory of motivation is general and powerful enough to encompass all human motives. As Cofer (1972, 158) cautioned, "monolithic motivational interpretations of behavior are far too simple, however complex and seemingly compelling, to give an adequate understanding of why behavior occurs when and where it takes place." This caveat notwithstanding, identity-confirmation and the more general need to experience self within an orderly, knowable social existence are probably among the most powerful of human incentives.

Motivation and Self

Thoits (1989) has criticized affect control theory and other formal, deductive theories of emotions, including those of Kemper (1978), Collins (1981), and Scheff (1979), for ignoring the role of self in motivation. She alleges that such theories "treat affects as mechanical motivators: positive affect leads to some types of behavior, negative affect to others "(1989, 333). Her prescription:

> Incorporating the meaning of emotions for the self (and others) into theory helps specify when (and what) actions will follow from feelings. Emotions [and, by extension, affect in general] may provide impetus for action, but concerns about impression management and self-esteem direct that action. (1989, 333).

This section addresses Thoits' criticism by connecting the affect control/identity theory of motivation just presented to the interactionist concept of self.[14]

The idea that identities play a critical role in the constitution, organization, and functioning of a person's self connects symbolic interactionism with self-concept theory and research. Self-concept, however, is an all-encompassing theoretical construct, comprising all cognition and affect pertaining to the self as an object of consciousness (Rosenberg 1979, 7; cf. Rogers 1951, 136–7). To render it a more manageable construct, self-concept theorists distinguish between self-image and self-esteem. *Self-image* refers to the cognitive component of self-concept, the characteristics and qualities a person attributes to self as an object of cognition; *self-esteem*, the affective component of self-concept, the sentiments an individual maintains toward self as an object of evaluation.

Now, as argued earlier in this chapter, objects must be cathected or invested with affect before they motivate. Therefore, the motivational implications of self-concept must be conceptually located in self-esteem, the affective reaction to self-image.[15] Rosenberg (1979, 54–57) proposed that self-esteem is not merely a state of self-consciousness, but a universal motive of the self which is not reducible to other drives or motives; and Hewitt (1990, 142), that self-esteem is "a motivational state" which people "bring to each new situation of social interaction."

The link between self-image and self-esteem, on the one hand, and social identities, on the other, can now be stated. To begin, if self-images are based on the characteristics and qualities attributed to self (Hewitt 1990), then social identities can be viewed as general "self-schemata" (Markus 1977), cognitive structures in terms of which these more elemental self-conceptualizations are cognitively organized and processed. (This idea is elaborated in Chapter 8). A mother, for example, is supposed to be kind and supportive; a doctor, competent and caring. Moreover, because people often perceive themselves at the level of these general self-schemata, social identities are important constitutents of self-image in their own right. Thus, as the affective response to self-image, a person's self-esteem depends upon the validation of salient identities, those that organize and help constitute his or her self-image. As Stryker and Gottlieb (1981, 455) assert, "it does not seem unreasonable to believe . . . that self-esteem is tied to behaving in accord with a salient identity."

Identities can be either *situated* or *biographical* (Hewitt 1990). In addition to a repertoire of situated identities, every person has a number of biographical or situationally general ones (e.g., gender, ethnic, occupational). These are connected to past situations and performances through memory and to future ones through anticipation. By implication, self-image and self-esteem also have a biographical or core dimension, providing a sense of continuity and integration to a person's self and constituting more deeply–rooted sources of personal motivation (Hewitt 1990, 134–138).

In this respect, Rosenberg (1979, 21) described the self–concept as a "complex hierarchical order" of elements, and global self-esteem as "the product of an enormously complex synthesis of elements which goes on in the individual's phenomenal field." Drawing upon the principal of psychological centrality, he proposed that the significance of particular self-concept components for overall self-esteem depends upon their location in an individual's self-concept structure, that "a person's global self-esteem is based not solely on an assessment of his constituent qualities but on an assessment of the qualities that count" (Rosenberg 1979, 18).

As will be discussed further in Chapter 5, identity theorists view the identities that constitute the self as arranged in a hierarchy of "salience" (Stryker 1968) or "prominence" (McCall and Simmons 1966/1978). Similar conceptualizations of self have been proposed by Rose (1962) and Turner (1978). As conceived by Rose, with explicit reference to Meadian constructs, a "me" is simply a social role subjectively viewed, and the self is built up from a complex of "me's" or internalized roles. A person perceives his or her repertoire of "me's," Rose argues, not as a discrete set of objects, but as an integrated whole in the phenomenal field, and in a hierarchy according to their strength as "reference relationships" to the individual.

While all these authors propose a hierarchy of cognitive salience structuring a person's global self-image, they also imply a corresponding hierarchy of affective salience defining a person's global self-esteem. For example, Stryker (1968, 562) proposed that "the more a given identity is invested with a positive cathectic response, the higher will be that identity in the salience hierarchy"; McCall and Simmons (1978, 75), that an individual's commitment to an identity, the degree to which he or she has staked self-esteem upon living up to or validating it, is "paramount among . . . determinants of prominence." Moreover, as implied by the general discussion of motivation earlier in this chapter, the cognitive salience of an identity would be motivationally impotent unless it evoked an affective self-response.

The idea that people act to confirm cognitively and affectively salient identities is consistent with the notion of the self as a unified object in an individual's phenomenal field. A person can contemplate self and its constituent identities simultaneously. At times, he or she may consider the consequences for self-esteem of claiming and validating one or another social identity through identity-confirming action. More often than not, a person preconsciously and automatically invokes identities, guided by affect control processes monitoring the situation with respect to potential consequences for overall self–esteem and constrained by the current definition of the situation and the overall context of the social act. Looming in the background of the phenomenal field in which the rehearsal of action takes place can be found the unified self of the individual. Its cognitive meaning corresponds to a person's biographical or global self-image, its affective meaning to his or her general level of self-esteem. Unless an individual valued or cathected self as an integrated object in this phenomenal field, there would be little motivation to claim or validate particular identities.

Affect control theory provides a way of conceptualizing and operationalizing the relationship among identities, self-image, and self-esteem and connecting these constructs with motivated action. A situated identity defines a person's self-image at any particular time and place. The fundamental sentiments attached to this identity, operationalized as evaluation, potency, and activity ratings on the semantic differential, defines his or her situated self-esteem. And, to the extent that the situated identities constituting a person's global self-image evoke positive sentiments, a person will have high global self–esteem.[16] By implication, a person should be motivated to validate positively evaluated identities in order to optimize self-esteem.[17]

The theory recognizes, however, that even when a person wants to confirm a positive identity or discard a stigmatized one, he or she might be compelled to act in ways that belie identity aspirations. This might occur, for example, when a positive identity that is continually disconfirmed or a stigmatized one that resists extinction sets up a vicious cycle between low self-esteem and anxiety (Hewitt 1990, 143–144). A person approaching situations with anxiety and trepidation is more vulnerable to the real or imagined criticism of others. This militates against the validation of positively evaluated identities, or the shedding of stigmatized ones, resulting in self-condemnation and an incremental reduction in self-esteem with each encounter.

Affect control theory also recognizes that identity-validation does not occur in a social vacuum; that is, the situated identity of each person is part of an integral definition of the situation that includes the identities of other interactants. As a result, people must consider each other's identities in order to effectively construct and sustain a social act. Moreover, because identity-validation depends upon the attributions, imputations, and confirmatory actions of others, people must generally support each other's identity claims and aspirations to confirm their own. This is a core idea in affect control theory that employs social events, the basic elements of social acts, as its units of analysis.

Summary

This chapter has addressed two general issues raised by introducing affect into the cognitive framework of Mead and traditional symbolic interactionism: the relation between cognition and affect and human motivation.

With respect to the first issue, I argued that cognition and affect are inextricable and complementary modes of human consciousness viewed as structure or cybernetically related phases of human consciousness viewed as process.

With regard to the second issue, I argued that an adequate theory of human motivation must account for both the mobilization and direction of behavior; must circumscribe the full range of human consciousness; and must be grounded in language, identification, and control. The motivational assumptions of affect control theory were then assessed in these terms. I identified the fundamental motivational principle of affect control theory as the confirmation of meaning through the minimization of affective deflection. I then showed how this general incentive takes the form of identity-confirmation when the self is actor and how this idea integrates the motivational assumptions of affect control theory with the interactionist concept of the self.

While independently conceived, the affect control/identity theory model of motivation presented in this chapter coincides in most respects with Turner's (1987) articulation of the interactionist model of motivation, including a consideration of the alleged human needs for personal identity and adjustment to others, self-conceptions (identities) in both their situational and dispositional (biographical, global, or core) sense, and the incentive value of self-conceptions as related to both self-esteem and self-consistency. And, while I have related the affect control/identity theory model to Collins' interactional ritual/solidarity theory of motivation, additional theoretical work is required to integrate it with the other models of motivation (the exchange, ethnomethodological, and psychoanalytic) formalized by Turner (1987).

Chapters 2 and 3 have presented a comprehensive delineation and discussion of affect control theory, paying particular attention to its affinity with symbolic interactionism. The next chapter continues this theme by drawing an explicit comparison between affect control theory and the social psychology of George Herbert Mead.

4

AFFECT CONTROL THEORY AND THE SOCIAL PSYCHOLOGY OF GEORGE HERBERT MEAD

This chapter advances a central theme of this book—the portrayal of affect control theory as an extension of symbolic interactionism—by drawing an explicit comparison between the theory and the social psychology of George Herbert Mead. One-sided exaggerations of Mead's ideas have resulted in quite dissimilar theories flying the banner of symbolic interactionism, each claiming loyalty to his original thought. Moreover, as discussed in Chapter 1, symbolic interactionists have largely ignored some of Mead's most important ideas—specifically, language and control. For these reasons, I have chosen to preface my comparison of affect control theory and Mead with a personal, straightforward account that stays close to his own writings, rather than trying to reconcile conflicting interpretations of his work by adherents to different schools of symbolic interactionism.

Psychological social psychologists in recent years also have been discovering the relevance of Mead, as their image of the person has shifted from one of a passive organism determined by contingencies of reinforcement and other external influences to one of a more active, reflexive, and self-regulating agent (Bandura 1977, 1982; Jackson 1988). Thus, Mead serves as a theoretical point of reference for integrating affect control theory not only with symbolic interactionism in sociological social psychology but also with theories in psychological social psychology that have adopted, if often only implicitly, a Meadian perspective.

In the first half of this chapter, I discuss the role of affect in Mead's social psychology. I begin by examining Mead for the rare instances where emotions are explicitly discussed. Next, I develop the thesis with which I introduced this book: that Mead ignored affect because he based his social psychology on a cognitive theory of language that rendered his major constructs ('mind,' 'self,' and 'society') affectively, and hence, motivationally lifeless. This is a critically important point because affect control theory assumes that a great deal of symbolically mediated thought consists of affective processing. In the second half of this chapter, I compare Mead's social psychology with affect control theory. A concept-by-concept comparison reveals that, despite Mead's views on affect, his emphasis on language and his model of 'mind' as a system of cybernetic control anticipate central features of affect control theory.

Emotions in Mead's Social Psychology

The extent to which Mead developed a theory of emotion has become a point of controversy among symbolic interactionists and other scholars interested in Mead's ideas. Meltzer (1972, 21) concluded that "the importance of sentiments and emotion manifested in personal relationships are given no recognition in Mead's position;" and Gerth and Mills (1964, xvii) that "Mead had no adequate notion of emotions and motives, no dynamic theory of the affective life of man." Franks (1985) observed correctly that Mead's discussions of emotion are adjunct to his debate with contemporaneous schools of psychology, especially parallelism and radical behaviorism (cf. Morris 1934, xii). On the other hand, Hochschild (1983, 212) concluded that although "Mead did not talk about emotion . . . [he] cleared a path for doing so from an interactional perspective." Denzin (1985, 223) included Mead with James, Cooley, and Dewey as one of those early interactionists who "give emotions serious attention in a significant number of places" (1985, 223). And, Baldwin (1985) suggested that Mead developed a rather coherent theory of emotions that is consistent with modern behaviorism.

Notwithstanding these conflicting evaluations of emotion in Mead's work, one thing is clear: Mead associated emotion with the early, preparatory stages of the act—impulse and perception, rather than its later stages—manipulation and consummation (Franks 1985; see also Baldwin 1985 and Scheff 1985b, 253). In Mead's words, "it is in the preparation for action that we find the qualitatively different emotional tones" (1895, 164). These emotional overtones of impulses, according to Mead, result from the inhibition of action as interactants adjust themselves to each other's responses. Behind the process of mutual adjustment

> lie the emotions which the checking of the acts inevitably arouse. Fear, anger, lust of hunger and sex, all the gamut of emotions arise back of the activities of fighting, and feeling, and reproduction, because these activities are for the moment stopped in the process of readjustment (1910b/1964, 124–5).

Mead described the physiological and behavioral manifestations of emotional experience—"the vasomotor preparations for action, such as the flushing of the blood vessels, change in the rhythm of breathing and the explosive sounds which accompany the change in the breathing rhythm and circulation" (1910b, 123. See also 1895, 163). In addition, he recognized the "sensory aspects [of emotion] connected with the central nervous system" (1934, 19), the "feel of the emotion" (1903/1964, 32) that occurs when a person senses the physiological manifestation of emotional experience. This basic kind of emotional experience is independent of language and consciousness and is characteristic of animals and very young children before verbal socialization takes hold (cf. Baldwin 1985, 267).

Mead's view on the external expression of emotion can be found in his criticism of Darwin's (1872/1955) theory that the function of primitive animal gestures, such as facial expressions and animal sounds, is to express emotion (1934, 15–18, 43–4; 1910b/1964, 124–5). For Mead, this implied that a state of consciousness precedes the display of emotion; and because he found it inconceivable to think that animals consciously express their emotions, he dismissed Darwin's theory outright. While gestures may "release" animal emotions, thereby revealing them to an observer, Mead argued, this is not the reason for their survival or existence.

Instead, Mead argued that emotional displays, like all gestures, are part of the organization of the social act. The gesture of one organism initiates a social act by evoking instinctive responses from the other organism, these responses become stimuli for the readjustment of each organism, and the process continues until the social act is consummated. To illustrate, Mead provided the example of a dogfight, in which the aggressive gestures of each animal stimulate mutually adjustive responses. He also considered boxing and fencing as examples of human acts dominated by instinctive response to primitive gestures. In such acts, the movements of protagonists are generally unreflective, evoking instinctive and non-conscious adjustments from each other. While he recognized that "emotional attitudes" often lie back of these instinctive acts, he maintained that "these are only part of the whole process that is going on" (1934, 45). For Mead, "the function of the gesture is to make adjustment possible among the individuals implicated in any given social act" (1934, 36), not to express their internal emotional states.

Now, when an idea lies behind a gesture and arouses the same idea in the other person, then the gesture becomes a significant symbol (Mead 1934, 45–46). However, like primitive gestures, the function of significant symbols is to stimulate the adjustment of one organism's actions to the actions of the other in the social act—"an adjustment which takes place through communication" (1934, 75). Even in human interaction, where significant symbols or language replace in large part the conversation of gestures that characterizes animal communication, Mead maintained that the natural function of language is to convey the cognitive meaning of adjustive responses, not to express emotional states (1934, 147–8). This is an extremely important point in understanding Mead's position on the role of emotion in social life, and is the basis upon which I build my argument concerning his failure to develop a social psychological theory of affect.

In conclusion, while it is difficult to weave a systematic fabric out of the disarray of theoretical fiber that constitutes Mead's treatment of affect, the overwhelming impression one gets is that he viewed emotion as a physiological and sensory phenomenon, rather than a social psychological one.

In the following section, I return briefly to my argument in Chapter 1 that Mead's failure to develop a social psychological theory of emotion can be traced directly to his cognitive theory of language. I then consider the profound consequences this had for his conceptualizations of mind, self, and society.

Language

Recapitulating and expanding my discussion in Chapter 1, Mead settled upon language, or the significant symbols that constitute language, as the universal, objective principle upon which to develop his social psychology, one that could deal with mind and consciousness without falling into the solipsistic trap of disintegrating into a branch of individual psychology. For Mead, the characteristic of significant symbols that made all this possible is their logical status as universals (1934, 125):

> Our symbols are all universal. You cannot say anything that is absolutely particular; anything you say that has any meaning at all is universal . . . a symbol is a universal of discourse; it is universal in its character . . . A person who is saying something is saying to himself what he says to others; otherwise he does not know what he is talking about (1934, 146–7).

As universals, significant symbols communicate the social meaning of objects, the concepts people share by virtue of having the same language.[1]

For Mead, however, meaning is not something located in the minds of individual people (1934, 127). Instead, the meaning of significant symbols, like all gestures, consists of the symmetry of response they evoke in self and others: "Such a response is its meaning, or gives it its meaning (1934, 145)." Mead's social behavioristic account of the significant symbol is captured in his concept of "attitudes"—shared behavioral dispositions that are the "beginnings of acts" (1934, 5).[2] Significant symbols evoke a symmetry of response—an attitude in both the symbol user and the recipient, a common behavioral disposition and implicit plan of action that is the foundation for the coordination of activity required in social acts.

The perception of these common behavioral dispositions evoked by significant symbols is the stuff of which social cognitions are made. Hence, Mead's behavioristic account of language is, at the same time, an account of the origins of social cognitions. While Mead's great contribution was to show the relevance of significant symbols to communication and the evocation of those common behavioral dispositions that make human intersubjectivity possible, he failed to extend the universal social character of cognitive communication to emotional expression. This resulted from his belief that the communication of affect lacks the symmetry of response that characterizes the communication of cognitive meaning. "On the emotional side, which is a very large part of the vocal gesture, we do not call out in ourselves in any such degree the response we call out in others as we do in the case of significant speech (Mead 1934, 149)." As we shall see, Mead did not deny the capacity of language to elicit emotions, only that emotion-eliciting words necessarily evoke the same response in different people.[3]

Because emotions lack the symmetry of response characteristic of cognitive acts of communication, they cannot be universally shared, hence are not social.[4] They are by nature private, subjective experiences. If emotions are not social phenomena, there cannot be a social psychology of emotions so long as one remains within the conceptual framework of Mead.[5] The asymmetry between arousal of self and others characteristic of "emotional attitudes" (1934, 147) denies affect a significant role in Mead's social psychology.[6]

Notwithstanding his position regarding the asymmetrical nature of emotional communication, Mead contemplated an apparent exception. This occurs in his discussion of aesthetics. The challenge for the artist, according to Mead, is "to find the sort of expression that will arouse in others what is going on [emotionally] in himself" (1934, 147). A lyric poet, working from a palette of words, as it were, "is seeking for those words which will answer to his emotional attitude, and which will call out in others the attitude he himself has" (1934 147–8). Similarly, an actor who is aware of the emotions his performance is designed to evoke in an audience often responds emotionally in the same way as the audience does.

However, Mead dismissed such instances of emotional symmetry as artificial and contrived. While acknowledging that "we do at times act and consider just what the effect of our [emotional] attitude is going to be and we may deliberately use a certain tone of voice to bring about . . . the same response in ourselves that we want to arouse in somebody else," he cautioned that this "is not a natural situation; one is not an actor all the time" (1934, 147). While recognizing that language can sometimes arouse in ourselves the same emotions as it arouses in others, he maintained that generally "we do not deliberately feel the emotions which we arouse [in others]. We do not normally use language stimuli to call out in ourselves the emotional response which we are calling out in others . . . as we do in the case of significant speech" (Mead 1934, 148).[7]

Mead's cognitive, emotion-free theory of language has some startling implications for his concepts of mind, self, and society. Because he conceptualized these phenomena as linguistic processes, while restricting the natural function of language to the communication of cognitive meaning, he was compelled to define them in cognitive terms as well. I now elaborate this point, beginning with Mead's concept of mind.

Mind

For Mead, the mind is not a spatial, material structure identified with the central nervous system, but a functional process relating individual and environment,[8] with language providing the field for this process.[9] "Out of language emerges the field of mind (1934, 133)." The intimate connection between mind and language is explicit in Mead's definition of mind as an "internalized or implicit conversation of the individual with himself" (1934, 47). By implication, mind develops in step with an individual's acquisition of the significant symbols or language of a society.[10]

The acquisition of language enables the individual to take "the attitudes of other individuals toward himself and toward what is being thought about" (1934, 192). Moreover, because language enables the individual to take the role of the "generalized other"—that hypothetical, abstract composite of specific others which in its most abstract sense constitutes the societal community—the individual assimilates the social processes of experience and behavior as a whole.[11] "When this occurs the individual becomes self-conscious and has a mind" (1934, 134), becoming aware of relations to the social process as a whole and to particular others participating in it.

The generalized other is indispensable for the development and functioning of mind for two reasons. Viewed objectively as the societal community, it provides the symbolic medium (language) for the internalized conversation that constitutes mind, as well as the content of thought in the form of social cognitions and attitudes. Viewed subjectively as the internalization of the societal community, it serves as a perspective from which to address ourselves in this inner conversation. In Mead's words, "the conversation which constitutes the process or activity of thinking is carried on by the individual from the standpoint of the 'generalized other'" (1934, 155). Or, phrased differently, "thought is the conversation of the generalized other with the self" (1922/1964, 246).[12] Thus, for Mead, the mind is profoundly social.

The implications of Mead's cognitive theory of language for his concept of mind can now be stated. Because mind is conceptualized as a socially engendered, internal linguistic process, while the function of language is restricted to the representation and communication of cognitive meaning, the mind must be an exclusively cognitive phenomenon as well. But where in the psychological experience of the individual does emotion reside? Surely, Mead would not deny that people have the capacity to consciously experience their emotions. To answer this question, we must examine Mead's concept of consciousness.

The constructs of mind and consciousness are closely related in Mead's social psychology and often are used interchangeably. Like mind, consciousness is not a substantive thing, but a functional process of symbolically mediated thought located in the objective social world. What takes place in the brain, according to Mead, is "the physiological process whereby we lose and regain consciousness: a process which is somewhat analogous to that of pulling down or raising a window shade" (Mead 1934, 112). The meaning of an object does not disappear when a particular individual ceases to be aware of it, in this physiological sense of consciousness, because "meaning is present in the social act before the emergence or awareness of meaning occurs" (1934, 77).[13]

As discussed above, Mead defined meaning in terms of the shared behavioral dispositions or attitudes evoked by significant symbols. The consciousness of meaning, then, consists of a person's cognitive awareness of a behavioral disposition to act toward an object: "The feelings of readiness to take up or read a book, to spring over a ditch, to hurl a stone, are the stuff out of which arises a sense of the meaning of the book, the ditch, the stone (Mead 1910b/1964, 125)." Mead (1910a/1964, 110) referred to consciousness of meaning thus defined as "reflective consciousness." Such cognitive images of unconsummated acts are the basis of reflective thought (cf. Shibutani 1968, 333).

Mead's social behavioristic account of reflective consciousness is his front line of defense against solipsism. Through communication and role-taking, individuals can verify the extent to which their subjective experience is shared by others. Without language, individuals would be confined to their own subjective worlds. However, because reflective consciousness logically requires the symbolic mediation provided by language, these would be phenomenal worlds of which individuals could have little or no conscious awareness. Thus, in this sense, solipsism is a logical impossibility within the conceptual framework of Mead. The "solipsistic spook" that would "reduce one's world to a nutshell" (Mead, 1910a/1964, 106) cannot logically take hold in his theory of consciousness.[14]

The implications of Mead's construct of consciousness for his treatment of emotion parallels those flowing from his construct of mind. Because reflective consciousness is a linguistically mediated process, while the natural function of language is restricted to the representation of cognitive meaning, it would appear that there is no place for the emotions in human consciousness. If excluded from reflective consciousness, the emotions cannot be considered social phenomena; and, thus, a social psychology of emotions is not possible within Mead's conceptual framework.

However, Mead identified a second kind of consciousness in which he created a place for the emotions. This kind of consciousness refers to "the sense qualities of things . . . the affections of the body of the sentient organism, especially those that are painful and pleasurable, the contents of the images of memory and imagination, and of the activities of the organism, so far as it appears in its experience" (1924–5/1964, 271). This is a private subjective world comprising "objects which the individual possesses from the inside, so to speak" (1924–5/1964, 274). Along with imagery, it includes "pleased palates and irritated or suffering members . . . straining muscles . . . fearful objects, or a turned stomach, or an attractive thing" (1924–5/1964, 273).[15]

In this way, Mead admits emotions to human consciousness through the back door of bodily sensations. This kind of consciousness, however, refers to "the private or subjective aspects of experience as contrasted with the common social aspects" (1934, 112) of reflective consciousness. The kind of consciousness wherein emotions dwell is individual and subjective; that wherein cognitions lie is social and objective.[16] This suggests an interesting implication. Since human consciousness is not coextensive with reflective consciousness where symbolic representation takes place, the mind cannot be coextensive with language (cf. Reck 1964, xxviii).[17] So, in his attempt to make a place for the emotions in consciousness, Mead inadvertently casts doubt on the adequacy of his model of mind to fully encompass the psychological life of the person.

Self

Parallel to Mead's theory of mind, the self develops in consciousness through language, communication, and role-taking: "Such is the process by which a personality arises . . . a process in which a child takes the role of the other . . . essentially through the use of language" (Mead 1934, 160).[18] However, if the natural function of language is restricted to the representation of cognitive meaning, the self must be an exclusively cognitive phenomenon. Mead stated this explicitly:

> Emphasis should be laid on the central position of thinking when considering the nature of the self. Self-consciousness, rather than affective experience with its motor accompaniments, provides the core and primary structure of the self, which is thus essentially a cognitive rather than an emotional phenomenon (Mead 1934, 173).

In short, Mead's self is coextensive with "self-image"—the cognitive dimension of self-concept, as opposed to "self-esteem"—its affective dimension. Thus, "self–conscious activity consists of a succession of responses to a series of self-images" (Shibutani 1968, 334), rather than self-feelings. In this regard, Mead took issue with Cooley and James, who attempted to establish the self on "reflexive affective experiences," those involving "self-feeling." He argued that "the individual need not take the attitudes of others toward himself in these [affective] experiences . . . and unless he does so, he cannot develop a self" (1934, 173). As a result, he reasoned, a model of self based on affect cannot account for its social origin.

Mead distinguished between two analytically distinct phases of the self viewed as reflexive process: the 'I' (its subjective phase) and the 'me' (its objective phase). Of these, only the 'me'—that organized set of others' attitudes toward oneself—can exist as an object of consciousness. In Mead's words, "the self-conscious, actual self in social intercourse is the objective 'me' or 'me's' with the process of response continually going on and implying a fictitious 'I' always out of sight of himself" (Mead 1912/1964, 141).

While Mead employed the 'I' and 'me' to refer to two phases of the self-process and avoided using these terms to refer to substantive entities, they often have been used to refer to structural aspects of self by subsequent commentators on his work. The 'me' has been employed to refer to the social aspect of self; the 'I', to its biological aspect. In these terms, it has been said that Mead relegated emotion to the 'I', the biological individual where other primitive human impulses are to be found, rather than to the 'me' where the socially engendered cognitions of self are located (Scheff 1985b, 243). And, "just as identity [the cognitive modality of self-response] is related to the 'me' aspect of Mead's concept of the self, the conative and cathectic modalities of response are related to the 'I' aspect" (Stryker 1968, 560n.). Again, as with mind, analysis of Mead's concept of self reveals that he did not consider emotions to be social phenomena, making it impossible to develop a social psychology of emotions within his conceptual framework.

Society

Mead's position on the nature of society is relativistic, defying classification as exclusively one of social realism or social nominalism. On the one hand, he maintained that the mind and self are social, both in genesis and function. The societal community provides the symbolic medium (language) for the internalized conversation that constitutes mind. It also provides the content of mind in the form of attitudes or social cognitions, along with a perspective (the internalized audience of the generalized other) for reflective thought. The societal community also provides the individual with a definition of self, as well as a perspective for treating the self as an object of reflective consciousness.

On the other hand, Mead held that human society as we know it could not exist without reflective minds and reflexive selves, because "its most characteristic features presuppose the possession of [such] minds and selves by its individual members" (1934, 227). The relation between society, on the one hand, and mind and self, on the other, can best be described as an ascending evolutionary spiral, culminating in a society populated by individuals with reflective minds and reflexive selves. In Mead's words, mind and self "emerged out of the human social process in its lower states of development," but thereafter "the rate of development or evolution of human society . . . has been tremendously accelerated as a result of that emergence" (1934, 227).

What, then, binds acting individuals together in cohesive social groups, organizations, and societal communities? What principle of organization ensures some degree of concerted action or cooperation among individual actors? Mead found the answer to the Hobbesian problem of order (Parsons 1937) in significant symbols or language. In contrast to the physiological specialization that characterizes the social organization of non–human organisms like insects, Mead proposed that "language gives an entirely different principle of organization which produces not only a different type of individual but also a different society" (1934, 244). Organized activity among humans is based upon the symbolic consensus provided by language (cf. Meltzer 1972, 7).[19]

For Mead, however, language is not simply an abstract system of communication. Instead, its acquisition coincides with the learning of a whole complex of attitudes:

A person learns a new language and, as we say, gets a new soul. He puts himself into the attitude of those that make use of that language. He cannot read its literature, cannot traverse with those that belong to that community, without taking on its peculiar attitudes. He becomes in that sense a different individual (1934, 283).

Thus, it is not simply upon language that the organization and integration of human society is based, but more fundamentally on that elaborate set of behavioristically defined meanings or attitudes embedded in language. However, because attitudes refer exclusively to cognitive meaning, the psychical cement that holds society together consists of social cognitions sterilized of affect. Hence, like mind and self, Mead conceptualized society as a strictly cognitive phenomenon.

The Social Psychology of Mead and Affect Control Theory

In the first part of this chapter, I have tried to show that a social psychology of emotion is not possible within Mead's conceptual framework, at least not without some dramatic revision. Because Mead's entire social psychology is predicated upon an exclusively cognitive theory of language, a revision must begin there. In the second part of this chapter, I show that once Mead's social psychology is modified by recognizing the affective significance of language, his conceptualizations of mind, self, and society coincide with those supposed by affect control theory. I also show how the introduction of affect into Mead's social psychology yields a theory of motivation that is identical to the affect control/identity theory model of motivation discussed in Chapter 3.

Language

In the formal statement of affect control theory presented in Chapter 2, Proposition 1 asserts that social interaction is conducted in terms of social cognitions; and Proposition 2, that language is the primary symbolic system through which social cognitions are psychologically represented, accessed, processed, and communicated. Taken alone, these two propositions simply reaffirm the cognitive, social symbolic position of Mead. The next two propositions, however, extend Mead's social psychology into the realm of affect. By proposing that all cognitions evoke affective associations, Proposition 3 expands Mead's theory of language to accommodate affect; and Proposition 4 simply specifies the dimensional structure of affective meaning assumed by affect control theory. Affect control theory also supposes that affective associations, because of their socially learned connections with the cognitions that evoke them, are intrinsically social. In fact, affect control theory supposes that affective communication is often more expeditious than cognitive communication, an idea that has become recognized in recent years (Etzioni 1988, 139–140, after Pieters and Van Raaij 1987).

Affect control theory extends Mead's theory of language in another important way. Modern linguistics recognizes two structural features of language that make the connections between symbols possible: semantics—the definition of the meaning of words in terms of other words with related meaning; and syntax—the grammatical structure of words that conveys longer sequences of thought.[20] Despite Mead's emphasis on language as the basis for self-conscious activity, he was not explicit about the structural features of language that make reflective thought possible. In contrast, affect control theory is conceptualized and operationalized in terms of the semantic and syntactic features of language.

With regard to semantics, the theory relates words to one another by locating them in the common semantic space defined by the evaluation, potency, and activity dimensions of the semantic differential. As a result, identities can be defined in terms of their implications for action, as proposed by identity theorists (Stryker 1968; Burke 1980), or in terms of one another. Employing EPA profiles, a "gangster" (-2.33 1.96 1.66), for example, can be defined as a "criminal" (-1.96 .92 1.49) whose characteristic acts in the pursuit of illegal goals are violent ones. This potential for violence, no doubt, accounts for a perception of greater evil, power, and liveliness than criminals in general (Canadian male data). In fact, it is because social identities, interpersonal acts, and other constituents of events can be represented in the same EPA semantic space that the modeling of affective reaction and affect control processes become mathematically possible.

As for syntax, affect control theory conceptualizes and operationalizes a social event "as a syntactically ordered conjunction of cognitive elements (usually culturally defined) designating actor, act, and object" (Heise 1979, 9). As discussed in Chapter 2, actor-persons (A) are dynamically related to object-persons (O) in social events by means of interpersonal acts (B). Cognitive complexities are taken into account by adding grammatical refinements to simple event structures (e.g., specifying settings and adjectivally-modifying social identities in the A and O positions of ABO events). Moreover, the theory supposes that social events are cognitively organized and processed in terms of the grammatical structure of language. In this regard, the impression formation equations that model the affective reaction to events reveal that the outcome impressions of participants are partly a function of their syntactic position in events. For example, a powerful act increases the potency impression of an actor-person, but attenuates the potency impression of the object-person.

Mind

In my comparison of Mead's model of mind and affect control theory, I begin with a feature they have in common: the conceptualization of mind as a process of cybernetic feedback and control.

According to Mead, mind emerged in the human species when, through the evolution of a complex central nervous system, humans acquired the capacity for reflexiveness—"the turning back of the experience of the individual upon himself" (1934, 134). From a developmental viewpoint, the emergence of individual minds through language acquisition and role-taking is predicated upon this capacity for reflexiveness. In short, reflexiveness is both the essential evolutionary condition and the defining feature of the human mind.

Because mind is inherently reflexive, Mead rejected the simple stimulus-response model of radical behaviorism as an adequate description of human behavior. He is very explicit here:

> It is the possibility of delayed response which principally differentiates reflective from non–reflective conduct in which the response is always immediate. The higher centers of the central nervous system are involved in the former type of behavior by making possible the interposition, between stimulus and response in the simple stimulus-response arc, of a process of selecting one or another of a whole set of possible responses and combinations of responses to the given stimulus (1934, 117–8).

Instead of describing human behavior in terms of stimulus-response, Mead did so in terms of the 'act,' a functional and time-bound unit of behavior that is less elementary than the stimulus-response unit of behaviorism.

Mead's concept of the act foreshadowed modern systems theory by explaining purposive behavior without resorting to the mysticism of teleology.[21] In Mead's words, "the statement of the act includes the goal to which the act moves. This is a natural teleology, in harmony with a mechanical statement" (1934, 6). Final causes are reduced to efficient causes through the negative feedback of the system's own anticipatory states:

> There is . . . an influence of the later act on the earlier act. The later process which is to go on has already been initiated and that later process has its influence on the earlier process. . . . the thing we are going to do is playing back on what we are doing now (Mead 1934, 72–3).

And, it is the reflexive nature of the human mind that is the basis for negative feedback and self-correcting response in the act.

However, while Mead's concept of the act provides a scientific explanation of the mechanics of purposive behavior, its exclusion of affect leaves open the question of what *motivates* individuals to initiate goal-directed or instrumental acts in the first place or to see an act through from impulse to consummation.[22] Cognitive processing alone cannot account for goal-oriented or purposive human behavior, nor can the pragmatist conception of mind "as constructive or reflective or problem–solving thinking" (Mead 1934, 308).

Instead, as discussed extensively in Chapter 3, cognized objects have to be cathected, invested with affective significance, desired or wanted before they mobilize action. In terms of my discussion of motivation in the preceding chapter, Mead's cybernetic model of mind explains the direction but not the *energization* of motivated behavior. Affect control theory vitalizes his construct of mind by supposing that all cognitions evoke affective associations, and that what is controlled in the construction of social action is the affective deflection produced by events.

Borrowing from Shibutani's (1968) description of Mead's cybernetic theory of motivation, deflection (the discrepancy between fundamental sentiments and transient feelings produced by an actualized or anticipated event) energizes response in the *impulse* stage of the act—a disturbance or momentary lack of adjustment between an organism and its environment. In the impulse stage of the act "an organism is set in motion by a disruption of its steady state; any discomfort leads to attempts to minimize it" (Shibutani 1968, 332). Cognitive awareness of deflection and conceptualization of actions that might minimize it take place in the *perception* stage of the act, a telescoped act consisting of anticipated actions and their consequences. While the direction of energized response begins with perception, it does not end there. Instead, direction is a product of an ongoing process of feedback and correction—from cognition to affective reaction and affect control and back again to cognition—in the *manipulation* stage of the act. This process continues until affective deflection is minimized, or affective balance restored, in the *consummation* stage of the act.

Finally, affect control theory assumes that cognition and affect are closely interrelated components of human consciousness and that affect, like cognition, is profoundly social. Hence, in contrast to Mead, who restricted reflective consciousness to cognition, affect control theory is not compelled to invent a second category of consciousness to contain emotion. This also was addressed thoroughly in Chapter 3, obviating further discussion here.

Self

Mead's 'I' has been criticized as a vague residual category of self—the nonsocialized or 'not-me' aspect—that "might include everything from biological urges to the effects of individual variations in life-history" (Meltzer, 1972, 19). Kolb (1944/1972) suggested that, by trying to explain individual differences in personality and in social attitudes, Mead

erred in attempting to explain these residual phenomena under one concept, the "I", and attempting to close his system by enclosing within it heterogeneous phenomena. The "I" becomes accountable for everything that cannot be explained by the organized set of roles [the "me"'s] which the individual takes over in the process of social interaction (1944/1972, 254).

I suggest that Mead also erred in relegating emotion to the non–social 'I' category of self. Again, because he did not believe affect to be a part of social experience, he had to find a residual category to contain it.

From the perspective of affect control theory, however, both affect and cognition are profoundly social. More generally, the social psychology of emotions that has developed in the last fifteen years or so has come to view emotion as produced by social relations (Kemper 1978) and influenced in its expression by human culture (Averill 1980; Shott 1979; Gordon 1981; Hochschild 1983). This suggests that a great deal of affective human experience should be moved conceptually from the residual, non-social category of the 'I' to the social category of the 'me.' While affect occurs on the response side of human behavior (the 'I'), it also occurs on the stimulus side (the 'me'). Perhaps this is what Hochschild (1983, 12) had in mind when she observed that "had Mead developed a theory of emotion he would have begun by elaborating his idea of the 'I.'"

Without this relocation of affect within Mead's conceptual framework, we are faced with a thorny problem. If the 'I' cannot be an object of consciousness, how would we account for cognitive awareness of emotional experience including affective self–response? Indeed, not at all. Because Mead's cognitive view of self is a logical extension of his cognitive theory of language, the conceptual relocation of emotion from the non-social 'I' to the social 'me' can be effected only by recognizing the affective significance of language.

Mead's analysis of the self centers upon "the characteristic of the self as an object to itself" (1934, 136). For Mead, the meaning of self as object in a person's consciousness is cognitive; otherwise, in his view, the origin of the self could not be social (1934, 173). However, as discussed in Chapter 3, a conceptualization of self based solely upon cognition ("self–image") ignores the affective dimension of self-concept ("self–esteem"). And, just as there is no motivation without affect, a person's concept of self would be motivationally impotent without self-esteem. Again, the theory of motivation that incorporates these ideas was developed thoroughly in Chapter 3.

Finally, as also discussed in the preceding chapter, affect control theory operationalizes the affective meaning of the identities that constitute the self as evaluation, potency, and activity scores on the semantic differential. In this regard, and notwithstanding Mead's exclusion of affect from self-concept, Schwartz and Stryker (1970, 36) suggest that there is a great deal of similarity between the psychological theory of meaning underlying Osgood's semantic differential and Mead's notion of self-development.

Society

As discussed earlier in this chapter, Mead proposed that the learning of a language is coincidental with the learning of a society's culture—an entire complex of attitudes or cultural meanings. Through acquiring language and taking the role of the generalized other, the individual internalizes its culture. It is in this sense that Mead identified language as the principle of organization and social integration in human society. While this must be counted among his important contributions to social psychology, Mead made a number of critical errors in articulating this idea.

His first mistake was to identify culture with language. As recognized by anthropologists, sociologists dealing with culture, and affect control theorists alike, while language is part of culture and reflects much of the content and organization of culture, *it is not equivalent to culture.* Discussed in Chapter 1, this point requires no further elaboration here.

Mead's second mistake was to restrict the culture of a society to social cognitions. Today, we generally recognize that cultural structure, including that part of it reflected in language, comprises both cognitive and affective processes—"people perceiving, thinking *or feeling* things together" (Wallace 1983, 29. Emphasis added). Again, once we revise Mead's theory of language by acknowledging the social significance of its affective dimension, we can consider the emotional side of culture and its role in social integration. This includes the part played by social values, which, after all, are nothing more than social cognitions permeated by affect (Collins 1986; Etzioni 1988), as well as the emotional energy of social groups that is the basis for social solidarity in the Durkheimian sense (Collins 1981).

Mead's third mistake was to assume a single generalized other, ignoring the cultural pluralism of complex modern societies (Meltzer 1972, 20). Even in a unilingual society, words do not always convey precisely the same meaning, cognitive or affective, to different individuals. While the 'other' plays a critical role in Mead's theory, he did not give the concept the same analytical attention he gave to the mind and self of the actor (Kuhn 1964a/1972, 172). The work on reference groups since Mead's time, of course, has largely remedied this theoretical shortcoming (Meltzer 1972, 20).

In step with this refinement of Mead, affect control theory acknowledges the multiplicity of reference groups and cultural perspectives that exist within any society. Based on the affective sentiments of particular cultures and subcultures, affect control predictions are admittedly culture-specific, although evidence accumulated to date suggests that affect control principles themselves are culturally universal.

Mead's fourth mistake was his failure to specify the mechanism by which the complex of shared, cultural meaning embedded in language gets translated into concerted action and social organization. For Mead, joint action simply "happens" as individuals sharing a common system of symbols and meanings take account of each other's roles and align their actions accordingly. "For Mead and the pragmatists," as Collins (1985, 223) laconically observes, "there is no problem of how society is put together; we simply work it out."

In this regard, ethnomethodologists have pointed to the over-taxation of the cognitive system implied by the infinite reflexivity of role-taking assumed by Mead and symbolic interactionists. In contrast, ethnomethodologists argue that people simply assume the most conventional understandings in particular situations, becoming aware of their preconscious assumptions only when disturbing events disrupt the routine flow of interaction. And, even then, according to ethnomethodologists, people make the minimum repair necessary to enable social interaction to get under way again (Collins 1985, 222–3). Despite its appeal, however, the ethnomethodological argument falls short of identifying a principle of social organization and integration. Collins (1986) identifies emotion as the "mysterious x-factor" in the ethnomethodological account of social order.

Thus, by focusing upon emotion, affect control theory, like Collins'(1981) theory of interactional ritual chains, specifies a mechanism by which the shared symbolic system of meaning emphasized by Mead and symbolic interactionists becomes translated into cooperative action and social integration. Affect control theory proposes that the conventional understandings of people are contained in their social sentiments for social identities, interpersonal acts, and other constitutents of social events, and that EPA profiles code information on social sentiments. Employing EPA profiles as inputs, impression formation equations model the affective reaction of people to events; and impression management equations model the control processes triggered by those that do not square with social convention. The concept of affective deflection provides a precise, quantitative measure of the disruption in the flow of interaction produced by culturally unexpected events; and affect control models show how socially disruptive events are repaired through restorative acts or reconceptualizations so that some functional level of social order and integration generally prevails.

Summary

In the first part of this chapter, I discussed how Mead's cognitive theory of language prevented him from developing a social psychology of emotions. Because all his major constructs—mind, self, and society—are defined in terms of language, they must be considered cognitive phenomena as well. Mead made no place for affect and the emotions in social experience. Instead, he proposed a *physiological*, rather than a *social*, psychology of emotion, relegating affect to the biological substratum of human consciousness. Without revision, the exclusively cognitive slant of his social psychology presents an insurmountable obstacle to a symbolic interactionist theory of emotion.

In the second half of this chapter, I suggested how Mead's social psychology can be revised to accommodate affect. Beginning with his cognitive theory of language, I argued that once his gratuitous and restrictive assumptions concerning the emotional significance of language are abandoned, affect automatically floods his other constructs—mind, self and society. This proposed revision of Mead paves the way for an interactionist social psychology that encompasses both cognition and affect and, by implication, motivation as well. Such a theory was proposed in Chapter 3. Because affect control theory maintains Mead's emphasis on language and control, while vitalizing his emotionally sterile constructs, I have portrayed the theory as an extension of Mead's social psychology into the realm of affect.

If affect control theory can be construed as an extension and revision of Mead, then by implication the theory can also be considered an extension and revision of symbolic interactionism, the self-proclaimed heir to Mead's social psychology. The following four chapters, beginning with the next chapter on identities, apply affect control theory to substantive issues with which symbolic interactionists traditionally have been concerned.

5

IDENTITIES AND ROLES

This is the first of two chapters applying affect control theory to role theory and analysis. This chapter lays the theoretical foundation by articulating the relation of affect control theory to identity theory, an application of the symbolic interactionist perspective to role analysis (Stryker and Statham 1985). The following chapter describes the affect control theory model for role analysis, illustrates its application with a straightforward presentation of simulation results, and compares the affect control theory of learning and retrieving roles with other theories.

Sociological role theories attack the study of roles with the conceptual armament of norms—those culturally expected or scripted behaviors and personal attributes that constitute social roles. Affect control theory approaches role analysis from the symbolic interactionist perspective of identity theory: "[P]eople behave within the framework of their situated identities and the implied social structure, and experiences that confirm fundamental sentiments about these identities are attained by engaging in role appropriate acts" (Heise 1988, 15). From this perspective, to cite Cancian (1975, 137), "norms are collective prescriptions or beliefs about what actions or attributes will cause others to validate a particular identity. An individual conforms to norms in order to validate an identity."

However, affect control approaches the study of roles at an even more elementary level than most identity theorists; that is, in terms of language and its affective meaning. Moreover, the theory is singular in its rigorous mathematical formalization of the identity theory approach to role behavior.

Following a concise statement of the concepts of *identity* and *role*, this chapter discusses the sociological and interactionist approaches to role theory, showing how identity theory is the theoretical offspring of their union. A brief review of the early statements of identity theory by Stryker (1968, 1980, 1981) and McCall and Simmons (1966/1978) sets the stage for drawing on explicit comparison between affect control theory and two later versions of identity theory—Burke's model of role-identity processes (Burke 1980; Burke and Tully 1977) and situated identity theory (Alexander and Wiley 1981). Besides embodying essential ideas from Stryker and/or McCall and Simmons, these two theories bear a strong resemblance to affect control theory in important respects. The purpose of this theoretical work is to present affect control theory as an important extension of identity theory and the symbolic interactionist tradition.

The Conceptual Framework

The early literature in role theory is characterized by much conceptual confusion (see Biddle and Thomas 1966; Gross et al. 1958; Heiss 1981; Wallace 1983). The conceptual work of Gross, Mason, and McEachern (1958) clarified matters considerably. Gross et al. defined a role as "a set of expectations . . . a set of evaluative standards applied to an incumbent of a particular position" (1958, 60), where "expectations" refer either to the behavior or the attributes for position incumbents, and where "position" is defined as the location of an actor in a social relationship. Gross et al. distinguished further between role expectations and the actual role behavior and attributes manifested by particular incumbents of social positions. Several implications and refinements of this definition of role are important for this and the following chapter.

First, a role refers to expected, rather than actual behavior.[1] To incorporate expectations and behavior into a single concept would be to confound *explanans* and *explanandum* and reduce explanation to description (cf. Heiss 1981).[2]

Second, as evaluative standards, role expectations are normative rather than descriptive (Gross et al. 1958, 58–9); thus, a role consists of a complex of normative expectations or norms.[3]

Third, as psychical phenomena, role expectations are part of a society's *cultural structure* (Wallace 1983, 110–115). As physical phenomena, role performances are a part of a society's *social structure* (Wallace 1983, 74–77).

Fourth, *social positions*, which convey the bundles of cultural expectations we call roles, can be considered from either an objective or subjective viewpoint—either from a sociological or a social psychological perspective. When internalized, social positions become *identities* (Stryker 1968, 1980) or, when considered together with their associated roles, *role-identities* (McCall and Simmons 1966/1978).

Two Schools of Role Theory

Two opposing schools of role theory are generally recognized in sociology and sociological social psychology. These have been assigned various appellations, but for the purposes of this discussion, I will refer to them as the *sociological* and the *interactionist* schools of role theory.[4]

From the sociological perspective, roles are institutionalized scripts constraining an actor's performances. From the interactionist viewpoint, roles are packages of behavior from which actors selectively sample, creating highly personalized and improvised performances. In the sociological model, an actor en-

gages in *role playing*—a more or less preconscious and automatic enactment of socially defined roles. In the interactionist model, an actor engages in *role-making*—
a self-conscious and creative process of constructing performances within the loose
organizing framework of a role (Turner 1962; Hewitt 1990, 98–99).

As ideal types, these two approaches to role theory embody diametrically opposed conceptualizations of the relation between person and society. From the traditional sociological viewpoint, society is a relatively structured, stable, and
consensual system consisting of more or less passive and receptive organisms. This
view is caricatured in Wrong's (1961) concept of the "oversocialized conception
of man." From the interactionist perspective, society is something emphemeral,
and consensus an occasional and precarious thing. The person is active and reflexive, creating social reality through personal and shifting definitions of the situation; social structure is, at best, a framework within which social interaction
takes place. In its extreme form, the interactionist perspective might be said to pro-
mote an "undersocialized" conception of man.

The same one-sided exaggerations of structure and process, of constraint
and creativity, that distinguish the sociological and interactionist schools of role-
theory characterize a long-standing schism in symbolic interactionism itself. One
side is defined by those who attempted to introduce social structural concepts from
conventional sociology into the dynamic, processual framework of symbolic interactionism; the other, by those who discarded structural concepts in favor of a
near Heraclitean model of social interaction. These two "denominations," so to
speak, have become known, respectively, as the "Iowa" and "Chicago" schools of
symbolic interactionism (Meltzer and Petras 1972) because of the institutional affiliation of their respective exemplars—Kuhn (1964/1972) and Blumer (1969). In
the discussions that follow, I will refer to these as the *structure* and *process* schools
of symbolic interactionism, respectively.

I introduce this complexity because any attempt to integrate the sociological and interactionist schools of role theory has implications for reconciling
the structure and process schools of symbolic interactionism itself. And, as we
shall see, this is important to my portrayal of affect control theory as a general
symbolic interactionist theory that incorporates both structural and dynamic
elements.

Now, as is frequently the case in a discipline's paradigmatic squabbles, caricaturing and mindless attack give way with the passing of time to mature reflection, an appreciation of the other's viewpoint, and a recognition of common
ground. The battle lines become less sharply drawn and the issues over which the
early battles were pitched become more diffuse. For example, Heiss (1981) observed an implicit description of interaction operating "just below the surface" of
structural analyses in sociological role theory (1981, 98); and, on the other side
of the paradigmatic front, a softening of the anti-structural position of the interactionist school.[5]

The most ambitious attempt to integrate the sociological and interactionist schools of role theory, and by implication, the structure and process schools of symbolic interactionism itself, can be found in Stryker and Statham (1985). In an encyclopedic review of both literatures, Stryker and Statham document the development of an emergent integrative framework which they identify with the generalized symbolic interactionist model proposed by Stryker (1968) and embodied in identity theory (Stryker 1968, 1980, 1981; McCall and Simmons 1966/1978). According to Stryker and Statham, this emergent framework manifests a dual focus on societal constraint and personal construction—"imposition" and "improvisation" (Powers 1980)—that characterizes the respective emphases of the sociological and interactionist approaches to role theory. Moreover, it assumes that society and person are reciprocally related influences on individual behavior.

Identity Theory

As articulated by Stryker (1968, 559), identity theory begins with the generalized symbolic interactionist premise that "symbols [are] used to designate the stable, morphological components of social structure usually termed 'positions,' and it is these positions which carry the shared behavioral expectations conventionally labeled 'roles.'" This early statement illustrates the continuity between identity theory and the sociological conceptual framework of Gross et al. (1958) discussed above. While accepting the objective nature of positions and roles as units of social and cultural structure, identity theory approaches these structural concepts from the subjective viewpoint of the self; people employ social positional designations to name themselves, and these "reflexively applied positional designations . . . create internalized expectations with respect to their own behavior" (Stryker 1968, 559).

Stryker's (1968) statement of identity theory incorporated two important ideas from symbolic interactionists. First, while social behavior is initiated by internalized expectations, it develops through a process of "role-making" (Turner 1962) that continually reshapes the ensuing interaction (1968, 359). Second, because identities exist only insofar as a person participates in social relationships, requiring a coincidence of person's identity claims and others' placements, identities "situate" a person in social relations (Stone 1962).

Stryker proposed that social identities are arranged in a hierarchy of salience, where salient identities are those that have a high probability of being invoked in a variety of situations. While viewing identity salience as largely a cognitive matter, he acknowledged the role played by cathectic and conative modalities of self-response to identities (1968, 560–562). In this regard, he proposed that the greater the investment of positive cathectic response in an identity, or the greater its instrumental value to a person's desires, the higher that identity will be in a person's salience hierarchy. The motivational implications of this proposition were discussed in Chapter 3 of this book and need not be repeated here. In addition to providing organization to the self, according to Stryker, identity salience is an important predictor of behavior, especially in structurally complex situations where multiple identities become candidates for invocation.

Stryker contends that his concept of "commitment" makes the connection between person and society, and specifies the relevance of social structure for interaction. A person is committed to an identity and corresponding role to the extent that his or her social relationships depend upon "being a particular kind of person." Hence, commitment is operationally defined as the "costs" entailed in foregoing relations based upon the appropriation to self of a given identity (1968, 560).[6] Stryker (1968, 561) identified two dimensions of commitment—*extensivity*, the sheer number of relationships, and *intensivity*, the depth of relationships, premised on a particular identity. Stryker gathered his concepts of identity salience, commitment, and behavior in his general proposition that "commitment affects identity salience which, in turn, affects behavioral choices" (1981, 24). He then derived a set of testable hypotheses from this general proposition (Stryker 1968, 1980, 1981).

A second version of identity theory was independently developed by McCall and Simmons (1966/1978) about the same time as Stryker's (1968) early programmatic statement. Their concept of *role-identity*—"the character and the role that an individual devises for himself as an occupant of a particular social position . . . his imaginative [and often idealized] view of himself . . . as an occupant of that position" (1978, 65)—captures the essential ideas in Stryker's conceptualization of *identity*, while emphasizing that identities "are likely to be role-specific" (1978, 84). Like Stryker, they propose that role-identities are arranged in a hierarchy of "prominence," albeit conceived as perhaps more "loosely patterned" and "plastic" (1978, 74) than Stryker's concept of identity salience. McCall and Simmons also imply, like Stryker, an affective as well as a cognitive component in the hierarchy of role-identities that help organize a person's self. Among the determinants of prominence, they include the amount of support provided by self and others to sustain a particular role–identity, a person's commitment and investment in it, and the intrinsic and extrinsic gratifications derived from related performances.

However, role-identity prominence is not the only personal determinant of behavior. The actual performances enacted in a situation depend as well on a "very fluid hierarchy of identities" they refer to as "salience." The referent of salience is the "situational self" (1978, 84), in contradistinction to *prominence*, whose referent is the "ideal self." While prominence is relatively stable, salience shifts as gratification obtained from related performances leads to temporary satiation.

McCall and Simmons distinguish further between the "situational self" and "character." While "the situational self constitutes merely the person's own preferences as to the set of role-identities he will enact in a given situation . . . his character—being a social object—represents the subset that is actually interactively negotiated and ratified for him in the situation by all the participants" (1978, 84).

In addition to a more elaborate set of distinctions that captures the active, situationally fluid and phenomenal nature of the self, the version of identity theory proposed by McCall and Simmons departs from Stryker's by drawing heavily upon exchange theory and the dramaturgical metaphor.

Affect Control Theory and Identity Theory

Referring to the generalized symbolic interactionist framework articulated by Stryker and, by implication, identity theory, Heise claimed that affect control theory "has these features and can be considered a version of symbolic interactionism" (1979, 36). Moreover, Stryker (1981; Stryker and Statham 1985, 357) accepted this claim. Heise (1979, 36) also observed the indebtedness of affect control theory to the role-identity theory of McCall and Simmons 1966/1978), whose influence can be found throughout his first major statement of affect control theory (1979).

In view of the acknowledged affinity of affect control theory and the early identity theories of Stryker and McCall and Simmons, it would be somewhat superfluous to pursue a detailed comparison here. Instead, I compare affect control theory with two later versions of identity theory that extend important ideas from the work of Stryker and/or McCall and Simmons: (1) Burke's model of role-identity processes (Burke 1980; Burke and Tully 1977); and (2) situated identity theory (Alexander and Wiley 1981). While the second of these falls short of identity theory's objective of relating microinteraction to social structure (Stryker and Statham 1985, 343), it draws heavily from McCall and Simmons (1966/1978) and other important symbolic interactionists, including Stone (1962) and Mead (1934) himself, as well as Goffman's (1961) closely related work on situated activity. Comparing affect control theory to these two versions of identity theory enables me to demonstrate its continuity with identity theory, while highlighting the particular features of affect control theory that contribute to its development and refinement.

Burke's Model of Role-Identity Processes

Integrating ideas from both Stryker (1968/1980) and McCall and Simmons (1966/1978), Peter Burke (1980) extended identity theory by delineating five theoretical properties of identities from an interactionist view of the self: (1) identities are self-meanings; (2) identities are relational; (3) identities are reflexive; (4) identities affect behavior indirectly; and (5) identities motivate. While Burke intended these five properties to define an adequate measurement of identities as meanings attributed to the self, they also serve as a concise statement of identity theory itself, with which affect control theory can be efficiently compared. In the following discussion, I first describe each property and then draw an immediate comparison with affect control theory.

First, the idea that identities are meanings a person attributes to the self has become a truism in interactionist theory. People learn self-meanings from the responses of significant others to their words, acts, and appearances, and from the identities others impute to them on this basis. What is novel about Burke's work is his imaginative and creative attempt to measure identities with quantitative precision, while remaining true to the theoretical properties of self-meaning supposed by interactionism. Embracing Schwartz and Stryker's (1970, 36) proposal that the psychological theory underlying the semantic differential—what Osgood et al. (1957) called the "representational mediation process"—is consistent with the symbolic interactionist view of the self, Burke conceptualizes the meaning of identities as their location in a multidimensional semantic space.

Similarly, "in a theory of roles obtained by applying the affect control model, a role is defined by the meaning of the role-identity—especially its evaluation, potency, and activity associations" (Heise 1979, 105). However, while both theories employ Osgood's semantic differential to measure identities, Burke questions whether the established EPA structure of the semantic differential employed by affect control theory necessarily includes the most relevant dimensions of meaning. In lieu of the *a priori* approach of affect control theory, therefore, he opts for an *a posteriori* procedure that empirically defines the underlying dimensions of meaning for particular sets of identities and counter-identities. I examine the implications of this difference in procedure below.

Second, Burke identifies three ways in which identities are relational. First, identities are related to roles. To make this connection explicit, he employs the "role-identity" concept of McCall and Simmons (1966/ 1978). Second, identities are related to other identities in the salience hierarchy proposed by Stryker (1968), those nearer the top organizing those lower in the hierarchy. Third, by learning the social structure of a society, the individual learns how to relate to other people. Just as roles in the external social structure are given meaning by their relation to "counter-roles," identities in the internal structure of the self derive their meaning from their relation to "counter-identities."

Of these three ways in which identities are relational, Burke emphasizes the third. He proposes that identities cannot be adequately measured in isolation, that they must be assessed in terms of their commonalities and differences with counter–identities. He observes that this presents little problem for identities nearer the top of the hierarchy (e.g., age, sex, occupation)—the "sociologically interesting ones" representing the "great structural divisions of society" (1980, 19). However, he acknowledges that measuring the relational meaning of identities lower on the hierarchy becomes more problematic, presumably because the identification of counter–identities in these cases is more difficult. (For example, what

are the counter-identities structurally related to a "fink," a "buddy," an "egghead?")
This is a major limitation in Burke's procedure, which I discuss below.

Like Burke, affect control theory conceptualizes identities as inherently relational: "[T]he constraints on identity–confirming actions shift, depending on
the feelings attached to others' identities, so that generally an actor's behavior
varies across relationships" (Heise 1979, 105). However, while Burke incorporates
the relational property of identities into his measurement procedure by employing dimensions of meaning that maximally distinguish identities from counter-
identities,[7] affect control theory builds this property into the affect control model
itself. For a given identity in the actor position of social events, the model predicts
different behaviors for different counter-identities in the object position.[8]

The difference between the two procedures derives from relative emphases
in their respective research programs. While Burke is far from disinterested in
identity-meaning as independent variable (Burke and Reitzes 1981, 1991), his
model is devoted to describing the meaning of identities in the theoretical property space supposed by the interactionist concept of self. In contrast, while affect
control theory is not unconcerned with the descriptive applications of identity
measurement, the theory focuses on predicting and modeling interaction from
simple and direct measures of identity meaning.

Burke's requirement that counter-identities be employed to define the di-
mensionality of the semantic space containing identities points to a serious practical limitation in his measurement procedure. As intimated above, his procedure
is restricted to measuring identities with clearly identifiable counter-identities,[9]
while the range of social identities measured in affect control research is virtually
unlimited. "Fink," "buddy," and "egghead" pose no greater problem for measurement than standard sociological identities like "mother," "student," and "doctor."
Moreover, even for those identities having clearly identifiable counter-identities,
the pair-by-pair requirement of Burke's procedure would require massive research
expenditures and place unreasonable demands on research subjects to collect data
on more than a small number of social identities.

Third, for Burke, "reflexivity is nothing more than feedback to the self"
(1980, 20) from one's performances and other's reaction to them. Identities influence behavior and, in turn, behavior has implications for the identities people
are trying to confirm through their actions. The *feedback identity*—the "image" of
the self in role—that results from a person's behavior is monitored and compared
with the *actual identity* the person is trying to confirm in a situation. A person con-
trols the feedback identity by modifying his or her actions until some correspondence is reached between the ephemeral "image" and the stable "identity."
According to Burke, there are two measurements that are consistent with the reflexiveness of self: first, measuring the strength of a "corrective response" when a
person's performance is "off target" with respect to the confirmation of a particular identity; and second, an assessment of what gets corrected.

Like Burke's model, affect control theory supposes that a reflexive self underlies the identity-confirmation process. In Chapters 3 and 4, I discussed how the theory embraces Mead's concepts of the reflective mind and the reflexive self, and his view of social action as a cybernetic process of "corrective responses" to "off target" performances. In affect control theory, affective deflection is a precise quantitative measure of the consequences of "off-target" performances for identity-confirmation; and what gets corrected through restorative action is the transient impression of a person until it corresponds optimally with the fundamental sentiments of the identity he or she is trying to confirm. In the process, successive images of the self in role approach the identity an actor is trying to confirm; but for affect control theory, this cognitive convergence is mediated by affect control processes.

Like the relational property of identities, reflexivity is built into Burke's measurement procedure,[10] while in affect control theory it is embodied in a theoretical principle (affect control) external to the measurement procedure. Thus, while Burke conceives of identity-confirmation as a process of reducing cognitive discrepancies between "feedback identity" (image) and "actual identity," affect control theory views identity-confirmation as a process of achieving correspondence between transient impressions and fundamental sentiments evoked, respectively, by present and earlier cognitions of the same identity-situated self.

The fourth theoretical property of Burke's model of role-identity processes, the indirect effect of identities on behavior, addresses the dual nature of the self as "structure" and "process." Burke claims that the distinction between identities (the stable components of self-meaning derived from social structure) and images (the ephemeral components of self-meaning derived from social process) bridges the theoretical divide between the structure and process schools of role theory. Because the relative stability of identities renders them unresponsive to the instantaneously shifting demands of interaction, according to Burke, identities affect performances only indirectly through the images they create.

Of particular relevance to affect control theory, Burke's model incorporates an element of cybernetic control. This consists of a small return effect of image on identity, along with a small feedback effect of performance on image. In addition, his model specifies that the effect of one person's performances trickles through the interactional process depicted by the model, thereby affecting the images and subsequent performances of other interactants. The cybernetic nature of Burke's model is made conceptually more explicit in Burke and Reitzes (1991), where it is likened to affect control theory.

Returning to Burke's proposition that identities influence performance indirectly through the images they create, affect control theory makes no formal distinction between "identity" and "image." Yet, the idea behind the distinction—that identities are subject to variations in situational demands—is embodied in the impression management equations of the theory (Proposition 8, Chapter 2). Affect control analysis begins with identities in the Actor and Object positions of ABO events. The fundamental sentiments of identities in affect control theory correspond to the stable meanings of identities in Burke's framework. However, once identities become paired in A-O frames, their meanings become mutually adjusted in the impression management equations that generate the unknown behavioral expectations for actor and object-person. These mutually adjusted meanings reflect the situational demands posed by the presence of specific others and are functionally similar to images, the "working copies" of identities in Burke's conceptual framework.

Moreover, the implementation of an act by either participant creates additional situational demands and further adjustments in the fundamental sentiments for identities. These transient feelings serve as a new "working copy" of each identity for the next event. In affect control theory, as in Burke's model of role-identity processes, the initial meanings of identities shift continually as events unfold. The reidentification model of affect control theory (Chapter 8) shows how identities become modified by traits and other kinds of attributions as events create transient impressions of participants that depart from the fundamental sentiments of their situated identities, or are replaced by entirely new identities (labels) when events produce such massive deflections that the initial identities of participants cease to be cognitively sensible. Hence, the theory does not find it necessary to distinguish between identities and images to account for process and change in social interaction. The theory is inherently dynamic.

Finally, drawing upon Stryker (1968), Burke proposes that identities motivate. This property of identities as self–meanings, according to Burke, has important implications for identity measurement. First, identities and behaviors can be located in the same semantic space. Second, the set of dimensions defining this space can be employed as a coordinate system for locating identities and behaviors in that space. By computing the distances between points, the researcher can assess the behavioral implications of particular identities and, conversely, the identity implications of particular acts. This enables the researcher to get an empirical handle on the reflexive nature of identity processes. Third, in line with the interactionist notion of meaning, and in order for meaningful social interaction to take place, the underlying dimensions of this semantic space must be culturally defined, and there must be some consensus on the relative locations of particular identities and acts within it.[11]

With respect to the proposal at hand, I argued in Chapter 3 that in order to motivate behavior, identities must first be invested with affect. By measuring identities and behaviors in terms of the evaluation, potency, and activity dimensions of the semantic differential, affect control theory captures the affective meaning of identities and, hence, their motivational implications for action. By rejecting the EPA structure of the semantic differential in favor of more content-specific and cognitive dimensions of meaning, Burke discards the dynamic principle of affect.

And, having done so, his model cannot account for the motivational significance of identities.

In this regard, Burke's entire model of role-identity processes is cast in cognitive terms—identity as "a kind of idealized picture of the self-in-role which provides the motivation for performances" and image "as a map for role-taking or role performance . . . a guide in role-making and construction" (1980, 21). For affect control theory, it is the affective meaning of identities that mobilizes action, not "cognitive maps" and "images." In terms of my discussion of motivation in Chapter 3, Burke's model accounts for the *direction* but not the *energization* of response in motivated behavior—the same criticism levied against Mead's cognitive model of mind in Chapter 4.

Situated Identity Theory

While developed in response to the allegedly pervasive and contaminating effect of the social desirability factor in experimental research, situated identity theory (Alexander and Wiley 1981) is an important theoretical development in its own right. Moreover, it bears a striking resemblance to affect control theory and to identity theory in general.

Situated identity theory integrates attribution theory with symbolic interactionism, the work of Heider (1958) with Mead (1934), Goffman (1959, 1961a), Stone (1962), and McCall and Simmons (1966/1978). Affect control theory developed out of the same theoretical roots (Heise 1979). For both theories, the unit of analysis is the social act, whose "defining properties . . . are situated identities" (Alexander and Wiley 1981, 270). In addition, both theories stress that the definition of the situation changes with the unfolding of events and the shifting of perspectives as an actor interacts with different others.

Combining ideas from Heider (1958) and Mead (1934), situated identity theory proposes that people learn through role-taking to see themselves in terms of the dispositional imputations made by others, and to view their conduct as expressions of these attributes. The actual or presumed presence of others stimulates, in Heider's terms, a readiness to perceive the relation between self and environment in terms of personal dispositions imputed by others or, in Mead's terms, a readiness to take the attitudes of others toward oneself through role-taking.

Following McCall and Simmons (1966), situated identity theory distinguishes between mere human *behavior*, wherein a person is "psychologically oblivious to others' presumed or potential presence," and human *conduct*, wherein "an actor orients himself to a field in which others are psychologically present" (1981, 273). Carrying this distinction one step further, situated identity theory distinguishes between conduct and *situated activity*. In conduct, others may not be actually present, only potentially so, and an actor may remain unaware of the fact that he or she has taken the actual or potential presence of others into account. In situated activity, on the other hand, an actor perceives particular others, or classes of others, and more or less consciously incorporates their perspectives into his or her orientation to conduct. "Conduct becomes situated activity when it is anchored outside the self and constrained by presumed monitoring (1981, 273)."

Situated activity provides the basis for identity formation and social behavior. Out of situated activity emerge situated identities, "the attributions that are made from salient perspectives about an actor's presence and performance in the immediate social context" (1981, 270). Situated identities are properties of the social field of interaction and define the relation between an actor and his or her environment at any point in the flow of situated activity.

To systematically discuss the affinity of situated identity theory and affect control theory, I offer the following formal statement of situated identity theory, comparing each of six propositions in turn to affect control theory.

1. According to the most basic assumption of the theory, "identity formation is the fundamental process of social perception and the cornerstone of interaction" (1981, 274).

Similarly, affect control theory supposes that people try to experience events that confirm fundamental sentiments (Proposition 8, Chapter 2), and that they accomplish this by validating the identities of self and other. Applied to social perception, the theory proposes that identity-confirming events are more likely to be recognized (Proposition 12, Chapter 2) and that identity-disconfirming events instigate the reidentification of participants through labeling or attribution processes (Propositions 9, 21, and 22, Chapter 2). Applied to social interaction, the theory proposes that people are more likely to implement interpersonal acts that confirm the identities of self and other (Propositions 16 and 17, Chapter 2).

2. As "an ongoing process of establishing, confirming, modifying, and sometimes destroying situated identities," situated activity "provides the conditions under which identity formation occurs" (1981, 273).

Like situated identity theory, affect control theory views social interaction in terms of its consequences for the situated identities of participants. Interactional events produce transient impressions of each person that often are at variance with the fundamental sentiments of their situated identities. And, again, identity-disconfirming events that cannot easily be undone through restorative action instigate reidentification processes that modify or transform the original identities of participants. In fact, the empirically-based reidentification equations in affect control theory reveal that "a person's action is mostly what determines the identities the person achieves" (Heise 1979, 89).

3. "Actors enter settings with portions of their identities already established," their social characteristics or locations, such as age, gender, and occupation, and these "culturally established summaries of previous events and actions . . . function in the same manner as information about past events" (1981, 287).

Similarly, affect control theory proposes that the definition of the situation establishing the initial identities of participants is the outcome of complex cognitive processing that takes into account the social characteristics and classifications people bring to the situation (See Proposition 6, Chapter 2, and Heise 1979, 78; 1988, 2–4). Like situated identities, these biographical and general social identities (Hewitt 1990) convey information about the potential actions of participants.

4. "Identity claims set the pattern for status, affective, evaluative, and power relationships that prevail during any activity sequence (1981, 274)."

According to affect control theory, the identities claimed by participants evoke affective associations which determine the status, power, and liveliness of their initial actions, setting the pattern for social relationships in the ensuing sequence of events. Affect control theory not only embraces the proposition at hand, it operationalizes it through its impression management equations.

5. Because an actor perceives that his or her conduct has implications for the dispositional attributions made by others, and thus his or her situated identities, "actors will prefer an alternative to the extent that it is more socially desirable than the others available" (1981, 288).

While not formally incorporated into affect control theory, the theory accepts that "much of the time—perhaps most of the time—people are operating with situational definitions [and hence situated identities] that have been provided by others" (Heise 1979, 6). Despite the inclination of people to confirm identities presumed to be monitored by others, affect control theory recognizes that many other factors determine which identity becomes invoked and actualized in any situation. Not the least of these is an identity's personal "salience" (Stryker 1968, 1980) or "prominence" (McCall and Simmons (1966/1978). Affect control theory also recognizes, as McCall and Simmons (1966/1978), Collins (1975), and numerous other authors have noted, that the identity a person tries to implement in a situation often is at odds with those imputed and reinforced by others, giving rise to power plays and identity negotiations (Heise 1979, 6–7). Put another way, people are not always willing participants in what Weinstein and Deutschberger (1963) call "altercasting" processes.

This brings us to the rub in situated identity theory: its scope is restricted to sequences of normatively structured action—those involving consensus on the attributional dimensions in terms of which acts are to be assessed; how to characterize particular acts along each dimension; and, by implication, the consequences of particular acts for the attribution of situated identities (Alexander and Wiley 1981, 275). While affect control theory assumes that people universally agree on the relevant dimensions for assessing acts (evaluation, potency, and activity), and that people within a given culture or subculture agree on the approximate positions of acts on these dimensions, its predictions are not limited to situations of normative consensus.

Affect control research has already generated a number of cultural data sets (American, Irish, Canadian, Japanese, and German), and separately by gender within each culture. Hence, it can simulate situations involving "multiple, possibly conflicting perspectives that define the situated identities associated with a given response alternative" (Alexander and Wiley 1981, 289), which remains a self-proclaimed aspiration for the development of situated identity theory.

6. With respect to others' expectations for a person's conduct, situated identity theory proposes that, "in the absence of any other criteria, normative expectations about conduct should be a function of the social desirability of alternatives" (1981, 276).

This proposition, as well as the preceding one, follows from the assumption that the underlying dimensions of situated activity are evaluative in nature. Due to the supposed overwhelming salience of the evaluative dimension of meaning, the theory proposes that an actor's choices among actionable alternatives, as well as others' expectations for his or her selection, are a function of their social desirability. Since affect control theory recognizes that power and activity are also important dimensions of meaning, it views an actor's behavioral choices and others' normative expectations as a function of the powerfulness and liveliness of available actions as well.

In conclusion, while there is a striking affinity between situated identity theory and affect control theory, there are also a number of important differences. In addition to those differences identified in the preceding discussion, a principle of control is at best implicit in situated identity theory, in its assumption that actors continually monitor their actions from the perspectives of others.

Nor does situated identity theory make explicit the role of affect in situated activity. Despite its emphasis on social desirability as a pervasive influence on situated activity, the theory does not explicitly deal with the evaluative dimension of meaning in terms of affect. The theory supposes that the social desirability of actionable alternatives in normatively structured situations gets translated into personal preferences. However, it fails to recognize that an actor's choices are motivated by a desire to confirm situated identities that have become appropriated to self and invested with affect. By default, the theory implies that an actor's conduct is motivated simply by its anticipated consequences for the dispositional imputations made by others.

Finally, affect control theory operationalizes situated activity at a more micro level than situated identity theory; that is, at the level of language—the syntactic structure of situated activity and the semantics of interpersonal acts, social identities, and other components of social events.

Summary

This chapter began with a discussion of how identity theory integrates the sociological and interactionist approaches to role theory and, at the same time, the structure and process schools of symbolic interactionism itself. Following a review of the program statements of identity theory by Stryker (1968, 1980, 1981) and

McCall and Simmons (1966/1978), two later versions of identity theory were explicitly compared with affect control theory—Burke's model of role-identity processes (Burke 1980; Burke and Tully 1977) and situated identity theory (Alexander and Wiley 1981). The objective of this theoretical work is two-fold: to demonstrate systematically that affect control theory is an important extension and refinement of identity theory in the symbolic interactionist tradition; and to lay the theoretical foundation for the following chapter on role analysis.

If, as claimed in the present chapter, affect control theory is an offspring of the generalized symbolic interactionist framework articulated by Stryker (1968), and hence a sibling of identity theory, then its predictions should span both the sociological and interactionist schools of role theory, as well as the structure and process schools of symbolic interactionism itself. That is, the theory should be successful in predicting role behavior in both routine and novel situations—those reflecting socially and culturally structured patterns of interaction and those requiring role creativity and improvisation on the part of interactants.

6

ROLE ANALYSIS

Affect control theory proposes that people engage in role–appropriate behavior in order to validate cognitively and affectively salient identities (Proposition 17, Chapter 2). The preceding chapter laid the conceptual and theoretical foundation of this proposition. Applied to role research, "the applicability of affect control theory . . . is demonstrated best by showing that a variety of analyses conducted in the framework of the theory yield sensible results" (Heise 1979, 106). This is the task of the chapter at hand.

Simulations of standardized events across a number of conventional institutionalized settings are presented first to illustrate the applicability of affect control theory to a wide range of socially and culturally structured interaction. These are followed by example simulations of unstandardized events, those that challenge the role creativity of participants. These analyses demonstrate that affect control theory is applicable to the central concerns of both the sociological and interactionist schools of role theory, or the structure and process schools of symbolic interactionism. The chapter concludes with a discussion of how roles are learned and later retrieved in memory, comparing the account of these processes provided by affect control theory to the social learning theory of Heiss (1981) and the associative addressing theory of Wallace (1983).

The Affect Control Model for Role Analysis

Role analysis is conducted in affect control theory by applying the model for *event construction* (Heise 1979, cpt. 3; 1988, 21–23; 1992, 4–7). While the mathematical formalization of the model is complex, a brief verbal description should convey what the mathematics accomplish.

Using EPA profiles of identities for the actor and object–person of a possible event as inputs, the model searches for interpersonal acts that would optimally confirm the known identities. The numerical EPA behavior profile defining optimal, identity-confirming acts is derived from an equation maximizing the subjective likelihood or normality of events (Heise 1979, 1988) or, equivalently, minimizing its subjective unlikeliness or uniqueness (Heise 1992). In turn, the subjective likelihood (or unlikelihood) of events is defined as a function of deflection—the squared discrepancy between the *fundamental sentiments* for the known identities and unknown behavior of a possible event and the *transient feelings* that would occur if this event were realized. Events generating small deflections appear more likely; those producing large deflections seem more unlikely (Heise and MacKinnon 1988). Hence, because maximizing event likelihood involves minimizing affective deflection, the optimal EPA behavior profile derived from the likelihood equations maximally confirms the known identities in an event. Applied to role analysis, empirically measured interpersonal acts whose fundamental EPA profiles come closest to fitting the optimal EPA behavior profile generated by the model define role-appropriate behavior.

The *generative* model of affect control theory contrasts sharply with the *inventorial* approach of traditional role analysis (Heise 1979, 135–140). Epitomized in the person–behavior matrices of Biddle and Thomas (1966), inventorial models specify a role empirically by cataloging the behavioral expectations for an incumbent of a social position. Because this involves judgmental sampling of behaviors from an often indeterminate universe, the inventorial approach to role analysis is an operationally inadequate procedure (Heise 1979, 135–136).[1]

Role Analysis

In the role analyses that follow, pairs of identities were drawn from various institutional settings. Each dyad was analyzed by INTERACT (Heise 1978; Heise and Lewis 1988a), employing equations and cultural data from the Canadian study.[2] For simplicity, actors were assumed in each case to agree on the definition of the situation (their respective identities and the nature of the relationship, as explained below).

Each simulation in the following tables contains a row of numbers. This is the model-generated EPA behavior profile specifying the kinds of interpersonal acts that would optimally confirm the identities in each dyad, thereby defining role–appropriate behavior. The interpersonal acts that follow each optimal profile are those that come closest to fitting it. These are listed according to the order in which they were retrieved; that is, in terms of their ability to confirm the fundamental sentiments of identities in a given dyad.[3]

Certain acts (e.g., physical, touching ones, especially those of a sexual nature) are appropriate only in particular institutional contexts. Institutionally inappropriate acts are suppressed in INTERACT analyses by activating one or more cognitive filters. The ones used for these analyses were: verbal (acts with a verbal emphasis); physical (acts with a physical emphasis); primary (interpersonal acts like "love" and "abandon"); exchange (economic acts like "pay" and "hire"); managing (controlling acts like "deter," "coerce," and "arrest"); fixing (therapeutic acts like "rehabilitate," "cure," and "medicate"); and training (socialization acts like "teach," and acts like "marry" and "adopt" that initiate new roles). Either verbal or physical acts, or both, must be specified in each analysis, along with at least one of the remaining kinds of acts. In most cases, supplementary analyses revealed that the employment of cognitive filters made little difference to the behavioral re-trievals based on EPA profiles alone, except to remove the occasional institution-ally anomalous act.

Family Roles

According to the role expectations reported in Table 6.1, good, nice acts are culturally expected in family interaction. A husband and wife, for example, should compliment and enjoy one another. In addition, he might applaud, adore, dance with, invite, and nuzzle her; and she, uplift, massage, kiss, and alert him. A father is expected to welcome, assist, comfort, please, and uplift both sons and daughters; to console and aid a son; and to coach, gratify, encourage, thank, and praise a daughter. A mother is expected to perform similarly good but less powerful acts toward her children. As the most powerful family member, a father can expect to be consulted, accommodated, admired, honored, gratified, complimented, in-vited, and greeted by both sons and daughters; talked to, answered, appealed to, and delighted by a son; and thanked by a daughter. A mother can expect compa-rably good acts from her children, but also acts that are slightly less deferent and somewhat more lively than those directed towards a father. A brother is expected to implement somewhat more powerful and lively acts than a sister towards sib-lings of either gender.

It must be emphasized that the role expectations reported in Table 6.1 have been generated from the fundamental sentiments of males, and that somewhat dif-ferent results occur when female sentiments are employed. For example, the ideal profile generated by the model for sister-to-sister acts is [2.1 .9 1.1] for females, as compared to [1.8 .6 .7] for males, revealing that women expect sisters to interact in a somewhat more positive, powerful, and lively fashion then men do. While there is overlap between male and female expectations, women also expect sisters to amuse, flatter, aid, defend, warn, and encourage one another.

It must also be pointed out that physical, touching acts have been filtered out from simulation results for all but the husband-wife relationship. This serves the function of eliminating institutionally-inappropriate acts of intimacy for other relationships, but it also results in the suppression of normatively acceptable acts of physical affection among family members. For example, employing female sen-timents and deactivating the cognitive filter for physical acts, a father is expected to embrace and caress a daughter—appropriate, non–sexual physical behavior for a loving father.

TABLE 6.1

Role Expectations of Canadian Male University Students for Nuclear Family Roles,
Generated Analytically from the EPA Profiles for Actor and Object-Person Identities[a]

	Actor			
Object	Husband or Father	Wife or Mother	Son or Brother	Daughter or Sister
Husband or Father		[2.2 .9 .5] compliment enjoy uplift massage kiss adopt alert	[1.8 .1 .1] consult accommodate admire honor talk to answer gratify compliment invite greet appeal to delight	[2.0 .1 .1] accommodate consult honor gratify compliment admire thank invite greet
Wife or Mother	[2.1 .5 .3] compliment applaud enjoy adore dance with invite adopt nuzzle		[1.7 .4 .5] appeal to invite greet entertain talk to acclaim charm compliment delight admire	[2.0 .5 .6] compliment invite appeal to delight greet alert entertain uplift warn
Son or Brother	[2.6 1.3 .1] welcome assist comfort please uplift compliment console aid	[2.4 .7 .2] compliment please gratify encourage invite thank uplift	[2.2 .9 .8] alert compliment delight uplift invite warn appeal to aid	[1.9 .5 .6] invite appeal to compliment delight greet entertain alert

TABLE 6.1 (continued)

Actor

Object	Husband or Father	Wife or Mother	Son or Brother	Daughter or Sister
Daughter or Sister	[2.4 1.2 .1]	[2.2 .7 .2]	[2.1 .9 .9]	[1.8 .6 .7]
	welcome	compliment	alert	appeal to
	please	please	delight	invite
	assist	invite	warn	entertain
	comfort	gratify	cheer	delight
	uplift	encourage	appeal to	alert
	compliment	thank	compliment	compliment
	coach	greet	invite	greet
	gratify	honor	uplift	
	encourage			
	thank			
	praise			
	invite			

a. The row of numbers before each set of acts is the optimal EPA profile generated by the model for the actor's behavior toward the object-person in each dyad. Physical, touching acts have been suppressed for all but husband-wife relationships.

Medical and Mental Health Roles

As reported in Table 6.2, the role expectations for a doctor toward a nurse are socioemotional and supportive in nature: gratifying, complimenting, encouraging, thanking, pleasing, and praising. Those for a doctor towards a patient include similar socioemotional and supportive acts, but also functional ones like talking to and visiting a patient.

The role expectations for a nurse include complimenting, uplifting, or appealing to doctors and patients alike. In addition, a nurse might invite, alert, delight, please, and greet a doctor, and uplift, laugh with, massage, and assist a patient.

A patient might consult or esteem both doctors and nurses (coddle appears to be anomalous here), and notice, regard, ask about, or humor a nurse.

Most of the acts retrieved for medical roles appear to be quite sensible ones for initial encounters in social interaction. As reported above, a few functional acts (talk to, visit, assist) are sprinkled among the many supportive and socioemotional ones in the culturally expected behavioral repertoires of doctors and nurses. Nonetheless, core medical acts like cure, medicate, and rehabilitate do not show up in the initial retrievals.

TABLE 6.2

Role Expectations of Canadian Male University Students for Selected Medical and Mental Health Roles, Generated Analytically from the EPA Profiles for Actor and Object-Person Identities[a]

Actor	Role Expectations	Object
Nurse	[2.1 .8 .4] compliment, invite, alert, delight, please, uplift, greet, appeal to	Doctor
Patient	[1.8 –.7 –.3] consult, coddle, esteem	Doctor
Doctor	[2.3 .4 –.0] gratify, compliment, encourage, honor, thank, accommodate, please, praise	Nurse
Patient	[1.4 –.3 –.3] consult, coddle, notice, esteem, regard, ask about, humor	Nurse
Doctor	[2.0 .9 .2] compliment, praise, encourage, gratify, consider, respect, talk to, visit, approve of	Patient
Nurse	[1.9 1.0 .7] warn, laugh with, massage, appeal to, uplift, compliment, interest, assist	Patient
Psychiatrist	[1.3 .9 .2] acclaim, talk to, greet, approve of, correct, guide, befriend, charm	Patient
Patient	[1.2 –.7 –.1] consult, admire, ask about, call, entreat, explain, placate	Psychiatrist
Neurotic	[–.7 –.3 .5] pooh–pooh, patronize, softsoap, doubt, beseech, awake, haze, disbelieve, confound	Psychiatrist
Psychotic	[–.9 .3 .8] dog, confound, haze, parody, disconcert, befuddle, overrate	Psychiatrist

a. The row of numbers before each set of acts is the optimal EPA profile generated by the model for the actor's behavior toward the object-person in each dyad. The relationship of doctor and nurse toward patient has been defined as verbal, physical, and fixing. Physical acts have been suppressed for all other relationships.

However, functional acts associated with occupational roles often appear in affect control theory simulations—and, presumably, in real life settings as well—only after a round or two of preliminary social interaction. For instance, consider a scenario involving a male doctor and a female patient, where the relationship is defined as verbal, physical, and therapeutic by the doctor, and as verbal and therapeutic by the patient. The doctor's role expectations for himself (his behavioral intentions) generated by INTERACT are to compliment, praise, encourage, gratify, consider, respect, and talk to the patient. His expectations for the patient include a single act—that the patient consults him. Now, if the event, "patient consults doctor," is implemented, his intentions for the next round of interaction become more clearly therapeutic in nature. At this point, according to predictions, he might assist and rehabilitate the patient. At the same time, the patient's expectations for a doctor become even more singularly therapeutic. Having consulted a doctor, she expects him to rehabilitate, uplift, educate, help, cure, teach, and warn her.

Turning to mental health roles, the role expectations for a psychiatrist's relationship with a patient include a mix of socioemotional and functional acts like greeting, talking to, correcting, guiding, and befriending. A patient's role consists of consulting, admiring, calling, entreating, explaining to, and placating a psychiatrist. According to simulations of a psychiatrist's interaction with particular kinds of mental patients (not reported in Table 6.2), a psychiatrist might also examine, interview, or urge alcoholics, neurotics, and psychotics. Table 6.2 does report how different kinds of mental patients might act towards a psychiatrist. A neurotic's expected behaviors include acts of mild disdain (pooh-poohing, slighting, patronizing, and softsoaping), as well as incredulity (doubting and disbelieving). As might be expected, those of a psychotic towards a psychiatrist are notably more powerful and lively: dog, haze, parody, disconcert, and befuddle.

Religious Roles

The role expectations for an evangelist's relationships with various counteridentities, real or imagined, are presented in Table 6.3. His relationship with God is one of admiration and personal communication, with expectations of divine comfort and assistance. His relationship with the Devil is characterized by opposition and lighthanded or mild bantering on his part and temptation (needle, pester) and entrapment (bait, ensnare, bamboozle) on the part of the Devil. While an evangelist might disagree with either a Christian or a sinner, he might hail, prompt, awe, glorify, address, question, or persuade the former, but oppose, contradict, disagree with, divert, rock, ravish, jest, coax, waken, josh, or eye the latter. In return, a Christian's relationship with an evangelist is one of communication, consultation, and admiration; a sinner's, one of evasion, mockery, and incredulity.

Roles in Other Institutionalized Contexts

Considerations of space preclude a detailed presentation of role analyses for more than a few conventional social contexts. However, before proceeding to an

TABLE 6.3

Role Expectations of Canadian Male University Students for Selected Religious Roles, Generated Analytically from the EPA Profiles for Actor and Object-Person Identities[a]

Actor	Role Expectations	Object
Evangelist	[1.2 .1 –.1] admire, consult, answer, agree with, ask, call, ask about, talk to	God
God	[2.6 1.6 .2] welcome, assist, aid, uplift, coach, comfort, please	Evangelist
Evangelist	[.4 .6 1.4] kid, oppose, disagree with, hail, glorify, rib, josh, chatter to	Devil
Devil	[–1.1 .9 1.3] bait, needle, ensnare, affront, accuse, criticize, renounce, pester, bamboozle	Evangelist
Evangelist	[.6 .6 .5] hail, prompt, awe, disagree with, glorify, address, question, persuade	Christian
Christian	[1.7 .3 .1] accommodate, talk to, honor, greet, consult, admire, answer, invite	Evangelist
Evangelist	[–.1 .7 1.0] oppose, contradict, disagree with, divert, rock, ravish, jest, coax, waken, josh, eye	Sinner
Sinner	[–.7 .2 .8] parody, evade, confound, elude, imitate, haze, dog, patronize, imitate, doubt	Evangelist

a. The row of numbers before each set of acts is the optimal EPA profile generated by the model for the actor's behavior toward the object-person in each dyad. Only physical acts have been suppressed for an evangelist's relationship with God and Christian. No cognitive filters were employed for the evangelist's relationship with a sinner. The relationship between evangelist and devil was defined as verbal, exchange, and managing.

analysis of criminal justice roles in the next section, I examine role relationships in a variety of additional settings to illustrate the broad applicability of affect control theory to role analysis.

According to the simulation results reported in Table 6.4, a prime minister might convince, persuade, reprimand, urge, enrapture, appoint, laud, correct, or awe a "backbencher." In turn, a backbencher might placate, ask about, query, en-

TABLE 6.4

Role Expectations of Canadian University Students for Miscellaneous Role Relationships, Generated Analytically from the EPA Profiles for Actor and Object-Person Identities[a]

Actor	Role Expectations	Object
Prime Minister	[.7 1.4 .4] convince, persuade, reprimand, urge, enrapture, appoint, laud, correct, awe	Backbencher
Backbencher	[.3 –.1 –.1] placate, ask about, query, entreat, explain, implore, call, cue, brief	Prime Minister
Athlete	[1.8 1.3 1.6] bed, amuse, thrill, cheer, inspire, undress, excite, play with	Coed
Coed	[1.6 .4 1.1] court, desire, dance with, bed, flatter, play with, humor (female expectations)	Athlete
Clerk	[.9 .1 .0] agree with, ask about, dress, address, oblige, contemplate, explain, join, consult (female expectations)	Customer
Customer	[.8 .5 .3] answer, pay for, speak to, join, cue, brief, notice, prompt (female expectations)	Clerk
Professor	[1.9 .6 .1] thank, gratify, greet, compliment, encourage, honor, praise, invite	Graduate Student
Graduate Student	[1.7 .5 .3] greet, talk to, invite, accommodate, honor, appeal to, acclaim, admire, compliment	Professor
Vampire	[–.5 .6 .7] confound, stall, prod, overrate, contradict, stymie, elude, divert, work, deter	Maiden
Maiden	[1.1 .1 .5] ask about, ask, join, nuzzle, answer, oblige, call, bed (female expectations)	Vampire

a. The row of numbers before each set of acts is the optimal EPA profile generated by the model for the actor's behavior toward the object-person in each dyad. Physical acts have been suppressed for Professor-Graduate Student and Prime Minister-Backbencher relationships. Exchange acts were filtered out for relationships between Vampire-Maiden. No cognitive filters were employed for Athlete-Coed and Clerk-Customer relationships. Expectations are based on male sentiments unless specified otherwise in the table.

treat, explain, implore, call, cue, or brief a prime minister. The more powerful and active role of prime minister, in conjunction with the more subservient, often obsequious role of backbencher suggested by these simulation results would appear to describe the Canadian parliamentary system rather well.

The relationship of an athlete and a coed is characterized by positive, powerful, and lively acts centering on romantic and sexual behavior. According to simulation results, an athlete might bed, amuse, thrill, cheer, inspire, undress, excite, or play with a coed. In turn, she might court, desire, dance with, bed, flatter, play with, or humor him.

The behavioral retrievals for clerk-customer interaction describe our common understanding of the relationship quite accurately. In line with the commercial adage that "the customer is always right," the first retrieval suggests that a clerk should agree with a customer. A clerk might also ask about, dress (perhaps appropriate in a clothing store), address, oblige, contemplate, explain, join, or consult a customer. A customer might answer, pay for, speak to, join, cue, brief, notice, or prompt a clerk.

A professor and a graduate student are expected to greet, honor, invite, and compliment one another. In addition, a professor might thank, gratify, encourage, or praise a graduate student; and in return he or she might talk to, accommodate, appeal to, acclaim, or admire a professor.

Mythology is no less a part of social life than family, religious, and other social institutions, and the identity lexicon of affect control theory contains many mythical identities. Our final example involves the relationship between a vampire and a maiden. Affect control theory predicts that a vampire might confound, stall, prod, overrate, contradict, stymie, elude, divert, work, or deter a maiden. In return, a maiden might ask about, ask, join, nuzzle, answer, oblige, call, or bed a vampire.

Criminal Justice Roles

As we shall see, analysis of criminal justice roles with Canadian cultural data generate behavioral expectations for judges and police identities that appear to be too nice and unassertive in comparison with their portrayal by U.S. television and movies and simulation results from the U.S. study. Before discussing these crosscultural differences, I present two sets of simulations from the Canadian study—one involving interactions among courtroom actors; the other, among cops, criminals, and victims.

Courtroom Roles. The role relationships generated among judges, prosecuting attorneys, attorneys, defendants, and witnesses are reported in Table 6.5. Each identity has a set of core role expectations, defined here as acts generated for at least three counter–identities. Those for a judge are highly positive, relatively powerful, and unlively—praising, thanking, pleasing, encouraging, greeting, considering, complimenting, inviting, and gratifying other courtroom actors. In addition, a

TABLE 6.5

Role Expectations of Canadian Male University Students for Courtroom Roles, Generated Analytically from the EPA Profiles of Actor and Object-Persons[a]

		Actor			
Object	Judge	Prosecuting Attorney	Attorney	Defendant	Witness
Judge		[0.9 0.9 0.2] correct urge ask speak to acclaim address befriend charm talk to	[1.3 0.9 0.0] talk to guide greet befriend praise approve of acclaim invite charm appeal to	[1.3 −0.7 −0.3] consult admire ask about call explain entreat extol placate	[1.7 0.5 0.0] accommodate honor talk to thank greet gratify praise compliment invite
Prosecuting Attorney	[1.5 0.9 0.0] talk to greet praise guide consider thank believe compliment please uplift invite encourage assist		[1.3 0.9 0.6] charm acclaim flatter appeal to enthral address entertain delight warn	[0.4 −0.3 0.0] ask about placate query entreat call explain extol	[1.5 0.7 0.2] talk to greet acclaim invite guide answer ask appeal to charm
Attorney	[1.9 0.8 −0.1] encourage thank gratify praise consider honor greet compliment please invite uplift	[1.0 0.9 0.5] address charm acclaim urge flatter enthral warn		[0.7 −0.3 0.0] ask about call entreat placate explain admire agree with compliment	[1.7 0.6 0.2] greet talk to invite praise thank honor accommodate appeal to

TABLE 6.5 (continued)

Actor

Object	Judge	Prosecuting Attorney	Attorney	Defendant	Witness
Defendant	[1.9 1.2 –0.1]	[0.8 1.3 0.6]	[1.2 1.3 0.8]		
	please	enrapture	enrapture		
	encourage	persuade	enthral		
	praise	awe	back		
	consider	urge	amaze		
	thank	enthral	charm		
	support	correct	flatter		
	gratify	address	negotiate with		
	honor	question	acclaim		
	greet				
Witness	[2.0 0.8 0.1]	[1.0 0.9 0.5]	[1.4 0.9 0.5]		
	compliment	address	acclaim		
	greet	urge	charm		
	praise	acclaim	appeal to		
	thank	charm	flatter		
	encourage	correct	invite		
	invite	awe	enthral		
	please	flatter	approve of		
	gratify	enthral	delight		
			warn		
			back		

a. The row of numbers before each set of acts is the optimal EPA profile generated by the model for the actor's behavior toward the object-person in each dyad. Physical and primary acts have been suppressed for all role relationships.

judge might talk to, guide, believe, uplift, and assist a prosecuting attorney; honor and uplift an attorney; and support or honor a defendant.

A prosecuting attorney's core role expectations are less positive but slightly more powerful and lively than those for a judge. The predictions suggest that he or she might address, urge, acclaim, charm, correct, awe, enthrall, or flatter other courtroom actors. A prosecuting attorney also might ask, speak to, talk to, or befriend a judge, and enrapture or question a defendant.

The core role expectations for an attorney are acclaim, charm, appeal to, flatter, invite, enthrall, and delight. In addition, he or she might talk to, guide, greet, befriend, praise, or approve of a judge; address, entertain, or warn a prosecuting attorney; enrapture, back, amaze, or negotiate with a defendant; and approve of a witness. An additional simulation (not reported in Table 6.5) reveals that an attorney might warn or defend a defendant who first asks about or calls him, illustrating again that functional acts of occupational roles often show up only after an initial round of interaction.

A defendant's role expectations are moderately positive, weak, and unlively toward a judge and slightly positive, weak, and unlively towards all other courtroom participants. In addition to calling, asking about, entreating, placating, explaining, extolling, and admiring other courtroom actors, a defendant might consult a judge, query a prosecuting attorney, and agree with an attorney.

As might be expected, a witness is predicted to act much more powerfully and not quite as unlively as a defendant. A witness is predicted to act more positively toward all other courtroom identities, particularly to a prosecuting attorney or an attorney. Besides greeting, talking to, inviting, accommodating, honoring, praising, complimenting, acclaiming, and appealing to other courtroom actors, a witness might gratify a judge and guide, answer, ask, charm, or delight a prosecuting attorney.

Crime Roles. Contrary to the classic sociological view that deviance results from a failure of socialization (Parsons 1951; Merton 1957, cpt.4), affect control theory views deviant roles as "organized by the same sociocultural system that defines normal roles" (Heise 1979, 118, after Nadel 1964, 49). Therefore, notwithstanding the fact that deviance also answers to subcultural variations in the larger sociocultural system, it is possible to analyze interaction involving deviant identities and roles with data from the dominant cultural system.

Table 6.6 reports role expectations for selected crime roles generated from the Canadian study. The core role expectations of a cop interacting with a thief, mugger, or pickpocket include rally, undress, rouse, dazzle, flatter, and debate with. A cop might also glorify a thief or a mugger (clearly anomalous), arouse or engage a thief or pickpocket, appeal to or charm a mugger (anomalous) and hail or persuade a pickpocket. Some of these behavioral retrievals appear to be quite sensible, especially rouse (as in startle), arouse, debate with, engage, and persuade. Even undress is a conceivable act, in the situation of searching a suspected criminal. Other behavioral retrievals (noted parenthetically above) appear to be singularly anomalous, belying the stereotypic relationships between "cops and robbers" conveyed by U.S. mass media. Again, I will address these anomalies below.

In contrast to the acts predicted for a cop's interaction with criminal types, those for a cop toward a suspect are immediately more plausible. According to simulation results, a cop might face, address, release, persuade, urge, flatter, charm, engage, or correct a suspect; in turn, a suspect might extol, obey, beseech, implore, watch, emulate, disbelieve, or doubt a cop.

The role expectations for criminal identities are stereotypically bad. Those for a mugger's interaction with a cop are particularly nasty and tormentive—upset,

TABLE 6.6

Role Expectations of Canadian Male University Students for Selected Crime Roles, Generated Analytically from the EPA Profiles for Actor and Object-Person Identities[a]

	Cop	Victim
Mugger		
As Actor	[−1.5 0.7 1.3] upset, vex, bamboozle, arm, bait, needle, pester, trick, bother, mislead	[−1.8 0.6 1.0] nag, bother, repulse, con, frustrate, embarrass, belittle, hoodwink, bamboozle, mislead, upset
As Object	[1.1 0.9 1.4] undress, rally, rouse, dazzle, flatter, debate with, glorify, appeal to, charm	[0.5 −0.3 −0.2] serve, obey, placate, explain, look at, entreat, query, watch, implore, beseech
Thief		
As Actor	[−1.0 0.4 1.0] dog, disconcert, criticize, parody, pester, tease, fool	[−1.0 0.7 0.9] disconcert, renounce, fool, dog, confuse, unnerve, affront, impede, fluster, arm, bait
As Object	[0.9 1.0 1.2] rally, undress, rouse, dazzle, flatter, arouse, debate with, glorify, engage, address	[0.1 −0.3 −0.4] query, watch, obey, placate, implore, overhear, explain, submit to
Pickpocket		
As Actor	[−1.2 −0.2 0.8] slight, wheedle, misjudge, tease, disturb, pooh–pooh, evade	[−1.4 0.2 1.0] aggravate, tease, disturb, slight, snub, ride, pester, goad, badger, antagonize
As Object	[0.8 1.1 1.2] rally, rouse, undress, arouse, dazzle, debate with, flatter, hail, engage, persuade	[−0.2 −0.1 −0.5] query, overhear, watch, implore, placate, obey, explain
Suspect		
As Actor	[0.1 −0.1 0.3] extol, obey, beseech, implore, watch, emulate, disbelieve, doubt	[0.2 0.5 0.6] coax, eye, waken, nudge, disagree with, beckon, reproach, question
As Object	[0.9 1.3 0.7] face, address, release, persuade, urge, flatter, charm, engage, correct	[0.4 −0.1 −0.5] explain, placate, look at, entreat, query, obey, serve, coddle, appease,

a. The row of numbers before each set of acts is the optimal EPA profile generated by the model for the actor's behavior toward the object-person in each dyad. The relationship between a cop and all other identities has been defined as verbal, physical, and managing. The relationship between a victim and all other identities has been defined as verbal, physical, exchange, and managing.

vex, bamboozle, arm, bait, needle, pester, trick, bother, and mislead. Those for a thief are generally less negative, less powerful, and less lively: dog, disconcert, criticize, parody, pester, tease, and fool. And those for a pickpocket, even less powerful and lively, include cowardly and furtive acts like slight, wheedle, disturb, pooh-pooh and evade.

The predictions for the interaction of criminals with victims comprise bad, nasty acts that vary in evaluation and power. The role expectations for a mugger are singularly bad, albeit not appreciably different in potency and activity than those for a thief. According to our simulations, a mugger might nag, bother, repulse, con, frustrate, embarrass, belittle, hoodwink, bamboozle, mislead, or upset a victim. A thief might disconcert, renounce, fool, criticize, dog, confuse, unnerve, affront, impede, fluster, arm, or bait a victim. The predicted acts for a pickpocket's interaction with a victim, less powerful than those for a mugger or a thief, include aggravate, tease, disturb, and pester. In reality, of course, a pickpocket would have little interpersonal interaction with a victim, success being predicated upon the victim's unawareness of the pickpocket's presence. Finally, the predictions for a suspect's interaction with a victim are near neutral on evaluation and less lively than those for the three genuinely criminal roles in our analysis. According to simulations, a suspect might coax, eye, waken, nudge, disagree with, beckon, reproach, or question a victim.

Finally, predictions for a victim's actions suggest that he or she might obey, placate, explain, or query either a mugger, thief, pickpocket, or suspect. A victim also might watch or implore a mugger, thief, or pickpocket; serve, look at, or entreat a mugger or suspect; overhear a thief or pickpocket; beseech a mugger; submit to a thief, and coddle or appease a suspect.

Discussion: A Cross-Cultural Comparison. The role expectations generated for criminal justice roles reported in Tables 6.5 and 6.6 are generally plausible, and often stereotypic, except for those of a judge toward a defendant and a cop toward criminal types. Our predictions portray judges and cops as far too nice and restrained in comparison with predictions from the U.S. study, contradicting stereotypic images of judges and cops promoted by U.S. mass media.

The optimal EPA profile defining the role expectations of a judge's interaction with a thief is [1.8 1.3 .2] in the Canadian study and [−.2 2.3 −1.2] in the U.S. study. A comparison of these profiles suggests that a judge in Canadian society might treat a thief in an extremely nicer, much less powerful, and much more lively fashion than a judge in U.S. society.

The optimal EPA profile defining the behavioral expectations for a cop's interaction with a thief is [.9 1.0 1.2] in the Canadian study and [−.1 1.4 −.0] in the U.S. study. The difference between these profiles suggests, again, that a cop in Canadian society might act in a much more positive, less powerful, and much more lively way towards a thief than a cop in U.S. society.

As a result of these differences in optimal behavioral profiles, simulations with the U.S. model and cultural data yield more stereotypic results. Here, a judge is expected to test a defendant and to summon, persuade, convict, reprieve, discipline, or sentence a thief. Comparable expectations can be generated with the Canadian model and data only by modifying identities with traits or moods, or by specifying a typical setting for the interaction scenario.[4] For example, an "angry" judge is predicted to judge, discourage, classify, humble, bluff, chide, and convict a "guilty" defendant, and test, laud, convince, psychoanalyze, exonerate, summon, or reprimand a "guilty" thief—plausible judge-like actions in both cases. Alternatively, casting the scenario in a courtroom setting and leaving identities unmodified by traits or moods, a judge is expected to test, exonerate, laud, summon, interview, examine, and convince a thief.

The behavioral expectations for a cop's interaction with a thief generated by the U.S. model and data are also quite stereotypic in the framework of U.S. television shows and movies—lure, stop, reprimand, dissuade, summon, discipline, rebuff, endure, evaluate, and quiet. As with simulations involving a judge, comparable results with the Canadian model and cultural data can be obtained only by modifying one or both actors with dispositional traits or moods, or by specifying a typical interactional setting. For example, a cop might outwit, dissuade, confront, challenge, convert, influence, or stop a "guilty" thief—one caught in the act, perhaps. Alternatively, the behavioral retrievals for a cop's interaction with a thief in a ghetto—arouse, debate with, challenge, astonish, dazzle, initiate, putdown, rally, rouse, and confront—approach predictions from the U.S. study. If, in addition, a cop is provoked by a thief (say, "insulted"), his or her behavior becomes even more stereotypic. In this scenario, a cop might restrain, catch, arrest, putdown, repel, or tackle a thief.

At the risk of caricaturing these results, we might say that they suggest that judges and cops in U.S. society "shoot from the hip," while those in Canadian society wait upon further information and/or provocation. In the Canadian case, stereotypic behavior is evoked only when attributions provide more information about participants—the guilt or innocence of a thief, for example; or when participants are situated in typical social settings: a judge in a courtroom, a cop in a ghetto; or, additionally, when an initial round of culturally scripted interaction has occurred. To what can we attribute these differences in role expectations for criminal justice roles?

Lipset (1986) has argued that Canada is a more elitist, conservative, and law-abiding society than the United States. If he is correct, this general cultural difference should manifest itself as observed differences in fundamental sentiments, and hence role expectations, for criminal justice identities. In fact, comparison of the fundamental sentiments for criminal justice identities between the two studies reveals that courtroom and police identities are generally more highly evaluated in

Canada, supporting Lipset's cross-cultural generalization. Additionally, both police and criminal identities are generally perceived as more powerful and lively in the Canadian study as well. If, as conventional wisdom would have it, the unusual appears more shocking, then the relatively greater powerfulness and liveliness of police and criminal identities in the Canadian cultural data may reflect the lower incidence of crime in Canada.[5]

Role Improvisation

If affect control theory exemplifies the generalized symbolic interactionist model embodied in identity theory (Stryker 1968, 1980; Stryker and Statham 1985), it must demonstrate the capacity to predict both role conformity and creativity. The simulation results reported thus far in this chapter demonstrate the ability of the theory to generate standard events in institutionalized settings. The simulations reported in this section illustrate the capacity of the theory to generate nonstandard events, those contradicting cultural expectations and demanding some measure of role creativity on the part of interactants. While some interactionists have suggested that role creativity may be personally idiosyncratic and acultural (Turner 1962, 23; McCall and Simmons 1966, 67), affect control theory supposes that the same cultural sentiments and affect control processes involved in role conformity are at work in role improvisation (Heise 1979, 140).

Role improvisation is demanded when an event challenges the identities claimed by or imputed to participants in social interaction. Affect control theory simulations reveal that behavioral expectations following a disturbing event are generally quite different than those for a first encounter. In some cases, behavioral retrievals suggest restorative action, in other cases, controlling and sanctioning behavior to bring the perpetrator of a disturbing event back into line with an initially claimed or imputed identity (Heise 1979, 126–127).

As an example of restorative action, the role expectations reported in Table 6.1 for a husband's relationship with his wife include acts of complimenting, enjoying, uplifting, massaging, and kissing. Now, if an act is implemented that creates a disturbing event (say, husband cheats wife), the behavioral expectations for the wife in the next event include acts that are even more positive than before, and extremely more powerful and lively. The model predicts that she might save, make love to, protect, and satisfy a husband who has cheated her—restorative acts that conceivably might save the marriage, rather than vengeful ones that probably would result in its further disintegration. (The latter kind of behavior can, of course, be implemented by INTERACT analysis to track the consequences of retaliatory action for the stability of the marriage.)

As an example of controlling, sanctioning behavior, the role expectations for a backbencher's interaction with a prime minister reported in Table 6.4 include placating, asking about, querying, entreating, and explaining. If, instead, one has a backbencher disobey a prime minister, the behavioral predictions for the next event suggest that a prime minister would negotiate with, astonish, debate, or challenge a renegade backbencher.

Finally, the role expectations for a clerk's interaction with a customer reported in Table 6.4 include agreeing with, asking about, obliging, and explaining. In view of these expectations, a clerk ignoring a customer constitutes a disruptive event. If implemented, simulations reveal that a customer might counter with restorative acts like interesting, alerting, or appealing to a clerk who has ignored him or her.

For affect control theory, role creativity is not confined to improvisational or adaptive response to culturally unexpected events. People also express their role creatively in response to disruptive events by reconceptualizing the identities of participants through attribution and labeling processes. Described briefly in Chapter 2, this kind of role creativity is the topic of Chapter 8.

Learning and Accessing Norms

The preceding section illustrates the capability of affect control theory to generate role expectations for given pairs of socially identified actors. While the analyses are occasionally marred by anomalous retrievals,[6] the overwhelming plausibility of predictions begs the question of how so much social structure can be generated from such limited information on cultural sentiments.

Part of the answer lies in the theory's approach to role interaction as a process of identity-confirmation. As discussed in Chapter 5, the meaning of social identities lies in their implications for action, such that identity-confirmation is achieved through implementing particular kinds of acts (Stryker 1968, 1980; Burke 1980). For affect control theory, identities and acts are located in a common affective space defined by evaluation, potency, and activity; and "a role exists specifically in the process of confirming [through action] fundamental feelings about the identities of the self and others" (Heise 1979, 104). Thus, knowing only the EPA profiles of social identities and interpersonal acts, the theory can predict role expectations with a considerable degree of accuracy. However, this does not explain how cultural sentiments get attached to social identities and interpersonal acts in the first place.

Heise (1979) speculated that cultural sentiments for social identities and interpersonal acts have evolved from interaction sequences that became standardized in role relationships. As salient beliefs, standard events characterizing particular role relationships generate sentiments for the social identities and behaviors implicated in them, so that over time these sentiments become consistent with the standard events from which they evolved. Once established, cultural sentiments become capable of regenerating the standard events that gave rise to them.

This idea—that standard events cause the formation of sentiments that regenerate these events—helps in understanding how EPA profiles code so much sociological information: the standard events are the original sources of the sentiments that regenerate these events (Heise 1979, 140).

From a developmental, as opposed to an evolutionary perspective, Heise (1979, 105–6) proposed that role socialization involves the acquisition of only a finite and manageable set of affective and cognitive meanings for social identities and acts—their EPA profiles together with their denotative and syntactic features.[7] Cognitive meanings are established in role socialization from verbal statements about the implied states and behavior of social identities; e.g., that a prostitute is a woman who engages in sexual relations for money. Besides providing cognitive information in the form of denotations and syntactic connections, such verbal statements establish affective associations along evaluation, potency, and activity dimensions. Extending the present example, knowing that sexual relations are intimate acts, we learn that prostitutes are usually involved in intimate behavior. Because we learn that intimate behavior is considered morally bad outside of certain strictly prescribed and controlled social contexts, a prostitute becomes an identity that takes on the negative affective associations of her morally proscribed behavior.

Thus, a small number of verbal statements establishes the cognitive meanings and affective associations of identities. These can be later accessed in memory to generate role expectations for interaction among many kinds of socially identified people. As discussed in Chapter 3, human consciousness oscillates rapidly between complementary cognitive and affective systems of meaning (Heise 1979, 94). Applied to role behavior, affective sentiments for social identities generate conceptualizations of role-appropriate acts which, if implemented, create transient feelings that confirm these sentiments. If affect control theory is correct, then, by implication, "role learning might even be largely auxiliary to language learning" (Heise 1979, 106.)

Since Heise (1979) proposed this explanation of role socialization and recall, other important theories dealing with these issues have appeared. One of these (Heiss 1981) focuses on role learning; another (Wallace 1983), accessing roles in memory. Both theories differ from affect control theory by approaching roles conceptually at the level of norms, rather than at the more elementary level of the cognitive and affective meaning of social identities. The next two sections outline these theories and evaluate them from the perspective of affect control theory.

Role Socialization: A Social Learning Approach

Jerold Heiss (1981) proposed a theory of role socialization based upon Bandura's (1977) social learning theory. Summarizing Heiss's discussion of Bandura, most learning takes place through observing the overt responses of others who serve as models. Observation does not automatically result in learning, however, because attentiveness on the part of the observer is also required. And, while Bandura does not consider external rewards necessary to acquire new responses, he supposes that their anticipation by an actor is a major determinant of his or her attentiveness.[8]

The retention of newly acquired responses is enhanced if they can be coded in vivid visual images that later can be evoked in the presence of appropriate stimulus cues. Verbal coding is an even more important aid to retention, especially when the behavior in question is complex. Overt practice and covert rehearsal are additional means for enhancing retention of newly acquired responses.

People implement only a fraction of the large repertoire of behaviors learned by these means. Some will be simply beyond the observer's skills. For learned responses within reach of an actor's skills, the theory assumes that people will implement those responses that have been reinforced. However, the theory does not assume an automatic connection between reinforcement and behavior; instead, it supposes that people themselves consciously make this connection. Moreover, reinforcement need not be external nor experienced directly by a person; it can be vicarious, self-administered, and anticipatory. Humans also have the capacity for creative modeling by amalgamating elements from different observational models. People also create opportunities for learning and determine partly what will be taught. Finally, through abstract modeling, humans can derive the underlying principles of observed behavior and generalize them to new situations. Applied to role theory, they "can develop a conception of a generalized role from the observation of concrete cases" (Heiss 1981, 104–5).[9]

While adopting social learning theory as a useful model of role learning, Heiss cautions that it only begins to explain role playing, "for the form that behavior takes depends upon the general role definition that actor starts with and events that occur within a particular situation" (1981, 111). Borrowing from identity theory (Stryker 1968; McCall and Simmons 1978), he proposes that "actors rank the various ways that they know to play a role along a hierarchy of prominence," and that a person "will be inclined to use the definition that is currently highest on the hierarchy if its preference rating is above an acceptable minimum" (1981, 111–112).

The problem then becomes one of accounting for the "preference level" of each role definition. By an extension of social learning theory, Heiss proposes that "the general preference level for a particular version of a role is a direct function of the anticipated total profit [reward less correlative costs] associated with its performance" (1981, 112). In this regard, he suggests that role versions that have been more frequently observed will be assumed to be more acceptable versions, commanding greater profit.

Among other factors affecting anticipated total profit, Heiss includes the reactions of self and others to past performances, vicarious reinforcement, the similarity of observed others, and the significance of others controlling rewards and punishments. According to Heiss, the person also considers the value of particular role definitions for self-reinforcement, including self-esteem, which may or may not coincide with their social acceptability. The costs entailed in obtaining reinforcement from any source also becomes an important parameter in the calculation of profit, including the facility with which a particular role version can be performed (e.g., time required) and its congruence with the actor's personality and the actor's competence.

Evaluation. Social learning theory reverberates with a number of core ideas in symbolic interactionism and affect control theory, not the least of which is its conception of the person as a creative, reflective, and self-reinforcing organism. In his application of social learning theory to role socialization, Heiss draws upon identity theory to define his concept of "preference ratings." In addition, he acknowledges that covert observational learning through role-taking provides important modeling information over and above the overt kind of observational learning stressed by Bandura. Finally, he recognizes that role playing is a function of both the general role definitions actors start with and events that transpire within a particular situation.

Like affect control theory, Heiss emphasizes the role of language, defining observation broadly to include such language–related processes as hearing and reading. He includes verbal instruction as a method of observational learning and verbal coding as a critically important mechanism in the retention of new responses. Unlike affect control theory, however, his theory of role socialization is formulated at the level of norms, rather than at the more elementary level of language. Further, it makes no explicit reference to either affect or control.

While the concept of "profit" and the exchange metaphor in general is foreign to affect control theory, Heiss's inclusion of self-esteem as an important reward in self-reinforcement, and social approval as an important reward in social reinforcement, suggests an important bridge between the two theories. Since self-esteem is based upon the confirmation of affectively salient identities, as discussed in Chapter 3, identity-confirmation becomes an important incentive in human motivation; and the reward of social approval simply reflects the requirement that one's identity claims be validated by others' acceptance—socially reinforced, if you will. Therefore, to propose that people enact those role definitions associated with the highest anticipated total profit is to propose, like affect control theory, that people engage in role behavior to confirm personally salient and, presumably, socially reinforced identities. Viewed this way, identity confirmation can be described as a personally profitable enterprise.

Accessing Roles in Memory: An Associative Addressing Model

While Heiss (1981) addresses the problem of role socialization and, to some extent, role playing, Wallace (1983) tries to explain how learned roles become stored and accessed in memory. Like Heiss and most other role theorists, he disaggregates roles into norms, their more elementary components. Every norm, according to Wallace, consists of an actor, situation, response, and consequence expectation. Every norm also evokes cognitive, cathectic, and conative orientations toward action. Bringing these two sets of concepts together, Wallace specifies that the actor and the situation expectations implicate a cognitive orientation; the consequence expectation, a cathectic orientation; and the response expectation, a conative (behavior readying) orientation.

Having analyzed the concept of norm in this way, Wallace proposed "that this description of a norm also provides for its being accessed (i.e., brought to consciousness) by the individual holding it" (1983, 104). That is, a norm can be accessed in memory through either its actor, situation, response, or consequence expectations because norms are "cross-filed or cross-indexed in four different ways within the mind of each participant" (1983, 104). Thus, when norms are called up at the actor "address," the individual also gets an idea of the situations, responses, and consequences associated with a particular actor: "Here is stored all the information about the kinds of lives 'burglars,' 'teachers,' 'students,' . . . and a host of other actor-types live (1983, 105)." When norms are called up at the situation address—the "definition of the situation" file—expectations for actors, responses, and consequences are also made available in consciousness. When norms are called up at the response address, expectations simultaneously occur as to who performed the behavior, where, and why. Finally, norms accessed at the consequence address—the "definition of the motivation" file—evoke expectations that explain why actors behave the way they do in particular situations.

While all this sounds very mechanical, what Wallace means to convey by his notion of "cross-indexed files" is the "associative addressing" method of information storage described by Powers (1973). In associative addressing, retrieval information consists of a fragment of what is recorded in more than one place in memory so that information may be retrieved from multiple locations. Moreover, Wallace disclaims any alliance with a normative determinism. Because people have multiple expectations for actor, situation, response and consequence, "norms can reduce but cannot eliminate the individual's cognitive, conative, and cathectic uncertainty" (1983, 108). For these reasons, norms are not mechanically retrieved as intact units, but rather situationally assembled by people " 'ad hocing it'—under a variety of non-normative influences . . . from a more-or-less connected actor, situation, response, and expectation modules" (1983, 108).

Evaluation. For Wallace, the meaning of identities ("actor-types") consists not only of their implications for action ("response expectations"), as in identity theory and affect control theory, but also their situational and motivational ("consequence") expectations. Although his treatment of normative expectations implicates all three orientations of the actor, what is stored and retrieved, by this account, is cognitive information *about* the affective and conative orientations of the actor. Affect and conation are not assigned an active role in his model of storage and retrieval of norms.

As discussed in Chapter 2, affect control theory recognizes that the kind of cognitive work described by Wallace precedes affective reaction and affect control processes. However, the theory proposes a different kind of associative addressing in which cognitive classifications of actors, behaviors, and the like evoke affective associations that are encoded and retrieved according to their "address" in EPA affective space. The associative addressing model of affect control theory suggests that role knowledge is stored and accessed in memory at a more fundamental level of meaning than Wallace supposes. In turn, as illustrated in this chapter, affectively coded information about actor's identities and situational settings generates expectations for actor's behavior. Moreover, affect control theory moves beyond Wallace's treatment of "consequence" expectations as cognitive information *about* the motivations of actors to a theory of motivation itself—viz., that people engage in role appropriate action in order to confirm their fundamental sentiments for the identities of self and other (see Chapter 3). In the process, they construct the norms that are retrospectively applied in sociological accounts of motivated behavior.

Summary

This chapter has illustrated the application of affect control theory to role analysis. Following simulations of role behavior for both institutionally standardized and unstandarized events, the chapter concluded with a discussion of how roles are learned and subsequently accessed in memory, comparing the affect control theory account of these processes with other theories.

Affect control theory's proposal that people construct role–appropriate action in order to confirm cognitively and affectively salient identities begs the question of how people know whether or not they have been successful. As outlined in Chapter 2, emotions provide this information in the form of those affectively rich cognitive signals we recognize as emotions. The next chapter examines the role of emotions in more detail.

7

EMOTIONS

Affect control theory distinguishes between affect (or emotion) as a general mode of consciousness pervading all our cognitions, and those situationally episodic and ephemeral affective experiences we call emotions. As discussed in Chapters 2 and 3, it is affect in the first sense that is the basis for affect control theory and its identity theory of human motivation. However, affect control theory also deals with affect in the second sense, as referring to the specific, short-lived emotions instigated by events.

This chapter opens with a discussion of the constructionist versus positivist debate in sociological social psychology (Kemper 1981) and establishes a partial reconciliation. The next two sections, respectively, present the affect control theory of emotions and illustrate the emotions model with simulations based on the Canadian data and equations programmed in INTERACT (Heise and Lewis 1988a). The concluding section of the chapter shows how affect control theory, by incorporating the production and management of emotions within a single model, contributes to the further reconciliation of positivist and constructionist theories of emotion.

The Constructionist Versus Positivist Debate

The paradigmatic battle between constructionists and positivists has been pitched along a number of fronts, with participants claiming allegiance to one side or another on fewer than the total number of fronts available, and occasionally defecting to the other side across one or more of the remaining lines of engagement. Inspired by cognitive theories of emotion[1] (Averill 1980; Schacter 1964; Schachter and Singer 1962), and largely indistinguishable from them, the constructionist position in sociological social psychology has been staked out and articulated by Gordon (1981), Hochschild (1979, 1983), Shott (1979), and Thoits (1984). Denzin's (1984) social phenomenological theory of emotions has also flown the banner of constructionism.[2] A comprehensive statement of the constructionist position can be found in the collection of papers edited by Harré (1986). While Kemper (1978, 1981, 1987) has been the leading spokesperson and advocate of the positivist position, Barchas (1976), Collins (1981), Mazur (1985), Scheff (1983), and others have displayed its colors along one or more lines of contention.[3] The following discussion builds upon Kemper (1981). A parallel debate between constructionists and positivists also has taken place in anthropology (Lutz and White 1986).

One major issue in the constructionist versus positivist debate concerns the conceptualization of emotion itself. Positivists tend to define the construct rather leanly, basically in biological terms, as "a relatively short-term response essentially positive or negative in nature involving distinct somatic (and often cognitive) components" (Kemper 1978, 47–48). Some constructionists propose much more inclusive definitions that incorporate both biological and cultural referents (Gordon 1981; Thoits 1984). For example, Gordon's concept of "sentiments" (a term designed to distance the constructionist position from the positivist concept of emotion) comprises not only physiological "sensations" and "expressive gestures," but also "socially constructed . . . cultural meanings" (1981, 516)—the vocabulary, norms, and beliefs that constitute "emotional culture" (1990, 152). Others exclude the biological referent from their definition of emotion altogether: "an emotion is not a feeling (or a set of feelings) but an interpretation . . . a system of concepts, attitudes, and desires, virtually all of which are context-bound, historically developed, and culture specific" (Solomon 1984, 248–9). From this viewpoint, the identification of emotion with physiological states and sensations becomes "an ontological illusion" (Harré 1986, 4).

Because constructionist concepts of emotion incorporate the major explanans of the constructionist theory of emotions (cultural structure) into the definition of the explanandum (sentiments) itself, they pose the danger of rendering the study of emotions a descriptive rather than an explanatory enterprise.[4] More potential than actual in Gordon (1981), this danger becomes fully realized in the work of cultural anthropologists like Lutz and White who proclaim that "the core of the attempt to understand the relation between emotion and culture lies in ethnographic description of the emotional lives of persons in their social contexts" (1986, 426). The restriction of the study of emotions to descriptive research and interpretation is also heralded as a virtue in Denzin's (1984) social phenomenology of emotions.[5]

While constructionists tend to limit their reach to ideographic analysis, favoring observations in natural settings and qualitative data analysis, positivists unabashedly proclaim the aspirations of a nomothetic science, preferring observations in more controlled experimental and survey settings and quantitative data analysis.

Because it has been more responsive to vested interest and ideological commitment than to dispassioned judgment, the debate over the relative merits of qualitative and quantitative methods defies resolution on objective grounds. Thus, aside from asserting the necessity of both kinds of research, I will seek reconciliation of the constructionist and positivist positions along the remaining lines of contention identified in this discussion.

A second major issue in the debate between constructionists and positivists, closely connected to their respective views on the relative importance of culture and biology, concerns whether the physiological correlate of emotional experience is undifferentiated or specific. Constructionists maintain that emotions are constructed above the surface of a relatively undifferentiated substratum of physiological arousal, implying that there are as many emotions as cultural definitions of affective states (Gordon 1981). In contrast, positivists suppose the existence of a small number of culturally universal "primary" emotions associated with specific physiological changes, onto which are grafted an indefinite number of culturally defined "secondary" emotions during affective socialization (Kemper 1978, 1987).

In my view, this issue is not as serious as some protagonists in the constructionist/positivist debate make it out to be. After all, positivists predicate only a small number of primary emotions corresponding to allegedly specific states of physiological arousal, the existence of which remains an empirical question with respect to which constructionists are in a no-lose situation. That is, even if future research eventually affirms primary emotions, the constructionist position will remain unscathed by virtue of the numerical predominance of terms for the "secondary" emotions in the affective lexicon of all societies.

In fact, while remaining skeptical about the importance and universality of physiological sensation in emotional experience, some constructionists have flirted with the possibility of primary emotions. Gordon (1990, 152), for instance, acknowledged that "we cannot assume human emotional nature to be infinitely malleable, and must search for any biological or psychological limiting conditions that constrain the social construction of emotions" (cf. Franks 1989, 100). Interestingly enough, some constructionists have implied the possibility of universal emotions based upon cultural rather than biological grounds. Despite their cautionary stance, I detect this in Lutz and White's statement that the "abstract generalizations of human problems" contained in their proposed comparative framework for the study of emotions "are meant to serve as initial comparative reference points . . . about universal situational causes of emotional experience" (1986, 428); and in Solomon's qualification that to proclaim the cultural specificity of emotions "is not to foreclose the probability that some emotions may be specific to *all* cultures" (1984, 249).

The third fundamental issue that has fueled the debate between constructionists and positivists concerns the extent to which cognitive interpretation mediates the effect of situational events on emotional response. Specifically, to what degree is emotional response to socially and culturally structured situations mediated by an extensive process of cognitive appraisal and decision-making, as constructionists propose, or more or less automatically triggered by relational stimuli, as positivists argue? For constructionists, the mediating role of cognitive appraisal and interpretation produces considerable variation in individual response to emotion-instigating situations, because of variation in the personal relevancy of situations and the appropriation of cultural grammars of emotion (Franks 1989, 98–99). For positivists, "the shaping influence of culture [and other external factors, including social structure] . . . is so powerful that it produces a modal emotional response to given social stimuli" (Kemper 1978, 18). For constructionists, cognitive awareness and processing is an essential component of emotional experience. For positivists, "cognitive awareness and labeling of the emotions are not necessary, although they are frequent components of the experience of emotion" (Kemper 1978, 47–8).

Again, this issue is one of relative emphasis. Recalling my discussion of cognition and affect in Chapter 3, we might say that positivists emphasize the lower level of cognitive awareness where events are more felt than recognized; constructionists, the higher level of consciousness where events are subjected to a process of symbolically mediated thought. Since human consciousness is a continuum of cognitive awareness, the positivist and constructionist positions with respect to the issue at hand are more complementary than irreconcilable.

The fourth point of contention concerns the relative causal impact of cultural structure and social structure on human emotion. For constructionists, emotions are culturally influenced social constructions: "[S]ince culture directs our seeing and expecting, it directs our feeling and our naming of feeling" (Hochschild 1983, 223). For positivists, emotions are more or less direct outcomes of socially structured social relations: "It is what our fellow participants do to us and what we do to them—the social relations that constitute the existing social structure—that evoke our emotions" (Kemper 1981, 344).[6] We might say, without inflicting too much violence to either position, that constructionists propose a theory of "cultural structuralism"; positivists, one of "social structuralism" Wallace (1983).[7] Correlatively, constructionists have tended to focus on the *management* of emotions, in response to emotion norms; and positivists, on their *production*.

Because cultural and social structure are inextricable components of social institutions, however, the constructionist and positivist positions are, again, more complementary than irreconcilable. A closer look at each position, in fact, reveals that neither neglects the face of social institutions emphasized by the other.

On the constructionist side of the debate, Gordon (1981) proposed that emotions are organized around social relations, and identified three interactional processes—emotion differentiation, socialization, and management—through which "the social structural effects on emotion flow" (1990, 151). His statement that "emotion is a reaction to a situation usually of social origin, such as a change in a social relationship" (1990, 152) is virtually indistinguishable from the positivist position. Social structure plays an important role in other constructionist theories of emotions as well. According to Hochschild (1983), for example, the relative positions of people in particular social structures determine the amount of "emotion-work" required of them.

Nor have positivists neglected cultural structure. Kemper (1978), for instance, identified culture as a major factor reducing individual differences in emotional response. Specifically, he proposed that culture influences and shapes the meaning of power and status for actors engaged in social relations, specifies the occasions for the occurrence of social relations, and defines the power and status implications of concrete behaviors and objects in the situation within which social relations occur (Kemper 1981).

In summary, I have delineated the constructionist versus positivist debate in the sociology of emotions along four lines of contention, and have attempted a preliminary reconciliation of these seemingly irreconcilable positions. Following the presentation and illustration of the affect control theory of emotions in the next two sections, I will identify the contributions of the theory to the further reconciliation of constructionist and positivist theories of emotion.

The Affect Control Theory of Emotions

Suppose that, in the course of a lecture, a professor has his or her competence challenged by a student, or commits a cognitive error in presentation or, perhaps, a social *faux pas*. Assuming that the professor is cognizant of others' challenge or his or her own faulty performance, we would expect the momentary disconfirmation of identity-situated self to be accompanied by a flash of emotion, which he or she might recognize as shame, embarrassment, anxiety, or perhaps a meld of these and cognate emotions.

But what if events have confirmed the professor's identity? Say that all students were attentive and enthusiastic and the professor delivered a flawless lecture, impressing everyone, including self, in the process. Would he or she experience no emotion, be rendered emotionless by success? Intuitively, we would expect that, under these circumstances, a professor would experience and recognize positive emotions like contentment or satisfaction, those befitting the confirmation of a positive identity like professor.

These imaginary scenarios describe precisely the affect control theory conceptualization of emotions. The theory assumes that people enter settings with presumed identities, like "professor," "mother," "father," or "doctor." What transpires in the ensuing interaction—the situated activity of self and others—will either confirm or disconfirm the identity-situated selves of interactants. Emotions register these outcomes for each person, and overt emotional expressions reveal each person's private emotional experience to others present. The emotions model in affect control theory simply duplicates this process.

The equations for predicting the emotional outcomes of events are an application of the attribution equations of the theory. In turn, the attribution equations are mathematically derived from the empirically-based amalgamation equations of the theory, which describe how modifiers such as traits and emotions combine with identities to produce outcome impressions (Averett and Heise 1988; Heise 1988, 1992). Affect control theory treats emotions as descriptive attributions or "transient particularizations" (Heise 1992) of a person's identity-situated self. What emotions describe are the *transient* self-feelings created by recent events in comparison to the *fundamental* sentiments for the identity-situated self. Given the fundamental EPA profile for a person's current identity and the transient EPA profile for the person built up by recent events, the problem becomes solving for an emotion-attribution which, in combination with the person's identity (e.g., an "angry professor"), produces the transient profile.

The parameters of the equations reveal that emotions are an outcome of two factors: the *transient impression* of a person created by an event—his or her momentarily felt goodness, powerfulness, and liveliness; and the *deflection* of this transient impression from the fundamental goodness, powerfulness, and liveliness of the person's current identity. The first factor directly captures the identity-confirming or disconfirming consequences of events; the second, the intuitively compelling notion that the discrepancy between the transient self and the fundamental identity-situated self should amplify the impact of events on a person's emotions. This two-factor theory of emotions is contained in Proposition 18, Chapter 2.

To the extent that events disconfirm a person's current identity, creating transient feelings that deviate from the fundamental sentiments of his or her current identity, the deflection factor becomes important in predicting a person's emotions (e.g., when a professor delivers a badly presented, poorly-received lecture). To the extent that events confirm a person's identity, the deflection factor diminishes in importance. In the extreme case, where events perfectly confirm a person's identity, the deflection term in the equation drops out and we are left with the transient term as the major predictor of emotions (e.g., when a professor delivers a flawless, enthusiastically-received lecture). However, because transient impressions would equal fundamental sentiments under this condition, a person's emotions would be determined solely by the fundamental goodness, powerfulness, and liveliness of his or her identity. Thus, a professor whose identity is perfectly confirmed by events should feel contented and satisfied because these emotions are consistent with the fundamental goodness, powerfulness, and liveliness of the confirmed identity.

In a nutshell, when events *disconfirm* a person's identity, then he or she will emote in cadence with the *transient impression* created by events and the magnitude of its *deflection* from fundamental sentiments. And when events *confirm* a person's identity, then he or she will experience emotions befitting the fundamental sentiments of his or her situated identity.

This implication of the emotions equations—that identity–confirming events produce emotions that are consistent with the identities maintained—connects with the affect control theory of motivation discussed in Chapter 3. To propose that people are motivated to confirm salient identities is to imply that they are motivated to experience emotions that are consistent with the identities they are trying to confirm. Proposition 19 (Chapter 2) of the affect control theory of emotions specifies this connection precisely and extends identity theory into the social psychology of emotions.

Two additional implications follow from the two-factor structure of the emotions equations of affect control theory.[8]

First, the transient factor that is important in both identity-confirming and disconfirming events implies that momentary impressions of goodness will contribute to the generation of positive emotions; momentary impressions of badness will generate negative emotions (*mutatis mutandis* for impressions of powerfulness and liveliness and their emotional consequences).

Second, the deflection factor that is important in only identity-disconfirming events suggests that transient impressions which exceed the fundamental goodness of a positive identity produce even more positive emotions; those exceeding the fundamental negativity of a deviant identity, even more negative emotions (*mutatis mutandis* for potency and activity). By implication, people with different identities will experience different emotions in response to objectively the same event. For instance, while a professor who has just delivered a stimulating and competent lecture might feel contented or satisfied, a lower status university teacher like a graduate student might feel thrilled; while a mugger who has assaulted a person might feel annoyed, a less nefarious felon like a pickpocket might feel outraged (cf. Smith-Lovin 1990).

The Kinds and Consequences of Emotions

According to the affect control theory of emotions just discussed, emotions register the identity-confirming or disconfirming consequences of social events. Within this general framework, emotions can be analytically differentiated according to whether they originate in a person's situated identity, a person's stable social relationships with specific others, or in the actual behavior of the person or others in social interaction. Figure 1 outlines the three kinds of emotions differentiated on this basis.

Characteristic emotions are those emotions people should experience when their situated identities are perfectly confirmed by social events. *Structural* emotions are those people will likely experience as a function of encountering specific others in socially structured relationships. *Consequent* emotions are those people should experience as a function of the actual behavior of self or other in social events. The first is a derivative of the affect control theory of emotions just discussed; the second and third correspond to Kemper's (1978) concepts of "structural" and "consequent" emotions.[9]

Characteristic emotions occur only in identity-confirming events, where the deflection factor in the emotions equations becomes negligible and where, by im-

FIGURE 7.1

A Classification of Emotions and Behavioral Consequences

Emotions

(1) Characteristic Emotions	those experienced when a person's identity is perfectly confirmed by social events (implication of the emotions model of affect control theory)
(2) Structural Emotions	those experienced in a particular social relationship (after Kemper 1978)
(3) Consequent Emotions	those experienced as a function of person and others' behavior (after Kemper 1978) (positivist emphasis on accounting for emotions)

Behavioral Consequences of Emotions

(1) Compensatory Behavior	actions implemented by a person to reaffirm an identity in the wake of experiencing an out-of-character emotion (an implication of the general affect control principle)
(2) Mood-Induced Behavior	actions implemented to confirm a composite identity consisting of person's current identity and an enduring affective state (an implication of the affect control theory of motivation)
(3) Emotional Goal-Induced Behavior	actions anticipated to bring about the experience of a desired emotion in response to an identity–disconfirming event or an emotion norm. (Constructionist emphasis on emotion management)

plication, the transient factor converges with the fundamental sentiments of a person's situated identity.

Structural emotions may occur either in identity-confirming or disconfirming events. That is, while many socially structured relationships are identity-confirming (e.g., the relationship between a husband and wife in a culturally "ideal" marriage), others confirm identity-situated selves only imperfectly, or, perhaps, not at all (e.g., the relationship between a craftsman and a production-oriented manager). In the first case, the deflection factor becomes negligible, the transient self converges with the fundamental self, and structural emotions approach the characteristic emotions of a person's identity. In the second case, both the transient and deflection factors become important in the production of emotions, no longer does the transient self coincide with the fundamental self, and there may be considerable difference between structural and characteristic emotions. Whether identity-confirming or not, social relationships are sufficiently structured and stable that one can predict the emotions experienced by each person with some accuracy.

Like structural emotions, consequent emotions may occur in either identity-confirming or disconfirming events. The predominance of the transient and deflection factors in the production of consequent emotions depends upon whether the actual behavior of interactants produces identity-confirming or disconfirming events. Additionally, to the extent that behavior optimally confirms the identities of both participants in a social relationship, consequent emotions will converge with structural emotions. To the extent that behavior confirms the identity-situated self of a particular person, consequent emotions will converge with the characteristic emotions of that person's identity-situated self.

This implies that all three kinds of emotions are, in effect, consequent emotions. Nonetheless, the analytical distinctions drawn here serve the purpose of relating emotions to the identity-situated self, on the one hand, and socially structured interaction, on the other, while acknowledging that the actual behavior of people often creates discrepancies between the way they ought to feel, by virtue of either current identity or social relationship, and the way they actually feel.

Figure 7.1 also classifies the behavioral consequences of emotions. These include *compensatory behavior*—the attempt of interactants to bring consequent emotions back into line with the characteristic emotions of their situated identities; *mood–induced behavior*—that which occurs when emotions become more enduring affective states, producing a qualitative transformation in the original identities of participants and motivating new identity-confirming actions; and *emotional goal-induced behavior*—actions designed to bring about the experience of a desired emotion—for example, one characteristic of a currently salient identity, or one prescribed by emotion norms. Because the behavioral consequences of emotions implicate the event–construction model of affect control theory, rather than the emotions model directly, I will defer further discussion until I encounter each type in the following section.

Emotion Analysis

This section illustrates with INTERACT simulations each of the three types of emotion and three types of behavioral consequences distinguished above.[10]

Characteristic Emotions

As defined above, characteristic emotions occur when events perfectly confirm a person's identity-situated self.

Table 7.1 reports the characteristic emotions predicted by the emotions equations of affect control theory for a selection of social identities. These predictions were obtained by assuming that events have optimally confirmed the identities in question, and are listed in Table 7.1 according to the order in which they fit the identity in question.

The results appear to confirm our common sense expectations of the way people with particular identities should feel when events confirm their identities. A child should experience positive, lively emotions like "elated" and "cheered"; a husband or wife, positive but quiet emotions like "calm" and "satisfied." While a professor, a particularly sedate socially identified person, is predicted to feel "satisfied," the youthful exuberance of a student gives rise to the prediction of a range

TABLE 7.1

Characteristic Emotions[a]

Identity	Characteristic Emotions
Child (F)	amused, elated, glad, cheered, delighted, satisfied, pleased
Husband (M)	calm, satisfied, proud, glad, in love
Wife (F)	calm, pleased, relieved, touched
Professor (M)	satisfied
Student (M)	relieved, glad, delighted, in love, passionate, cheerful, happy, elated
Adolescent (M)	anxious, amused, touched, satisfied
Mugger (M)	angry, mad, furious, outraged, anxious, annoyed
Victim (M)	melancholy, apprehensive, zip, sorry, awe-struck, displeased, lovesick
Prostitute (F)	anxious, zip
Policeman (M)	proud

a. Predictions based on male (M) or female (F) sentiments, as designated parenthetically in column one.

of positive, lively emotions—"relieved," "glad," "in love," "cheerful," and "happy." An adolescent should feel alternatively "anxious" and "satisfied," predictions that should ring true to any reader who has witnessed these emotional swings in adolescent children.

The characteristic emotions predicted for deviant social identities differ dramatically from those for positive identities. A mugger, for instance, is predicted to characteristically feel "angry," "mad," "furious" and the like; a prostitute, "anxious," or even more emotionally neutral (the meaning of "zip").

Structural Emotions

As just defined, characteristic emotions are those we would expect people to feel when events perfectly confirm their identity-situated selves. However, identity-confirmation is only imperfectly achieved in real-life circumstances because people are involved in social relationships with others whose identity-confirmation agenda compromises their own. As a result, people tend to pull each other's emotions in the direction of their own salient identities and characteristic emotions.

The structural emotions reported in Table 7.2 were generated by implementing behavioral predictions for counteridentities in the role set of each focal identity. Obtained from the event construction model of affect control theory, these predicted behaviors would, if implemented, optimally confirm the identities in each dyad.

Consider the focal identity, mother. Implementing an expected act of a father, son, or daughter toward a mother would make her experience positive emotions like "contented," "calm," and "pleased." If these structural emotions are consistent with how one might expect a mother to characteristically feel, it is because the culturally expected actions of family members are identity-confirming. In contrast, one would not expect a bill collector to confirm the positively evaluated identity of mother. Indeed, as reported in Table 7.2, a mother who is called by a bill collector is predicted to feel "irked," "heavy-hearted," "disgusted," "apprehensive," and so on.

A coed's social relationship with positively evaluated actors like athletes, professors, or other coeds produces positive emotions like "moved" or "contented." However, the structural emotions predicted for her relationship with a fink ("irked," "disgusted," and "heavy-hearted," as when a fink deprecates her) are uncharacteristic of how we might expect a coed to feel in most of her social relationships.

A minister provides a dramatic example of how a person's emotions change as he or she moves in and out of different social relationships. A minister's role set inludes both extremely good and bad identities, some embodied in real people (sinner, Christian), others a construction of imagination bolstered by religious faith (God, devil). The structural emotions that result from interacting with these alternatively good and bad counteridentities are equally contradictory. If a sinner acts

TABLE 7.2

Structural Emotions[a]

Object-Person	Actor	Behavior	Emotions Predicted For Object-Person
Mother (F)	father	snuggles	contented, moved, calm
	son	flatters	contented, moved, calm, touched, relieved, pleased
	daughter	assists	calm, at ease, proud, touched, satisfied, pleased, contented, relieved
	bill collector	calls	zip, irked, heavy-hearted, sorry, awe-struck, disgusted, lovesick, apprehensive
Minister (M)	sinner	doubts	zip, lovesick, displeased, disgusted, irked, resentful, dissatisfied
	Christian	consults	moved, zip, touched, charmed, satisfied, proud
	God	uplifts	melancholy, zip, moved, awe-struck
	Devil	dogs	zip, melancholy, displeased, apprehensive, disgusted, lovesick, irked, dissatisfied
Coed (F)	coed	entertains	moved, contented, calm, relieved, charmed, pleased, amazed, zip
	athlete	applauds	moved, zip, contented, awe-struck, calm, relieved, charmed
	professor	believes	zip, awe-struck, moved, contented
	fink	deprecates	zip, irked, disgusted, heavy-hearted, sorry, awe-struck, displeased, lovesick

a. Predictions based on male (M) or female (F) attitudes as designated parenthetically in column one. For mother as focal identity, physical acts have been suppressed for all counter-identities except father. For minister, physical acts have been suppressed for all counter-identities. For coed, physical acts have been suppressed for all counteridentities except athlete. The act implemented in each case was generally the first behavioral retrieval from INTERACT for a particular dyad.

in character and doubts a minister, or a devil dogs him or her, a minister feels "displeased," "disgusted," "irked," or "dissatisfied." If a Christian consults a minister, or God uplifts him or her, a minister experiences emotions like "moved," satisfied," and "awestruck.

Consequent Emotions

People do not invariably experience the structural emotions associated with their involvement in socially structured relationships because they frequently act out of character. In order to simulate identity-disconfirming behavior, we must "force" behaviors to obtain a full range of consequent emotions for any dyad.

The consequent emotions reported in Table 7.3 for the relationship between a man and a woman were generated by forcing prototypical acts for all possible EPA configurations. Since there are few behaviors that are high on evaluation and low on potency, prototypical acts are closer to neutral on potency for (+−+) and (+−−) configurations. In addition, because behavior is inherently lively, some EPA configurations include acts close to neutral on activity.

The following are behaviors that best match the eight possible configurations of high (+) and low (−) values on evaluation, potency, and activity. Because a perfect match between particular configurations and actually existing words cannot always be found, the prototypical acts for some EPA profiles overlap. Behaviors are listed separately by gender because males and females do not always agree on which acts represent particular EPA profiles.

(+++)

Males: thrill, make love to, excite, inspire, amuse, cheer, save, bed
Females: cheer, rescue, excite, thrill, kiss, applaud, laugh with, make love to

(++−)

Males: forgive, heal, pray for, appreciate, calm, console, soothe, understand
Females: pray for, soothe, counsel, cuddle

(+−+)

Males: desire
Females: dance with, court, desire sexually, desire

(+−−)

Males: consult, baptize, admire
Females: visit, coddle, sing to, confide in, oblige, address

(−++)

Males: horrify, seize, terrorize, prevent, capture, threaten, bawl out, hassle
Females: outrage, hassle, swindle, force, drug, kick, reject, enrage

(–+–)

Males: oppress, manipulate, reject, scorn
Females: flunk, disillusion, deprive, ignore, forsake, deprave, browbeat, sentence

(--+)

Males: fear, mimic, flee, envy, hide from
Females: beg, submit to, follow

(---)

Males: beg, submit to, envy
Females: beg, submit to

Table 7.3 reports the emotions that result when a prototypical act representing each of the above EPA configurations is implemented for the relationship between a man (actor) and a woman (object-person).

The consequent emotions predicted for actor and object–person vary dramatically with the evaluation and potency of behavior. Moving from good, powerful to bad, powerful behavior, for example, a man is predicted to feel "in love" as he cuddles a woman; but "furious" or "angry" as he scorns her. In turn, her emotions swing from "moved" and "contented" to feeling "uneasy," "discontented," and "ill at ease." Moving from good, powerful to good, less powerful behavior, a man might feel "delighted" and "elated" as he thrills a woman, but only "charmed" and "contented" as he admires her.

The liveliness of actions has less impact on consequent emotions. While this results in considerable overlap between emotions predicted for different prototypical acts, closer examination reveals subtle differences. For example, whether fleeing (--+) or begging (---) a woman, a man is predicted to feel "upset" and "shaken." But, in the first case, these emotions are melded with mildly angry emotions—"aggravated," "bitter," "agitated," "irritated," and "resentful"; and in the second case, sad emotions—"heart-broken," "hurt," and "ashamed." The difference between a woman's emotional response to each of these two events lies in her experiencing displeasure and disgust at the sight of a man begging her. Thus, the appearance of different emotions in the list of predictions for a particular event may not represent imprecision in prediction, but rather the mix and meld of emotions and opportunity for feelings that occur naturally in response to real events.

It is noteworthy that the consequent emotions for the actor are consistent with the actions he is implementing, but that those for the object-person are of much less intensity, albeit in the same direction as the actor's emotions. This difference in emotional response is a function of the asymmetrical transient impressions created by events for actor and object-person. According to the impression formation equations discussed in Chapter 2, thrilling a woman makes a man appear nicer, more powerful, and more lively; but this powerful and lively act creates an impression of momentary impotency and inactivity for the recipient. Thus, while a man is predicted to feel "delighted," a woman is predicted to feel only "moved" or "contented." Similarly, while a man is predicted to feel "angry" as he seizes a woman, she is predicted to feel "uneasy." In general, the consequent emotions of the object-person of an event are more muted than those of the actor.

TABLE 7.3

Consequent Emotions for Man > Woman Events[a]

Emotions Experienced

EPA Profile	Act	By Man (M)	By Woman (F)
(+++)	thrill	delighted, relieved, elated, overjoyed, joyful, excited	zip, moved, contented, calm
(++−)	cuddle	in love	moved, zip, contented, charmed
(+−+)	desire	charmed, touched, satisfied, pleased, glad, amused, calm	zip, moved, contented, awe-struck, calm
(+−−)	admire	charmed, contented, satisfied, calm, touched, moved, pleased	zip, awe-struck, moved, contented, lovesick
(−++)	seize	angry, mad, furious, outraged	uneasy, deflated, homesick, regretful, discontented, ill at ease, self-pitying
(−+−)	scorn	furious, angry, outraged, mad, annoyed, bitter, irate	uneasy, discontented, ill at ease, remorseful, apprehensive, regretful, anguished
(−−+)	flee	shaken, aggravated, bitter, agitated, upset, irritated, resentful	zip, irked, awe-struck, heavy-hearted, sorry, lovesick
(−−−)	beg	heart-broken, broken-hearted, sickened, upset, shaken, hurt, ashamed	irked, zip, heavy-hearted, disgusted, sorry, displeased, dissatisfied

a. The emotions predicted for the actor (man) are based on male attitudes; those for the object-person (woman), on female attitudes.

In summary, these simulations illustrate three analytically distinct kinds of emotions. These are differentiated according to the relative importance of a person's identity-situated self (characteristic emotions), a person's social relationships (structural emotions), or the actual behavior of participants (consequent emotions) in the production of emotions.

However, emotions are not only products of social behavior; they, in turn, engender behavior. I now discuss and illustrate the three kinds of behavioral consequences of emotions outlined in Figure 1. Because compensatory and mood-induced behavior represent two sides of the same coin, I consider them together. I then deal with emotional goal-induced behavior.

Compensatory Behavior and Mood-Induced Behavior

According to conventional wisdom, emotions motivate emotion–sustaining actions. Anger is presumed to evoke angry behavior; happiness, benevolent behavior. The affect control theory of emotions does not share this commonsense view of emotions embodied in many current theories. Instead, the theory supposes that people act to confirm their identity-situated selves, not to act out their emotions. From this perspective, out-of-character emotions signal a person that the process of identity-confirmation is not going well, cuing him or her to implement restorative, identity-confirming, rather than reactive, emotion-sustaining action.

While counterintuitive, this view of emotions is perfectly consistent with affect control theory. As discussed in Chapter 3, the incentive in the affect control theory of motivation is the confirmation of meaning through the minimization of affective deflection. In social interaction, this is effected by confirming the situationally salient identities of self and others. Thus, in the wake of identity-disconfirming events producing large deflections, the theory predicts that an actor will implement restorative action, rather than action that sustains the emotions signaling the deflection.

> In affect control theory, subsequent behaviors compensate for emotions. Since behaviors are chosen to reduce deflection and to maintain meaning, the behaviors, in general, must be opposite to deflections (and therefore the emotion labels) (Smith-Lovin 1990, 259).

At the same time, affect control theory is sufficiently general to accommodate the commonsense view of emotion as motivating actions in kind. In affect control theory, emotions motivate behavior only when they develop into more enduring affective states or moods, transforming an actor's identity—in effect, only when an actor is attempting to confirm an emotionally qualified or composite identity like an "angry doctor."

In short, affect control theory proposes that emotions *inform*, identities, including those transformed by affective moods, *motivate*.

Emotional experience allows us to monitor the impacts of social interaction, but emotions have no real force of their own. Behavior is driven and controlled [energized and directed] not by emotions but by the penchant to confirm fundamental sentiments about oneself and others, to maintain identities (Heise and Lewis 1988a, 50).

The distinction between emotions and moods drawn by affect control theory begs the question raised by Smith-Lovin (1990, 260): "[W]hen do emotions exist as a quick flash of feeling and when do they get absorbed into identity as a situationally stable mood?" Smith-Lovin suggests that when a person becomes cognizant of unintentionally engaging in an identity-disconfirming act, then the restorative action that follows would quickly evaporate the consequent emotion. On the other hand, when a person is the recipient of an identity-disconfirming act, especially if a sequence of such acts is built up in a situation, he or she would be more likely to incorporate the consequent emotion into his or her identity as a mood—happy, angry, or depressed depending on the transient impression of the person created by others' actions. In addition, the transition from emotion to mood would be more likely to occur where situational or institutional constraints create obstacles to resolving identity-disconfirming events through restorative action, or through reidentification of those whose actions have momentarily disconfirmed a person's identity.

Table 7.4 illustrates the *compensatory behavior* induced by emotions for a sample of events. In each case, a simulation was set up specifying a particular emotion for an actor as if it had just been produced by some event or built up from a sequence of events. Then, behavioral predictions for the next event were generated by INTERACT.

In line with the theory of emotions just outlined, a momentarily jealous husband does not initiate jealous behavior, as the commonsense view of emotion would have it. Instead, according to predictions, he might "love" his wife, a restorative action serving to reaffirm his identity as husband. Similarly, it is predicted that a doctor who has experienced a flash of annoyance will "rehabilitate," "help," "forgive," or "cure" a patient; a cop who has momentarily been afraid will "catch," "overwhelm," or "arrest" a mugger; and a professor who has momentarily been angry will "assist," "console," or "comfort" a student.

Table 7.5 reports how people might act when their current identities are transformed by more enduring affective states. The incorporation of *moods* into the motivational system of actors is simulated by modifying identities with emotion terms, employing the amalgamation equations discussed above. Here, compensatory behavior is no longer predicted. Instead, in line with the commonsense view of emotions, predictions suggest that *people will act out their affective moods.* Referring back to Table 7.4, it was predicted that a doctor who momentarily felt annoyed with a patient would implement restorative acts like "rehabilitate," "forgive," and "cure." In contrast, when this ephemeral emotion has become incorporated into his or her identity as a mood (an annoyed doctor), it is predicted that he or she will engage in mood sustaining behavior, like "disbelieving," "reproaching," or "rebuffing" a patient (Table 7.5).

Examining several other examples from Table 7.5, an afraid cop might "obey" a mugger, or perhaps "watch," "extol," or "implore" him. An angry professor, according to female expectations, might "parody" a student or "awake," "disconcert," or "judge" him or her. (According to male expectations, not reported in Table 7.5, an angry professor might "refuse" a student or "confound," "admonish," "criticize," or "deride" him or her.) A jealous husband might "flee" or "hide from" his wife, or perhaps "peek at" or "follow" her. Rather than "saving" or "helping" a maiden after a flash of momentary fear (Table 7.4), a hero who continues to be afraid might "chatter to," "emulate," "josh," or even "flee" her (Table 7.5).

Table 7.4

Behavioral Consequences of Emotions[a]

Actor	Actor's Emotion	Object-Person	Actor's Compensatory Behavior
Doctor (F)	annoyed	patient	rehabilitate, help, forgive, cure, educate, assist, heal, reassure
Cop (M)	afraid	mugger	catch, overwhelm, rebel against, arrest, astonish, tackle, put down, incite
Professor (F)	angry	student	assist, console, comfort, bless, compliment, thank, please, appreciate
Clerk (M)	distressed	customer	acclaim, ask, charm, answer, address, talk to, agree with, flatter
Husband (M)	jealous	wife	love
Hero (M)	afraid	maiden	save, marry, make love to, help
Child (M)	sad	mother	assist, uplift, compliment, aid, welcome, please, comfort, cheer

a. Predictions based upon male (M) or female (F) attitudes as designated parenthetically in column one. For the purpose of behavioral retrievals, the relationship for each dyad was specified as follows: doctor-patient (verbal, physical, fixing); cop-mugger (verbal, physical, managing); professor-student (verbal, primary, training); clerk-customer (verbal, primary, exchange); husband-wife and hero-maiden (no cognitive filters employed—acts of any type permitted); child-mother (verbal, primary).

TABLE 7.5

Behavioral Consequences of Affective Moods[a]

Actor	Actor's Affective Mood	Object-Person	Predicted Emotion-Sustaining Actions for Actor
Doctor (F)	annoyed	patient	indulge, coax, reproach, eye, nudge, exalt, disbelieve, rebuff
Cop (M)	afraid	mugger	obey, watch, extol, emulate, query, chatter to, implore, beseech
Professor (F)	angry	student	parody, butter up, overrate, exalt, fool, awake, disconcert, judge
Clerk (M)	distressed	customer	implore, query, deprecate, beg, pooh-pooh, placate, patronize, soft soap
Husband (M)	jealous	wife	flee, hide from, peek at, follow, mimic, ogle, beseech, pooh-pooh
Hero (M)	afraid	maiden	chatter to, extol, idolize, idealize, emulate, josh, ogle, flee
Child (M)	sad	mother	extol, chatter to, query

a. Predictions based upon male (M) or female (F) attitudes as designated parenthetically in column one. For the purpose of behavioral retrievals, the relationship for each dyad was specified as follows: doctor-patient (verbal, physical, fixing); cop-mugger (verbal, physical, managing); professor-student (verbal, primary, training); clerk-customer (verbal, primary, exchange); husband-wife and hero-maiden (no cognitive filters employed—acts of any type permitted); child-mother (verbal, primary).

Emotional Goal-Induced Behavior

Beginning in early childhood socialization, people learn which events produce specific emotions, enabling them to anticipate the emotional consequences of future events. These are the *anticipatory emotions* described by Kemper (1978). Conversely, people should be able to anticipate events to bring about the experience of desired emotions. Even if never realized through action, the contemplation and rehearsal of future events may be sufficient to induce an emotional goal-state.

Consider, for instance, a woman who has been ostensively wronged by another and intuits that she should be justifiably angry, but for one reason or another the emotional experience eludes her. Perhaps another's actions have momentarily disconfirmed her situated identity, challenging her "place" in an encounter so that becoming angry would serve as a reaffirmation of identity, or "place claim" (Clark 1990). She might even buttress her belief that she should feel angry by invoking an emotion norm applicable to the kind of event that has just occurred. Or, maybe a third party, having brought all this to her attention, coaches her to reaffirm her identity or "place" through the expression of normatively prescribed indignation.

Whatever the particulars of the case, an emotion becomes a goal-state to be achieved through appropriate action. The task for a person is to anticipate actions that will bring about the experience of a particular emotion. The corresponding task for affect control theory is to predict actions that will produce emotions specified in advance. The connection between emotional goal-states and constructionist theories of emotion is discussed in the next section.

The predictions reported in Table 7.6 describe the kind of actions that might bring about the experience of specific emotions (angry, afraid, sad, and happy) by particular actors in several social relationships. At first glance, the acts a husband might do to his wife to experience anger do not appear to be particularly angry acts. But, one must consider that both husband and wife are very positive identities, and acts like "jest," "contradict," "josh," and "oppose" are quite uncharacteristic of a culturally defined husband-wife relationship. "Serving" his wife or "hiding from," "submitting to," "peeking at," or "fleeing" her might make a husband feel afraid. To "serve" her might make him sad. (According to female expectations, "obeying" a wife might also make a husband feel sad, predictions that might both titillate and depress the feminist reader.) Finally, "adoring" his wife, or "applauding," "dancing with," "enjoying," "complimenting," "kissing," "inviting," or "appealing to" her might make a husband happy.

The second panel of Table 7.6 reports how a husband might act toward a ladykiller to feel alternatively angry, afraid, sad, or happy. For instance, "refusing," "admonishing," or "diverting" a ladykiller might make a husband feel angry; "watching," "querying," or "imploring" a ladykiller might make him afraid. Some of the events that might make a husband feel afraid might also make him sad, suggesting the mix and meld of emotions that probably occur in real-life circumstances in reaction to a single event. However, "lulling," "coddling" or "explaining to" a ladykiller would clearly make a husband sad, while "hiding from," "imploring," or "beseeching" a ladykiller would render him afraid. Finally, according to predictions, a husband would feel happy only as he implements actions that are consistent with his positively evaluated identity—"applauding," "appealing to," "complimenting," or "admiring."

The last panel in Table 7.6 reports the actions a cop might undertake to feel angry, afraid, sad, or happy in interaction with a hooker. A cop is predicted to feel angry as he "criticizes" a hooker or "renounces," "disconcerts," or "deters" her. He might experience either fear or sadness by "watching," "obeying," "querying," or

Table 7.6

Behavioral Consequences of Emotional Goal States[a]

Emotional Goal State

Actor	Object Person	Angry	Afraid	Sad	Happy
Husband	Wife	jest	serve	serve	adore
		butter up	hide from		applaud
		contradict	submit to		dance with
		josh	peek at		enjoy
		oppose	flee		compliment
		divert			kiss
		stall			invite
		cajole			appeal to
Husband	Lady-killer	refuse	watch	query	applaud
		admonish	query	lull	appeal to
		stymie	submit to	submit to	compliment
		work	overhear	coddle	alert
		stall	hide from	overhear	delight
		prod	implore	watch	flatter
		bluff	beseech	explain	admire
		divert			charm
Cop	Hooker	criticize	watch	query	applaud
		renounce	obey	obey	appeal to
		disconcert	query	watch	alert
		deter	implore	coddle	delight
		refuse	hide from	explain	compliment
		affront	overhear	look at	warn
		dog	beseech	overhear	flatter
		fool	submit to	entreat	charm

a. Predictions made employing male attitudes. No cognitive filters were employed in the retrieval of behaviors for the husband-wife relationship. The relationship between a husband-ladykiller and a cop-hooker was defined as verbal, physical, managing.

"overhearing" a hooker; but "imploring," "hiding from," "beseeching," or "submitting to" her are associated only with fear, and "coddling," "explaining," "looking at," or "entreating" her are behavioral concomitants only of sadness.

Finally, we can connect the analysis of emotional goal–states to the constructionist emphasis on cultural variation in emotional response by examining how a cop can feel happy in interaction with a hooker. In the Canadian study, where police identities are generally positive, powerful, and lively, events like "applauding," "appealing to," "alerting," and "warning" a hooker are predicted to make a cop happy. By comparison, according to simulations with the U.S. data and equations, a cop would feel happy only when he "interviews," "analyzes," "dissuades," or "restrains" a hooker.

With a discussion and illustration of the affect control theory of emotions in hand, we can examine how the theory advances the reconciliation of constructionist and positivist theories of emotion beyond what was accomplished in the opening section of this chapter.

The Constructionist Versus Positivist Debate and Affect Control Theory

I have summarized the debate between constructionists and positivists along four major lines of contention: (1) the relative emphasis on biology and culture in the conceptualization of emotion, and the related issue of descriptive versus explanatory research; (2) the specificity or differentiation of the physiological component of emotional experience and the related issue of primary versus secondary emotions; (3) the extent to which cognitive appraisal mediates the relation between situational events and emotional response; and (4) the relative importance of cultural and social structure in the instigation of emotions. The position of affect control theory on the first three points can be dealt with quickly. Its position on the fourth requires more extensive discussion.

Affect control theory's conceptualization of emotions as affectively-rich cognitive signals cuing the confirmation or disconfirmation of salient identities in social interaction lies somewhere between the constructionist and positivist positions. While acknowledging that emotions, thus conceived, are culturally influenced and variable, the theory supposes that emotions, like all cognitions, manifest an underlying universal structure (the EPA structure of general affective response). Since the theory studies emotions indirectly, through emotion terms, there remains the larger question concerning the extent to which the EPA structure of general affective response measures the cultural metaphors and prototypes of emotions embodied in language, as opposed to the biologically-based, physiological component of emotional experience itself. Some discussion of this issue with respect to prototypes can be found in MacKinnon and Keating (1989, 81–83).

While the theory's conception of emotions promotes explanatory research by not confounding *explanans* and *explanandum*, it recognizes the importance— indeed, the indispensability—of descriptive research, including qualitative studies in natural settings. As evidenced throughout this book, affect control theory draws upon the rich insights of constructionist theorists to frame and interpret affect control simulations and predictions.

As to the second line of contention, affect control theory does not maintain that emotions themselves correspond to specific, qualitatively different kinds of

physiological arousal and sensation. Instead, it entertains the hypothesis of specificity only with respect to the EPA dimensions of general affective response. At the
same time, affect control researchers (Morgan and Heise 1988; MacKinnon and
Keating 1989) have contributed to resolving the issue of primary versus secondary
emotions by showing how the many terms for secondary emotions in the lexicon
of English-speaking cultures cluster in EPA affective space within a small number
of identifiable regions corresponding roughly to the primary emotions identified
by Kemper (1987).

   With respect to the third contentious issue in the debate between constructionists and positivists, affect control theory supposes that cognitive and affective
processing mediates the impact of events on emotional response, but does not
maintain that this mediation is necessarily either conscious or protracted. While
the theory acknowledges that the cognitive work involved in interpreting emotion-
instigating events can often be extensive, it supposes that cognitive processing is
routinely governed by a preconceptual system established in early childhood socialization (see Chapter 3). Because affect control theory applies equally to
emotion-instigating events that have been subjected to conscious, cognitive appraisal and to those that have not, the theory subsumes the respective emphases of
constructionist and positivist theories of emotion.

   In the rest of this section, I identify the contributions of affect control theory to resolve the fourth point of contention between constructionists and positivists, the relative impact of cultural and social structure on emotional experience.
I begin by showing how affect control theory incorporates the constructionist emphasis on cultural structure.

   One way the cultural structure of a society shapes emotional experience, according to constructionists, is through language. Language provides a vocabulary
of emotion-labels (Gordon 1981), bringing the other components of emotional
experience (situational cues, physiological sensations, and behavioral expressions)
into conscious awareness (Thoits 1984).[11]

   Affect control theory extends the constructionist position on the role of language in emotional experience by viewing language in general as an affectively
loaded medium; that is, the words with which we designate all kinds of phenomena—including identities and interpersonal acts, not just those for labeling emotions—evoke affective associations (Propositions 2 and 3, Chapter 2).

   Among other implications, this affective theory of semantics gives us a linguistic handle on the process of "empathic role–taking" described by Shott (1979).
She suggested that before empathy can occur, identification with others must first
be established through cognitive role-taking. Now, if cognitive role-taking is predicated upon shared cognitions, then empathic role-taking is predicated upon the
assumption that social cognitions evoke culturally learned sentiments. Because
language is the primary symbolic system by which social cognitions are learned and
subsequently brought to consciousness, empathic role–taking is possible only be-

cause language conveys affective meaning. Thus, affect control theory enables one to conceptualize, at the linguistic level, the connection between cognitive and empathic role-taking suggested by Shott.

Besides language, constructionists have identified a second way in which culture influences emotions, through social norms governing emotional experience and its expression. In this regard, affect control theory accepts the notion that people often invoke social norms to explain, justify, and control the thoughts, feelings, and behavior of self and others. However, as discussed in Chapters 5 and 6, the theory questions whether a finite number of social norms can cover the infinite possibilities and exigencies that confront the actor in social interaction, and whether individuals learn or access a great deal of cultural structure at the level of intact social norms.

Instead, affect control theory supposes that people learn and access the cultural structure of a society at the more elementary level of social cognitions and affective associations, and that this is accomplished in large part through learning a culture's language. Moreover, the theory supposes that action and interpretation are motivated by a desire to confirm salient identities, not to conform to social norms.

Despite these differences in assumptions and levels of analysis, affect control connects with the constructionist idea of emotion norms. Events producing large discrepancies between fundamental cultural sentiments and transient feelings should coincide with specific norms proscribing them and the emotions they would produce, if realized. This is why affect control models can generate emotional response to so many events that fall under "the imperial scope of social rules" (Hochschild 1979, 551). And, in this sense, "all of affect control theory's predictions about emotions define norms since they are the responses generated by consensually held meanings" (Smith-Lovin 1990, 254).

The existence of emotion norms implies that people can violate them by experiencing "deviant" emotions (Thoits 1984, 1985, 1990)—those considered socially inappropriate for particular situations and events. Emotional deviance implies, in turn, that people are required to manage their emotions in social interaction, as documented by Hochschild's (1983) analysis of the "emotion work" demanded of service workers.

Affect control theory also connects with the constructionist idea of emotional deviance and management. Indeed, "affect control theory not only seeks to predict emotions but also is premised on management of emotions" (Kemper 1990, 18). The theory predicts that emotion-management will occur when events challenge or disconfirm an actor's situated identity, generating emotions that deviate from those a person might expect to feel on the basis of his or her identity-situated self or particular social relationship.

Thoits (1990) has distinguished between behavioral and cognitive modes of emotion management. The simulations of emotion-induced compensatory behavior reported in Table 7.4 exemplify the behavioral mode. According to predictions, a doctor who has experienced a momentary flash of annoyance will reaffirm his or her situated identity and characteristic emotions by "helping," "forgiving," or "curing" a patient; a cop who has momentarily been afraid will "catch" and "arrest" a thief.

The simulations of behavior induced by emotional goal states reported in Table 7.6 illustrate the cognitive mode of emotion management. For example, according to predictions, a husband who believes that he should be angry with a ladykiller can effect that emotional state by anticipating events like "admonishing" or "stymying" him, even though he may never carry out these actions.

Alternatively, a husband might reidentify a ladykiller, making him out to be a more nefarious character—a "scoundrel," perhaps, or a "lustful" ladykiller. Or, if his self-perceptions allow, he might momentarily reidentify himself as someone quick to temper, say, a "hothead" or a "hotheaded" husband. Because reidentifications effect correlative changes in behavioral expectations and characteristic emotions, a husband could easily envisage a sequence of events involving himself and a "scoundrel," or a "hothead" and a ladykiller, or both, that would leave him feeling angry. This suggests a close connection between reidentification processes (see Chapter 8) and emotion–management.

In addition to "feeling rules" or "emotion norms" governing the covert, private experience of emotions, the constructionist treatment of emotion-management invokes the concept of "display rules" or "expression norms" pertaining to the overt, public expression of emotion (Thoits 1990, after Ekman, Friesen, and Ellsworth 1982; Hochschild 1979, 1983). As discussed in a preliminary way in Chapter 2 (Proposition 20) and expounded in the following chapter, the visible expression of emotion influences the labeling and attribution processes through which people reidentify one another. Because the reidentification model of affect control theory incorporates information on emotion-displays, it can simulate scenarios wherein people manage their public expression of emotion in order to sidestep the imputation of unwanted attributions or identity labels.

The simulations reported in the next chapter reveal the dramatic impact that the public expression of emotion can have on a person's identification by others. Anticipating a simulation result from this chapter, a woman who expresses no emotion while being kissed by a man might be reidentified as a "wallflower," a "bookworm," or a "weak," "boring," "dull" woman by those observing the event. However, a woman who appears visibly "moved" might be labeled a "darling," a "lady," or a "nice," "sincere," "friendly" woman. This example, and others reported in Chapter 8, attest to the importance of emotion management in securing the social validation of our identity-situated selves.

Turning to the effect of social structure on emotional experience emphasized by positivists, the production of emotions from socially structured interaction is at the explanatory core of affect control theory. In contrast to Kemper's social behavioristic approach,[12] however, affect control theory views consequent emotions from the perspective of identity theory. That is, social events produce emotions as they confirm or disconfirm identity-situated selves.

Yet, there is a close connection between the identity theory perspective of affect control theory and the social behavioristic approach of Kemper. For Kemper, it is not simply what people do to one another that produces emotions, but rather the consequences of these actions for an individual's status and power. As noted previously in this book, Kemper's concepts of status and power correspond, respectively, to evaluation and potency in affect control theory, two dimensions of affective meaning in terms of which identities are confirmed or disconfirmed in social interaction. Because affect control theory adds a third dimension, activity, which it identifies with the liveliness or expressiveness of social identities, Kemper's dimensions are a subset of those employed in affect control theory.

Nonetheless, because of its greater affinity with identity theory than with Kemper's social behaviorism, it might appear that affect control theory has both feet planted firmly in the interactionist-inspired constructionist camp. However, as discussed in Chapter 5, identity theory is a version of symbolic interactionism that emphasizes, like positivists, the importance of social structure. And, while affect control theory is a dynamic theory that spans the *process* school of symbolic interactionism as well, it clearly does not identify with the anti-positivist methodological position adopted by many constructionists.

To draw this discussion to a close, consider the emotional life of a person. On the one hand, we have the more or less automatic and vital emotional response to socially structured events in the primary emotion system, as emphasized by positivists; on the other hand, the culturally influenced construction and management of emotional response in the secondary emotion system, as emphasized by constructionists. Affect control theory handles both sides of a person's emotional life. If one wants to study the former, then one sets up an INTERACT analysis in terms of the person's private, salient, high-commitment identities and interprets simulation results as predicting what a person will do and feel. If one wants to study the latter, then one sets up an INTERACT analysis in terms of the person's public, socially-demanded identities and interprets simulation results as predicting what a person *thinks* he or she *should* do and feel.

Results from the first kind of analysis predict consequent emotions—those produced by others' actions in socially structured relationships. Results from the second kind of analysis predict emotion management—behavioral and cognitive response to identity-disconfirming emotions or to those that violate emotion-norms. Examples of the first kind of analysis can be found in my discussion of consequent emotions (Table 7.3); examples of the second, in my discussion of emotion-induced compensatory behavior (Table 7.4) and emotional goal-states (Table 7.6).

Summary

According to affect control theory, emotions inform an actor how the process of social interaction is going with respect to the confirmation or disconfirmation of salient identities. Within the general confines of this functional theory of emotions, this chapter has described and illustrated three kinds of emotions. *Characteristic* emotions are those an actor experiences when social interaction perfectly confirms his or her identity-situated self. *Structural* emotions are those typically experienced in social relationships with particular others. *Consequent* emotions are those instigated by actual social events, and are frequently different from characteristic or structural emotions.

Reversing the direction between behavior and emotion, this chapter also has delineated and illustrated three kinds of emotion-induced behavior. *Compensatory behavior* occurs when actors feel compelled to redress the experience of an out-of–character emotion and, hence, to reaffirm a salient identity. *Mood-induced behavior* results from the qualitative change in an identity that occurs when an emotion becomes an enduring affective state. Behavior induced by *emotional goal-states* takes place when an actor anticipates events that will bring about the experience of a desired emotion.

The affect control theory of emotions and emotion-induced behavior was then applied to the debate between constructionists and positivists discussed in the beginning of this chapter. Among other differences, positivist and constructionist theories of emotion place a relatively greater emphasis on, respectively, social and cultural structure. Because affect control theory brings both faces of social institutions under its theoretical purview, modeling both the production and management of emotions, the theory integrates positivist and constructionist theories in a more general theory of emotions.

Affect control theory clarifies two additional issues that are skirted by constructionist and positivist theories of emotion: the role of affect and emotions in *motivation*; and the role of *language* in affect and emotions.

Neither constructionists nor positivists have developed an explicit theory of human motivation. The affect control theory of motivation, based on the incentive of identity–confirmation, was presented in Chapter 3. The behavioral consequences of emotions delineated in this chapter link this identity theory of motivation to emotions and to the theory of motivation implicit in constructionist treatments of emotion management. Because affect control theory deals with identities in terms of evaluation and potency, the subjective meaning of Kemper's status and power, it also connects with the theory of motivation implicit in positivist theories of emotion. By clarifying the role of affect and emotions in motivation, affect control theory advances the social psychology of emotion beyond either the constructionist or positivist positions.

In analyzing the role of language in emotional experience, contructionists have generally focused on the symbolic designation of emotions, while positivists have hardly dealt with language at all. By treating language as an affectively loaded medium, affect control theory extends the constructionist view on the role of language in designating emotional experience to a full-blown affective theory of semantics. And, by operationalizing social events as syntactically structured combinations of elements, affect control theory imposes linguistic structure upon the positivist premise that emotions are produced by socially structured social relations.

In conclusion, this chapter has focused on emotions as privately experienced affective states and their connection to a person's identity-situated self. It has only hinted at the visible expression of emotion and its consequences. The overt display of emotion through facial expressions, body language, or verbal communication projects the covert emotional life of the person into the public domain. The next chapter attends to the consequences of expressing or communicating private emotional experience for the maintenance of salient identities.

8

REIDENTIFICATION

The affect control theory of reidentification was outlined in Chapter 2. According to Proposition 9, when people cannot confirm their fundamental sentiments through restorative action, they attempt to do so through cognitive revision of what has already taken place. Proposition 21 proposes that past events are made more credible by assigning new identities (labels) to interactants that help explain their actions; Proposition 22, that a similar outcome is achieved by modifying the original identities of interactants through the attribution of explanatory traits. According to Proposition 23, because attributions have the cognitive advantage of keeping the current definition of the situation relatively intact, they are probably a more common form of reidentification than the imputation of identity labels.

Attribution theory in psychological social psychology has approached the reidentification problem in terms of the imputation of personal traits; symbolic interactionism in sociological social psychology, the assignment of identity labels, usually stigmatized ones. Both traditions emphasize the idea that people draw inferences about each other's character from observed behavior.

As discussed in the preceding chapter, however, emotions inform a person whether he or she has experienced an identity–confirming or disconfirming event; and emotional expression reveals this privately recognized outcome to other people. Thus, it is likely that people do not base their attributions and labeling upon behavior alone; they check their inferences from behavior against a person's overt emotional reaction to events before deciding what identity a person is trying to maintain or confirm in a situation. Revealing remorse in the wake of a deviant event, for example, suggests that an actor has implemented an unintentional act and does not deserve to be tagged with a stigmatized identity. This line of reasoning lies behind Proposition 24, which asserts that the emotion displays of interactants affect the reidentifications they suffer as a consequence of events.

The established reidentification model of affect control theory (Heise 1979; Averett and Heise 1988) integrates attribution and labeling processes. Heise (1989a) subsequently extended this model to incorporate the effects of expressed emotions on reidentification outcomes. To avoid unnecessary complexity, I have partitioned this chapter into two parts. Part I deals with the established reidentification model; Part II, its extension to emotions.

Part I: The Established Model—Attributions and Identity Labels

This section discusses the relation between attribution theory and symbolic interactionism, introduces and illustrates the established reidentification model, and shows how affect control theory contributes to the integration of the two theories by combining attribution and labeling processes in a single theoretical and predictive model.

Attribution Theory and Symbolic Interactionism

Symbolic interactionism, of course, has already been discussed extensively in this book, including a brief discussion of labeling processes in Chapter 2[1]; attribution theory, however, has not. While the origins of the theory can be traced to Lewin's (1935) insight that behavior is a function of both person and environment, Heider (1958) laid the foundations of the theory in his classic work, *The Psychology of Interpersonal Perception.* As developed by Heider, attribution theory rests on the supposed need for people to understand, predict, and control their environment. He argued that the human sensitivity to causal relations—the tendency to invoke a "principle of invariance" conjoined with the overriding salience of behavior in perception—predispose people to exaggerate the intentionality, purposefulness, and controllability of human behavior. As a result, people explain each other's actions by making inferences about stable dispositions like traits, emotions, and motives. In Heider's view, every layperson is a "naive psychologist," applying a personal theory of human behavior to explain and predict the social world.[2]

Both House (1977) and Stryker (1977) singled out the similarity between attribution and labeling processes as a promising point of rapprochement between psychological and sociological social psychology. Stryker and Gottlieb (1981) developed this observation into a full-blown comparison between attribution theory and symbolic interactionism.[3]

Stryker and Gottlieb (1981) identify four points of similarity between attribution theory and symbolic interactionism:

1. Both theories adopt a phenomenological perspective, focusing on the subjective experience of people as the object of inquiry. This is evident in Heider's belief that an understanding of human behavior must begin with the person's perceptions embodied in commonsense reports and descriptions, and in Mead's extension of the behavioristic perspective to the inner experience of the actor.

2. Both theories view the person as a rational, problem–solving actor. Heider likened the naive psychology of ordinary people to the rational scientific method, and later attribution theorists employed rationality as the norm against which they

identify and explain the cognitive biases of lay psychologies. Mead showed how reflexiveness and the social origin of the human mind made reflective consciousness and rationality possible.

3. Both theories focus on everyday life and experience, which they try to explain with principles derived from this domain. For attribution theorists, the naive psychology of each person is a product of his or her everyday social experience. For interactionists, meaning emerges from and is modified by everyday social interaction.

4. Both theories propose that symbolic-cognitive processes simplify and make manageable the complexities of everyday social life. For attribution theorists, the psychology of the layperson contains simplifying principles for comprehending reality in more parsimonious form. For symbolic interactionists, the definition of the situation establishes the relevant identities and corresponding roles in any situation so that interaction can proceed smoothly.

Stryker and Gottlieb (1981) also identify important differences between the two theories, deriving from their different conceptualizations of cognitive meaning.[4] For attribution theory, cognitive meaning is the product of an *intra*personal process whose objective is an understanding of a supposed external, objectively definable world of stimuli. For symbolic interactionism, cognitive meaning is an *inter*personally negotiated product that has no necessary correspondence to an external, objectively defined world.

While Stryker and Gottlieb (1981) compared attribution theory and symbolic interactionism, achieving a partial synthesis, Alexander and Wiley (1981) combined the two perspectives in a single theory. As discussed in Chapter 5, situated identity theory integrates the insights of Heider and attribution theorists on *person*-perception with those of Mead and symbolic interactionists on *self*-perception. This is accomplished by taking several conceptual cornerstones of interactionist theory and reconceptualizing them in attribution terms. For example, they define role-taking as the process whereby individuals "see themselves in the same *dispositional* terms [as others] and . . . view their activities and actions as expressing these *attributes*"(Alexander and Wiley 1981, 272. Emphasis added); and "situated identities," as the "*attributions* made from salient perspectives about an actor's presence and performance in the immediate social context" (1981, 270. Emphasis added).

The integration of attribution theory and symbolic interactionism can be advanced beyond Stryker and Gottlieb (1981) and Alexander and Wiley (1981) by examining how later attribution theorists apply the concept of general schemata (or schemas) to person and self-perception. Generic schemas are cognitive structures that organize experience at both the perceptual and cognitive-interpretative levels of psychological experience (Mandler 1984, 55–60). Schemas are "bounded, distinct, and unitary presentations" of environmental events enabling us to comprehend sensory input. They are also cognitive processing mechanisms, operative "in selecting evidence, in pursuing environmental data, and in providing general or specific hypotheses." A cumulative product of interaction between individual and environment, their activation in particular situations is generally automatic and below the threshold of conscious awareness. When activated, schemas elicit all kinds of "preconscious cognitions" from a "preconceptual system" (Epstein 1984) established in early childhood socialization.

In this regard, Rosenberg (1977) proposed that people do not store and access information about each other as concrete bits of data, but rather as schemata consisting of implicit correlations among traits. Schemata simplify person-perception by serving as prototypic characterizations about people. Markus's (1977) construct of self-schemata ("cognitive generalizations about the self . . . that organize and guide the processing of self-related information") applied this notion to self-perception. While she discussed self-schemata in terms of individual personality traits, one can extend the construct to clusters of implicitly correlated traits, like Rosenberg's application of schemata to person perception.

It does not require a great conceptual leap to connect the idea of schemas to the symbolic interactionist construct of identities. As cognitive generalizations about the self, organizing and guiding the processing of self-relevant information, identities constitute self-schemata in Markus's meaning of the term. By extension, identities operate as important schemata in person perception as well.

As discussed in Chapter 5, identities have implications for actions (Stryker 1968; Burke 1980); and, as discussed in Chapter 7, identities are associated with "characteristic emotions," those experienced in identity-confirming events. It is but a simple extension of these ideas to consider identities as implying "characteristic traits" or clusters of traits. This is a particularly compelling idea when one considers that the emotions equations of affect control theory are attribution equations (Averett and Heise 1988). And, like characteristic emotions, characteristic traits would be those experienced when events confirm a person's identity. Having impressed a student with his or her brilliance, for example, a professor should *think* of himself or herself as "competent," just as he or she should *feel* "satisfied" (Table 7.1).

While this connection between self-schemata and identities has yet to be empirically explored in affect control theory, what makes it possible for the theory to incorporate trait attribution and labeling within a single model is its conceptualization of a personal trait as a "trans-situational particularization of identity" (Heise 1991, 12). How this becomes operationalized is addressed in the following section.

The Model

That part of the established reidentification model predicting labeling outcomes is derived from the event construction model described in Chapter 6. In event construction, the actor (A) and object-person (O) identities of ABO events are knowns and the mathematical problem involves solving for an interpersonal behavior (B) that optimally confirms the known identities. In reidentification, on the other hand, either the actor (A) *or* the object-person identify (O) *and* the behavior (B) are knowns, and the problem becomes solving for the unknown identity (either O or A). The solution optimally confirms sentiments for the known components of the event (AB or BO), yielding object-person and actor reidentifications, respectively. The reidentification model programmed in INTERACT generates an optimal EPA profile and then searches the database for matching identity labels.

In the case of trait-attributions, the reidentification model applies the attribution equations of affect control theory derived from the empirically-based amalgamation equations of the theory (Averett and Heise 1988). The latter describe how a trait like "strict" combines with an identity like "father" to produce an impression of a modified identity, a "strict father." Given a particular situated identity like "father," the attribution equations solve for an unknown personal trait that combines with the known identity to confirm an observed event like "father disciplines child."

To apply the attribution equations to traditional attribution research, one would restrict retrievals to personality traits like "hostile," "intelligent," and so on. However, as discussed in Chapter 2, the model generates other kinds of attributions. Retrievals from the *emotions* subset of identity-modifiers would stimulate an interpretation of the actor's conduct along the lines of "mood-induced behavior" discussed in the preceding chapter. Retrievals of *status characteristics* (e.g., "young," "rich") would lead to interpretations invoking notions of an actor's social position; *moral* retrievals (e.g., "good," "evil"), explanations based upon his or her moral character.

In *actor*-reidentifications, we are trying to determine, for example, what kind of man would beg a woman. Our answer can take the form of the imputation of an identity label or the attribution of an explanatory trait. Anticipating a finding reported below, reidentification analysis predicts that a "lush," "heel," "sponger," "weirdo," or "suicidal" man might beg a woman.

Extending this example event to *object*-reidentifications, we are trying to figure out what kind of woman would be or seek to be (depending on how salient the actor remains after the verb is put in the passive voice) begged by a man. Again, anticipating a prediction reported below, a "shrew" or a "betrayed," "abandoned" woman might seek to be begged by a man.

Reidentification Analysis: Attributions And Labels

The reidentification model programmed in INTERACT employs a classification system that allows the analyst to cognitively constrain the retrieval of identities. The categories of this system are: (1) gender specific—identities that are typically male or female; (2) casual—those that can be found across a number of institutional contexts (e.g., "buddy"); (3) ascribed—those based on the ascription of attributes like age or capability ("juvenile," "cripple"); (4) legal—those pertaining to criminal justice and deviant roles; (5) trade—occupational and other identities involving remuneration; and (6) sociosex—those pertaining to family and neighborhood life or sexuality. While provisional, this classification system filters out institutionally anomalous or meaningless results like those requiring a sex change in an interactant (e.g., "mother" for the reidentification of a person whose original identity is man.)

Table 8.1 presents reidentification results for events involving the identities man (as actor) and woman (as object–person). In order to explore reidentifications for a full range of actions, behaviors were "forced" to fit the prototypical EPA configurations (+++,++–, . . . ---) described in the preceding chapter on emotions.

Identities are reported first in Table 8.1, followed by trait attributions in parentheses. Where optimal EPA profiles generated by the model lie outside the range of empirically measured identities and attributes, this is designated by "unidentifiable" and "undescribable," respectively. Predictions based on both male (M) and female (F) sentiments are reported in Table 8.1; but, in the interest of brevity, I confine my discussion to male sentiments and invite the interested reader to examine gender differences in predictions on his or her own.

For actor reidentifications resulting from positively evaluated acts, the model predicts that a "teammate," "myself as others see me," or a "boyfriend" might *thrill* a woman; a "nursemaid," an "innocent," or "storyteller" might *cuddle* her; a "musician," "classmate," "sidekick," or a "vivacious," "lucky" man might *desire* her; and a "houseguest," "underdog," "neighbor," or a "passive" man might simply *admire* her.

For actor reidentifications resulting from negatively evaluated acts, the model predicts that a "brute" or "thug" might *seize* a woman; a "goon," "hood," or "thug" might *scorn* her; a "sinner," lout," or "cynic" might *flee* her; and a "hypochondriac," "lush," "clod," or "blockhead" might *beg* her. Attributions are out of range for three of these four negative events. For the remaining event, the predictions that a "suicidal," "homosexual," or "persecuted" man might *flee* a woman seem plausible enough.

According to object-person reidentifications resulting from positively evaluated conduct of the actor, a "victim," an "old maid," or a "wallflower" might be *thrilled* by a man; a "bystander," "bumpkin," or "bored," "sluggish," "gloomy" woman might seek to be *cuddled*; an "accomplice," "gambler," or "abusive," "nasty," "cruel" woman might seek to be *desired*; and "a servant," "newcomer," or "drowsy," "resigned," or "absent-minded" woman might seek to be *admired*.

According to object-person reidentications resulting from negatively evaluated conduct of the actor, a "rogue," "hooligan," or "fiend" might be *seized* by a man; a "witch," "cad," "adultress," or "cruel," "bitchy" woman, *scorned*; an "adultress," "scoundrel," "cad," or "cruel," "bitchy," "abusive" woman, *fled*; and a "sophisticate," "alumnus," or "rigid," "stingy," "secretive" woman might seek to be *begged* by a man.

These results fit the dynamics of the impression formation equations. Among other things, the equations reveal that a good person, like a woman, loses considerable status simply by being the object-person of an event, that her initial potency and liveliness contributes to a further loss of status, and that a powerful actor, like a man, makes her appear less powerful and lively. The equations also show that an actor's behavior has a profound effect on the impression of the object-person. Powerful acts like *thrill* and *cuddle* make the recipient appear less powerful and lively. A weak, lively behavior like *desire* creates an impression of impotency, though not inactivity. A weak and passive behavior like *admire* makes the recipient appear both impotent and inactive.[5]

While explicable in terms of impression formation dynamics, however, these object-person reidentifications seem too negative—and either too weak or too passive or both—to generalize to many women. Surely, an "old maid" or a "wallflower" are not the only kinds of women who might be *thrilled* by a man; "bored," "gloomy" women, the only kind who might seek to be *cuddled*. (We encounter the same problems of generalization when we analyze woman-to-man interactions).

However, consider the demands we are making of the established reidentification model. We are asking it to reidentify interactants on the basis of very limited information—their original identities and the actor's conduct. Obviously, a model's predictions are only as precise as the information input to the model is complete. What is missing, in the case of object-person reidentifications, is information concerning the feelings of a woman when she is thrilled, cuddled, desired, or admired—how she might feel about being the recipient of particular actions by a man. And, while predictions for actor-reidentifications are more plausible, providing information on expressed emotions should enhance their precision as well. In the absence of information on *consequent* emotions, the model assumes by default that interactants are experiencing emotions characteristic of the new or attribution–modified identities imputed to them.

Emotion analysis, for example, predicts that a woman who has been *cuddled* by a man will feel "moved," "zip," "contented," or "charmed." These consequent emotions correspond roughly to the characteristic emotions (zip, melancholy) of the new or trait–modified identities predicted for the recipient—a "bumpkin" or a "bored," "sluggish," "gloomy" woman. However, assume that she expresses a nicer, more powerful and lively emotion, say *cheerful*, while being cuddled. Would one not expect her emotional response to bring about the attribution of nicer, more powerful, and more lively reidentifications? Indeed, simulations reveal that a woman appearing *cheerful* as she is cuddled might be reidentified as a "lover."

Expressing any emotion at all, including a less powerful and lively one, in fact communicates to others that she is a feeling, animate person rather than an

TABLE 8.1

Reidentifications for Man > Woman Events[1]

EPA Profile	Act	Actor (Man)	Object-Person (Woman)
(+++)	thrill	(M) teammate, myself as others see me, boyfriend (undescribable)	(M) victim, old maid, wallflower (undescribable)
		(F) teammate, comedian, playmate (undescribable)	(F) wallflower, bookworm, old maid (undescribable)
(++−)	cuddle	(M) nursemaid, innocent, storyteller (undescribable)	(M) bystander, bumpkin (bored sluggish, gloomy woman)
		(F) (unidentifiable) (undescribable)	(F) (unidentifiable) (sluggish, unromantic, widowed woman)
(+−+)	desire	(M) musician, classmate, sidekick (vivacious, lucky man)	(M) accomplice, gambler (abusive, nasty, cruel woman)
		(F) lad, dandy, street-musician (playful man)	(F) sidekick, hick (insecure, hopeless, unambitious woman)
(+−−)	admire	(M) houseguest, underdog, neighbor (passive man)	(M) servant, newcomer (drowsy, resigned, absent-minded woman)
		(F) dandy, colleague, myself as others see me (cheerful, nice, affectionate man)	(F) underdog, servant, newcomer (unhealthy, narrow-minded, submissive woman)
(−++)	seize	(M) brute, thug (undescribable)	(M) rogue, hooligan, fiend (undescribable)
		(F) brute, bully, slave-driver (undescribable)	(F) bigshot, rival, vixen (cruel, hostile, abusive woman)
(−+−)	scorn	(M) goon, hood, thug (undescribable)	(M) witch, cad, adulteress (cruel, bitchy woman)
		(F) cutthroat, villain, evildoer (undescribable)	(F) cynic, scoundrel, accomplice (abusive woman)
(−−+)	flee	(M) sinner, lout, cynic (suicidal, homosexual, persecuted man)	(M) adulteress, scoundrel, cad (cruel, bitchy, abusive woman)
		(F) fanatic, neurotic, scamp (stoned, obnoxious, foolish man)	(F) accomplice, shrew, cynic (betrayed, unkind, prejudiced woman)

TABLE 8.1 *(Continued)*

Reidentifications for Man > Woman Events[a]

EPA Profile	Act	Actor (Man)	Object-Person (Woman)
(---)	beg	(M) hypochondriac, lush, clod, blockhead (undescribable) (F) lush, heel, sponger, weirdo (suicidal man)	(M) sophisticate, alumnus (rigid, stingy, secretive woman) (F) lookout, shrew, dike, accomplice (prejudiced, betrayed, abandoned, insensitive woman)

a. Reidentifications are provided for both male (M) and female (F) attitudes. Identities are presented first followed by traits in parentheses. "Unidentifiable" indicates that there are no identities that lie within the EPA profile generated by the model. "Undescribable" indicates the same thing for traits.

emotionless, lifeless object of a man's actions. For example, simulations reveal that a woman who appears *moved* while being cuddled by a man gets reidentified as a "patient," "gentle" woman, rather than a "bored," "sluggish," or "gloomy" one.

Before introducing the expanded reidentification model, which takes the emotion displays of interactants into account, I return to my discussion of attribution theory and symbolic interactionism, showing how affect control theory combines the two theoretical perspectives into a more general theory of reidentification processes.

Symbolic Interactionism, Attribution Theory, And Affect Control Theory

I structure the following discussion around the theoretical commonalities of attribution theory and symbolic interactionism identified by Stryker and Gottlieb (1981), discussed in the first section of this chapter: (1) a phenomenological perspective; (2) a conceptualization of the person as a rational, problem-solving organism; (3) a focus on everyday life and experience; and (4) an emphasis on symbolic-cognitive processes as simplifying the complexities of social life.

1. Insofar as its basic data consist of the self-reported subjective sentiments of people, rather than their objectively observed behavior, affect control theory can be said to adopt a phenomenological perspective. However, while both attribution theory and symbolic interactionism focus on cognitive meaning, affect control theory begins with the affective associations cognitions produce (Proposition 3, Chapter 2). Capitalizing upon the dimensional simplicity of affective meaning en-

ables the theory to efficiently model symbolic-cognitive processes emphasized by attribution theory and symbolic interactionism.

2. While accepting that human organisms are to some extent cognitive, rational "problem-solvers" or "intuitive scientists" (Nisbett and Ross 1980), affect control theory introduces affect and motivation into the cognitive-rational framework of attribution theory and symbolic interactionism. As discussed in Chapter 3, the theory supposes that there is no motivation without affect and that the consequence of cognition on behavior is mediated by the affective associations cognitions produce. This has already been discussed with respect to symbolic interactionism (Chapters 3, 4, and 5), but not attribution theory.

Attribution theory proceeds as if humans have only one kind of need—making cognitive sense of the world—and treats emotion as a kind of interference in cognitive-rational processing. Consider the "fundamental attribution error," the tendency to overestimate internal dispositions and underestimate external constraints when explaining the behavior of other people (Ross 1977). This bias has been explained cognitively in terms of the overriding salience of a person's behavior in conjunction with the tendency for observers to treat a person and his or her behavior as a natural perceptual and cognitive unit (Heider 1958).

It is noteworthy, however, that while people are predisposed to make *dispositional* attributions when assessing the behavior of others, they tend to make *situational* attributions when explaining their own (Jones and Harris 1967; Nisbett, Caputo, Legant, and Maracek 1973). This phenomenon has been explained, again in cognitive terms, by referring to the different perspectives people adopt as they shift from person to self-perception (Jones and Nisbett 1971). That is, in the role of observer, a person focuses on the behavior of other people. But in the role of actor, a person does not generally focus on his or her own behavior, but rather on the situation in which it occurs. Because one's own behavior is not very salient, an actor will tend to perceive the situation as causally more potent and to favor external over internal attributions in self-perception.

There is reason to suspect, however, that the failure of the fundamental attribution bias to generalize from person to self–perception may occur for other than cognitive reasons. It has been well documented that the tendency for people to make external attributions in self-perception holds true for unsuccessful performances only. While people tend to externalize their failures, they tend to internalize their successes. This suggests that the over-attribution to external forces in the case of self-perception may be motivated by non–cognitive factors like self-esteem and social approval (Monson and Snyder 1977). Thus, external attributions in self-perception may not constitute cognitively-based misattributions at all, but rather rational (albeit not necessarily conscious) impression management devices employed in the service of self-esteem maintenance and enhancement.

According to the affect control view of human motivation discussed in Chapter 3, an actor's self-esteem is predicated upon the confirmation of affectively salient identities. Hence, the tendency to over-attribute to external forces in the case of unsuccessful performances can be explained through the incentive of identity maintenance and confirmation.

3. Like attribution theory and symbolic interactionism, affect control theory focuses on the explanation of everyday social life—"common social actions, like those of a doctor toward a patient, a judge toward a thief, a mother toward a daughter" (Heise 1979, viii). And, like both theories, affect control theory derives its basic explanatory principles from analysis of everyday social experience: that people try to experience an orderly, meaningful social life; that they react affectively to social events; that they control affective disturbance.

4. Like attribution theory and symbolic interactionism, affect control theory focuses on the symbolic-cognitive processes that make everyday social interaction managable. Additionally, the theory accepts that symbolic-cognitive processing is simplified, organized, and driven by powerful schemas. As proposed earlier in this chapter, social identities are generic schemas that simplify and organize person and self-perception, because of their implications for behavior, emotions, and traits. And, as discussed in Chapter 3, identities motivate because they have been affectively appropriated to self. The function of identities as generic schemas in person and self-perception and as incentives in human motivation has enabled affect control theory to develop elegant and powerful models for simulating social behavior, reidentification processes, and emotional response to events.

Part II: The Expanded Model—The Effect of Expressed Emotions on Reidentification Outcomes

Because the established reidentification model did not consider emotions, it implied that a reidentified person must be experiencing the *characteristic* emotions of an imputed identity and, by implication, that the person has accepted his or her recharacterization by others. For example, if reidentified as a *victim*, then the model assumed that a person must be feeling "apprehensive" and "sorry" (Table 7.1, Chapter 7). However, a person may be trying to confirm an altogether different identity, or resisting the imputation of a stigmatized one. According to Proposition 24 (Chapter 2), a person's visibly expressed emotions convey this private motivational information to other people, thereby affecting reidentification outcomes.

The established reidentification model continues to be applicable to situations where the emotions of interactants are unrevealed and/or unknown (e.g., straightforward, written accounts of events) or where they are to be discounted (e.g., emotional displays of people known to be manipulative).

Yet when we are present at the events that stimulate reidentifications or when we observe a person narrating his or her own behavior, we have access to the expressive signaling system that our species has evolved (Ekman 1984), and we obtain information about what emotions the person feels as a result of the events. No longer is it appropriate to assume that the person feels whatever emotion follows from a character reassessment, because we can see what emotion he or she does, in fact, feel (Heise 1989a, 14).

The Model

In actor-reidentifications employing the expanded model, we are trying to determine what kind of person would act toward a particular object-person in a specified way *while feeling a certain emotion* (e.g., What kind of man would flee a woman and feel *guilty* about it?). In object-person reidentifications, we are trying to figure out what kind of person might be, or seek to be, the recipient of a specified act by a particular actor *while experiencing a certain emotion* (e.g., What kind of woman might be fled by a man and feel *happy* when he has done so)?

The expanded model is sufficiently general to accommodate the expressed emotions of *alter* (the interactant not being reidentified) as another input to the anaysis. Otherwise, the model assumes that alter is experiencing the characteristic emotions of his or her current identity. For example, consider the event, a *man flees a woman*, leaving her feeling visibly *happy*. We can seek an object-person reidentification for *woman* while introducing the additional constraint that alter (the actor, *man*) looks *guilty* as he flees her.

The expanded model brings together the established reidentification model described above and the emotions model described in Chapter 7. The mathematics of the expanded model and its properties are reported in Heise (1989a, 1992). While too complex to consider here, what the mathematics accomplish can be easily conveyed by a brief verbal description. For actor reidentifications, the model searches for a new or trait-modified identity that accounts for both an actor's *behavior* towards a specified object-person and the actor's *expressed emotion.* The solution involves finding an identity-label (or a trait-modified identity) for the actor that differs from the impression of the actor created by his or her conduct so as to produce the actor's observed emotion. For object-person reidentifications, the model solves for an identity-label (or trait-modified identity) for the recipient that differs from the impression of the recipient created by the actor's conduct so as to produce the recipient's observed emotion.[6]

Reidentification Analysis: Attributions, Labels, and Emotions

Tables 8.2 and 8.3 report the effect of emotion displays upon reidentifications for, respectively, a positive and negative event. In each case, simulation results are reported for "appropriate" and "inappropriate" emotions. Emotions are considered appropriate when they are hedonically positive in response to a positive event (e.g., a man appearing to be "in love" while kissing a woman) or hedonically negative in response to a deviant event (e.g., a man appearing "guilty" while ignoring a woman).

Each set of simulations is preceded by a reidentification analysis that ignores information on emotion displays (Event 1 in each table). This serves as a baseline analysis against which to assess the effect of emotion displays on reidentification outcomes. The reidentification analysis examines three kinds of events: where only the actor expresses emotion, where only the object-person expresses emotion, and where both interactants express emotion. This enables one to systematically explore how the emotional expression of alter (the interactant not being reidentified) affects the recharacterizations of the person being reidentified.

Obviously, given the comprehensiveness of this design, the analyses reported in Tables 8.2 and 8.3 can be only selectively discussed. I deal with, in turn, the effect of expressed emotions on actor and object-person reidentifications, including in each case the effect of the emotion-displays of alter (the person not being reidentified). I then analyze the situation where the expressed emotions of actor and object-person are simultaneously taken into account in reidentification analysis.

1. Actor Reidentifications. To illustrate the effect of an actor's expressed emotions on actor reidentification, consider the positive event analyzed in Table 8.2. A man's status increases slightly when he expresses an appropriate emotion (*in love*) while kissing a woman (Event 2) than when he displays no emotional response at all (Event 1). Besides appearing a bit nicer, he also appears dramatically more powerful, though notably less lively. He maintains his original identity, "man," but might be reidentified as a "companion" or a "friend." On the other hand, his status declines when he expresses an inappropriate emotion (*annoyed*) while kissing a woman (Event 5), and he appears considerably more powerful and a bit quieter. In this case, the retrievals suggest that a "coach," "star," or "mastermind" are fitting recharacterizations of the actor.

Event 5, Table 8.3, illustrates the consequences for actor–reidentification of revealing an inappropriate emotion in response to a negative event. Looking *cheerful* while ignoring a woman results in even greater stigmatization than revealing no emotion at all (Event 1). The retrievals suggest that someone like a "shyster" or "liar" might cheerfully ignore a woman.

Event 3, Table 8.2, illustrates the effect of alter's expressed emotion on actor reidentification. Kissing a woman and leaving her feeling *moved* does not significantly affect a man's status and liveliness, but it dramatically increases his potency compared to when she expresses no emotion at all (Event 1). Once again, the event confirms his original identity, "man," but it also suggests that he might be recharacterized as a "host," a "friend," or a "loved," "friendly" man. ("Employed" should seem anomalous to all but the cynical reader). In contrast, a man suffers a substantial loss in status, but appears somewhat more powerful and considerably more lively, when his act of kissing leaves a woman feeling ostensibly *annoyed* (Event 6), than when her emotions are unknown (Event 1). The reidentifications generated by the model suggest that a "playboy," "whizkid," or "heman" might perpetrate such an event.

TABLE 8.2

Effects of Emotional Expression on Reidentifications
for an Evaluatively Positive Event (Man Kisses Woman).[a]

Condition	Actor Reidentifications			Object-Person Reidentifications		
	E	P	A	E	P	A
Identity Profile before any Event	1.69	1.46	0.53	2.07	0.08	0.64
		Man			Woman	
1. Baseline Event (No Emotions Displayed)	2.2	0.4	1.0	1.0	−1.3	−0.7
	mate, pal, myself as I really am (nice, cheerful, generous man)			servant, wallflower, bookworm (weak, boring, dull woman)		
Display of Appropriate Emotions						
2. Actor (in love)	2.4	2.0	0.2	3.6	1.6	0.9
	companion, man, friend			buddy, truelove		
3. Object-Person (moved)	2.1	1.6	0.7	2.5	−0.1	0.6
	man, host, friend (loved, employed, friendly man)			darling, babysitter, lady (nice, sincere, friendly woman)		
4. Actor (in love) and Object-Person (moved)	2.5	1.8	0.2	3.9	1.7	0.8
	companion, friend, man			buddy		
Display of Inappropriate Emotions						
5. Actor (annoyed)	1.7	2.9	0.8	0.0	−2.3	1.3
	coach, star, mastermind			squirt, shrimp, ninny		
6. Object-Person (annoyed)	−0.0	0.9	2.3	−2.4	0.4	0.7
	playboy, whizkid, he-man			psychopath, wrongdoer, bigot		
7. Actor (annoyed) and Object-Person (annoyed)	−0.4	2.0	2.5	−4.7	−1.7	1.3
	roughneck, jock, rowdy			stool-pigeon, phoney		

a. Reidentifications reported are for *gender-specific* and *casual* identities, and are based on male attitudes. Explanatory traits are reported parenthetically when they are within the range of the EPA profile generated by the model.

TABLE 8.3

Effects of Emotional Expression on Reidentifications for an Evaluatively Negative Event (Man Ignores Woman).[a]

Condition	Actor Reidentifications			Object-Person Reidentifications		
	E	P	A	E	P	A
Identity Profile before any Event	1.69	1.46	0.53	2.07	0.08	0.64
		Man			Woman	
1. Baseline Event (No Emotions Displayed)	−2.4	0.7	0.9	−1.1	1.1	−0.3
	villain, madman, evildoer			ghoul, grind, witch		
Display of Appropriate Emotions						
2. Actor (guilty)	−3.2	3.0	−1.2	1.7	3.6	2.0
	(mobster)			(champion, winner, star)		
3. Object-Person (hurt)	1.6	0.6	−1.4	2.3	0.6	1.6
	fisherman, connoisseur, storyteller			clown, sweetheart, mate		
4. Actor (guilty) and Object-Person (hurt)	−3.0	2.6	−1.6	2.1	3.9	2.4
	mafioso			champion, winner		
Display of Inappropriate Emotions						
5. Actor (cheerful)	−4.5	0.5	0.0	1.7	5.3	0.1
	(shyster, bigot, psychopath, liar)			(mastermind, parent, wizard)		
6. Object-Person (ecstatic)	−3.1	3.0	1.7	−2.3	−0.8	−1.1
	slavedriver, brute			grouch, wretch, drudge		
7. Actor (cheerful) and Object-Person (ecstatic)	−6.2	1.5	2.7	−2.3	2.3	−2.2
	(mugger)			(mafioso)		

a. Reidentifications reported are for *gender-specific* and *casual* identities, and are based on male attitudes. Those that lie outside the range of the EPA profile generated by the model are reported parenthetically. There are no explanatory traits that lie within the range of the EPA profiles generated by the model.

Event 6, Table 8.3 shows how the expression of an inappropriately positive emotion by the recipient of a deviant act results in the stigmatization of the actor. Ignoring a woman and leaving her feeling *ecstatic* makes a man appear considerably worse, but much more powerful and lively, than when a woman expresses no emotion (Event 1). The reidentification analysis suggests that a woman might (understandably) feel *ecstatic* when someone like a "slavedriver" or a "brute" ignored her. On the other hand, he escapes the attribution of a negative identity when she appears appropriately *hurt* when he ignores her (Event 3).

2. *Object Reidentifications.* Because model-generated profiles for object-persons often strayed outside the range of actual identities in his analysis, Heise (1989a, 19) contemplated that perhaps "the potential for influencing labeling outcomes through emotion displays is not as great for the recipient of action as for the agent of action." In contrast, the analysis presented here strongly suggests that expressed emotions have a profound impact on the reidentifications of object-persons.

Recall the analysis reported in the preceding section (Table 8.1) which ignored the emotional reaction of interactants. There, the impression of stigmatization, impotency, and somnolence created in the recipient of positive actions generated reidentifications which portrayed the object-person as so dull and unfeeling that one would not feel comfortable in generalizing results to many women. (Event 1 in Tables 8.2 and 8.3 replicates this condition.)

In contrast, the analyses reported in Tables 8.2 and 8.3 illustrate how the recipient of an act springs to life upon reacting emotionally to events. Displaying appropriate emotions makes a woman appear nicer and more lively. Revealing that she is *moved* upon being kissed transforms her from a "weak," "boring," "dull" woman like a "wallflower" or a "bookworm" (Event 1, Table 8.2) to a "nice," "sincere," "friendly" one like a "darling" or "lady" (Event 3, Table 8.2). Revealing that she is *hurt* when ignored (Event 3, Table 8.3) transforms her from a bad, powerful, quiet person like a "grind" or a "witch" (Event 1, Table 8.3) into a good, still powerful, and lively person like a "sweetheart" or a "mate."

While inappropriate emotional reaction to a positive event, expressing *annoyance* upon being kissed, results in stigmatization (Event 6, Table 8.2), the recipient appears more powerful and lively than when she remains emotionless (Event 1, Table 8.2). Only when she responds inappropriately to a negative event—expressing *ecstasy* upon being ignored—does she appear not only worse, but also less powerful and lively (Event 6, Table 8.3) than when she expresses no emotion (Event 1, Table 8.3).

The analysis reported here also shows that an actor's emotional expression affects object-person reidentifications. By displaying an appropriate emotion in reaction to either a positive or negative event, an actor makes an object-person appear dramatically nicer, more powerful, and more lively than when he expresses no emotion. A man appearing to be *in love* while kissing a woman (Event 2, Table

8.2) transforms her from a "weak," "boring," "dull" woman, like a "servant," "wall-flower," or "bookworm" (Event 1, Table 8.2), into a more valued, potent, and lively one like a "buddy" or a "truelove." When he seems appropriately *guilty* while ignoring her (Event 2, Table 8.3), she sidesteps the imputation of negative identities like "grind" or "witch" (Event 1, Table 8.3) and is reidentified as someone like a "champion" or a "winner."

An actor's inappropriate emotional reaction to a negative event protects the object-person from stigmatization and makes her appear more powerful (Event 5, Table 8.3). Employing female sentiments, reidentification retrievals suggest that a man might *cheerfully* ignore a powerful woman like an "expert" or a "brain." On the other hand, the recipient loses status as well as potency when the actor reveals an inappropriate emotion in reaction to a positive event (Event 5, Table 8.2). However, she appears more lively. Reidentification results suggest that "squirt," "shrimp," or "ninny" are fitting recharacterizations.

In summary, the findings reported in Tables 8.2 and 8.3 largely confirm a set of empirical generalizations induced by Heise (1989a) from a systematic analysis of emotion displays and reidentification outcomes. The consistency of findings from the two analyses takes on greater significance when one considers that they are based on data from different cultures, different parameterizations of the reidentification model, and somewhat different sets of events and emotions.

3. Reidentification and Expressed Emotions: An Extension. There remains the situation, considered but not analyzed by Heise, where the emotional reactions of actor and object-person to events are *simultaneously* taken into account in reidentification analysis (Events 4 and 7 in each of Tables 8.2 and 8.3). This analysis is based on the notion that observers of an event would consider, if available, the expressed emotions of both actor and object-person in reidentifying either participant.

A comparison of Events 4 and 2 in either Table 8.2 or 8.3 reveals that when the expressed emotions of both interactants are appropriate, the object-person's emotions have a negligible effect on actor reidentification. To illustrate, when a *man kisses a woman*, leaving her feeling *moved* and him, *in love* (Event 4, Table 8.2), the reidentification profile for actor (2.5 1.8 .2) is virtually indistinguishable from that (2.4 2.0 .2) when he alone displays an appropriate emotion (Event 2, Table 8.2); and both events produce the same reidentifications ("companion," "friend," and "man"). A similar pattern of reidentification outcomes occurs for the negative event *man ignores woman* when he appears *guilty* and she, *hurt* (Event 4, Table 8.3), as compared to when he alone expresses an appropriate emotion (Event 2, Table 8.3).

The actor's expressed emotions overshadow those of the recipient in object-person reidentifications as well. To illustrate, when the event *man kisses woman* leaves him feeling visibly *in love* and her, *moved* (Event 4, Table 8.2), the optimal profile for object-person reidentification (3.9 1.7 .8) is virtually identical to that (3.6 1.6 .9) when only the actor emotes (Event 2, Table 8.2); and "buddy" is a common retrieval. A comparison of Events 4 and 2 in Table 8.3 reveals a similar pattern of reidentification outcomes and common retrievals ("champion" and "winner") for the negative event *man ignores woman.*

Where the expressed emotions of both interactants are inappropriate, however, the expressed emotions of the object–person manifest a substantial impact on the reidentification of the actor. A comparison of Event 7 with Event 5 in either Table 8.2 or 8.3 supports this empirical generalization. To illustrate, when the event *man kisses woman* leaves both interactants feeling inappropriately *annoyed,* a man remains a relatively powerful person but becomes a considerably more lively one, exchanging positively evaluated identities like "coach," "star," or "mastermind" (Event 5, Table 8.2) for stigmatized ones like "roughneck," "jock," or "rowdy" (Event 7, Table 8.2). Similarly, when a *man ignores a woman,* leaving him feeling inappropriately *cheerful* and her, inappropriately *ecstatic* (Event 7, Table 8.3), he appears extremely worse, somewhat more powerful, and dramatically more lively than when he alone reacts emotionally to the event (Event 5, Table 8.3).

The inappropriate display of emotions by both interactants has a similar impact on object-person reidentification. Here, as compared to the situation where the expressed emotions of both interactants are appropriate, the overshadowing effect of the actor's emotions no longer prevails, and the recipient's own emotional response has a notable impact on her reidentification by others. Again, a comparison of Event 7 with Event 5 in either Table 8.2 or 8.3 substantiates this empirical generalization. To illustrate, when a *man kisses a woman* and only the actor appears inappropriately *annoyed* (Event 5, Table 8.2), a woman seems neither good nor bad, quite powerless, and somewhat lively. Reidentification retrievals suggest that she might be recharacterized as something like a "ninny." If, however, the event leaves her feeling *annoyed* as well (Event 7, Table 8.2), she becomes increasingly more stigmatized. "Phony" is an approximation that seems to fit the substantive context of the event ("junkie" and "slut" are interesting approximations generated from female data). Similarly, when the negative event *man ignores woman* leaves the actor feeling inappropriately *cheerful* and the recipient inappropriately *ecstatic* (Event 7, Table 8.3), she becomes dramatically stigmatized, less powerful, and more unlively than when only he reacts inappropriately to the event (Event 5, Table 8.3).

Summarizing these results, when both actor and recipient express appropriate emotions in either positive or negative events, those of the recipient have a negligible impact on both actor and object-person reidentifications. When both actor and recipient express inappropriate emotions, however, those of the recipient become important in reidentification of both actor and object-person.

These observed patterns can be explained in terms of the implications of expressed emotions for identity confirmation. The display of appropriate emotions by both interactants suggests that they are trying to maintain their original identities. For instance, a man should feel *in love* when kissing a woman and *guilty* when ignoring her if, indeed, he is trying to maintain his positively evaluated identity, man. And, by the same token, a woman should feel *moved* upon being kissed or *hurt* upon being ignored. Under this condition, the usual overwhelming salience of the actor supposed by attribution theorists should prevail, and an observer would rely on the actor's emotional reaction in assessing the current identities of participants. Hence, an actor's emotions would be expected to eclipse those of the recipient in both actor and object-person reidentifications.

On the other hand, the display of inappropriate emotions by participants suggests that they are maintaining identities other than their original ones (man and woman). Under this condition, the recipient and her expressed emotions also become salient in object-person reidentifications because the display of inappropriate emotions by interactants challenges her identity as well. And because the actor's identity has also become problematic, the recipient's expressed emotions provide relevant information for making inferences about his current identity.

To add substance to these generalizations, expressing an appropriate rather than an inappropriate emotion (say *moved* rather than *annoyed*) when kissed might suggest to an observer that the woman has not picked up on the man's insincerity revealed by his expressed annoyance. Under these circumstances, an observer might ignore the recipient's emotion in determining actor reidentifications because, after all, "no real harm has been done." On the other hand, because an expression of annoyance on her part would suggest that she has become aware of the actor's insincerity, an observer might feel compelled to take her expressed emotions into acount when reidentifying the actor. Only someone like a "roughneck," "jock," or "rowdy" would kiss a woman and so flagrantly reveal his insincerity to her (Event 7, Table 8.2). By the same token, only a very bad man would *cheerfully* ignore a woman and leave her feeling *ecstatic* that he has done so (Event 7, Table 8.3).

Summary

Part I of this chapter began with a brief discussion of the affinity of symbolic interactionism and attribution theory that makes it conceptually possible to combine labeling and attribution processes within the same reidentification model. This was followed by a description and illustration of the established reidentification model of affect control theory and a discussion of the contributions of the theory to the integration of symbolic interactionism and attribution theory.

Part II introduced and illustrated the expanded reidentification model which considers the effect of expressed emotions on reidentification outcomes.

In conclusion, affect control theory provides a more general model of re-identification processes than either attribution theory or symbolic interactionism taken alone, albeit one that leaves plenty of opportunity for studying cognitive factors in these processes. By extending this model to take account of the emotional reaction of interactants to events, the theory establishes an important linkage between cognitive theories like attribution theory and symbolic interactionism, on the one hand, and the social psychology of emotions, on the other.

9

CONCLUSION

The introductory chapter of this book opened with a criticism, a promise, and an aspiration. The criticism added to the widely acknowledged neglect of emotion by Mead and symbolic interactionism, the failure of interactionists to adequately attend to Mead's emphasis on language and control as the basis for a social psychology. The promise was the presentation of a social psychological theory in the symbolic interactionist tradition that addressed these deficits. The aspiration was the production of an integrative social psychology that combines the symbolic interactionist perspective of affect control theory with other theoretical views in sociological and psychological social psychology.

A major theme throughout this book has been the theoretical scope and predictive power of affect control theory. Chapters 5 and 6 showed how the theory integrates the structure and process schools of role theory and of symbolic interactionism itself; Chapter 7, how it helps to reconcile the positivist and constructionist positions in the sociology of emotions; and Chapter 8, how it contributes to the integration of attribution theory and symbolic interactionism. The predictive power of the theory stems from its mathematical formalization and linguistic frame. By measuring all kinds of social phenomena (identities, interpersonal acts, emotions, and so on) in the same semantic space, and interconnecting them in syntactically organized events, the theory is able to shift back and forth between affective processes, on the one hand, and cognitive and behavioral processes, on the other.

The concluding chapter of this book discusses the relation of affect control theory to social psychologial theories that lie outside the symbolic interactionist tradition; examines the status of the theory as sociological explanation and as integrative social psychology; and provides a prospectus for future research and refinement.

Relation to Other Theories

This book has presented affect control theory as a continuity of symbolic interactionism, in both its structure and process versions. However, affect control theory is closely related to other theories that do not fall squarely in the symbolic interactionist tradition. I have selected two for brief discussion here, one from psychological social psychology—Kelley's (1984) theory of intersituational processes; the other, from sociological social psychology—Collins' (1981, 1990) microsociological theory of interactional ritual chains.

Kelley's Theory Of Intersituational Processes

As observed in Chapter 1, Kemper (1978) criticized psychological theories of emotion for their perfunctory treatment of the situation. Since then, however, psychologists have paid greater attention to specifying the characteristics of emotion–instigating situations (de Rivera 1984; Kelley 1984; Roseman 1984).[1]

According to Kelley, situational theories of emotion in psychological social psychology constitute an underlying "experience-to-affect-to-behavior" model, wherein "some components of affect are retrospective, being sensitive to past events, and others are prospective, being oriented toward unknown future events" (1984, 94–95).[2] This suggests a functional theory of motivation in which affect serves as adaptive response to interest-relevant situations.[3]

The starting point in Kelley's situational theory of emotions is the assumption that people inhabit a causal environment characterized by interest-relevant situations which they classify in both specific and general terms. The various psychological systems of a person provide adaptations to this causal environment. Such particular structures as reflexes and habits handle the more specific aspects of interest-relevant situations; more general adaptive action tendencies like approach and avoidance attend to their more general and abstract features.

While adaptive systems like these operate over the course of each situation, Kelley focuses on the incipient and terminating points of situational events where "intersituational processes" occur. Intersituational processes enable the individual to adapt to the interest-relevant causal environment by "recording experienced variations in one's outcomes, inferring causes for those variations, extrapolating these patterns to imminent and subsequent situations, and mobilizing and directing appropriate action" (1984, 92).

The following are the essential features of Kelley's theory of intersituational processes. First, he proposes that "affects constitute the core elements in . . . intersituational processes" (1984, 92), mediating one's past experience and one's orientation to subsequent events by serving as a general mechanism of adaptive response. Second, he concludes that "the adaptive value of affective reactions is nowhere stated more clearly than by Osgood" (1984, 95), who identified evaluation, potency, and activity as the three major dimensions of situational stimuli relevant to an actor's interests. Third, Kelley observes that the complementarity between the EPA structure of situations proposed by Osgood and the EPA structure of emotional states proposed by Russell and Mehrabian (1977) "shows the mirror that a person's affective response system holds up to the ambient, interest-relevant environment" (1984, 95–6). Fourth, while Osgood suggested that the mechanism underlying the adaptiveness of affective reaction is genetic, Kelley proposes that an important part of its adaptive value lies in experience: "[P]eople find their presituational expectations to be confirmed or disconfirmed and, at the post-situational juncture, react affectively to that fact" (1984, 97). Finally, moving from reaction to proaction, Kelley identifies "the affect-to-action step" with "the 'motivational' role of affect, as it instigates and directs the subsequent line of behavior" (1984, 94).

This capsule summary of Kelley's model reveals its striking resemblance to affect control theory. For affect control theory, situations are interest-relevant because they constitute the arena in which identity-confirmation occurs. The experience-to–affect phase of Kelley's model corresponds to *affective reaction* in affect control theory; the affect-to-behavior or motivational phase, to *affect control*. Like affect control theory, Kelley views affect as the central feature of adaptive response and the essence of motivation. His emphasis on interest-relevant situations suggests an incentive theory of motivation, but one that incorporates the dual functions of *energizing* and *directing* response. This squares with the affect control theory of motivation discussed in Chapter 3. Like affect control theory, Kelley identifies evaluation, potency, and activity as the relevant dimensions of both situational stimuli and affective experience. And, finally, his view that affect is the central feature of intersituational processes connecting social events is a defining feature of affect control theory.

The central role of affect in adaptive response and human motivation supposed by Kelley led him to ponder whether affect is a separate phase, or component, of intersituational processes or a global term that summarizes the various processes that take place there. "By the latter view," he suggests, "the affect a person 'feels' represents an overall picture of the phenomenal products of the valuating, attributing, mobilizing, and orienting processes" (1984, 96) of the overall intersituational mechanism. While Kelley declined to stake out a position on this issue, affect control theory treats affect in both specific and global terms. As discussed in Chapter 3, the theory views affect as a pervasive mode of human consciousness that can be only analytically distinguished from the cognitive and conative (behavior readying) modes of "intersituational processes" psychologically connecting events. And, as discussed in Chapter 7, the theory also deals with affect in the more specific sense of those situationally episodic and ephemeral affective experiences we recognize as emotions.

Collins' Theory of Interactional Ritual Chains

Collins tried to establish the microfoundations of macrosociology by grounding social structural concepts in empirical observations "of what people do, say, and think in the actual flow of momentary experience" (1981, 984). According to Collins, the repetitive actions that constitute social structure can be explained by "interactional ritual chains," sequences of microevents, mostly conversational, that establish emotional identification with groups. By creating and sustaining cultural symbols and emotional energies, Collins argues, interactional ritual chains generate *group membership* as well as two major structural features of social organization: *property*—the access to or exclusion from particular physical places and objects, including the physical bodies of other people; and *authority*—dominance-subordination relationships in micro-interactions.

Collins identifies two components of successful interactional rituals: *emotional energies*—a minimal degree of emotional solidarity built up from past interactional rituals; and *conversational* or *cultural resources*—common cognitive realities established by past chains of conversational rituals.

Collins distinguishes between two kinds of conversational resources. *Generalized* conversational resources refer to events and things (e.g., religion, politics) at some level of abstraction from immediate situations, personal relationships, and organizational ties; *particularized* conversational resources, to specific places, things, and persons. The former is the basis of horizontally organized group membership and participation; the latter, the basis of *property* and *authority*. By constituting and sustaining each member's "reputation," particularized conversation validates his or her property and authority claims and enactments.

Despite differences in theoretical objectives and conceptual language, Collins' theory of interactional ritual chains makes many of the same assumptions and claims as affect control theory. Both theories establish the motivational basis of micro events in affective processes, rather than cognitive ones like conscious adherence to social norms.[4] For Collins, "the underlying emotional dynamics [of routine social life] . . . centers on feelings of membership in coalitions" (1981, 997); and "people are motivated by their emotional energies as they shift from situation to situation" (1981, 1004). For affect control theory, affect attaches to the identity-situated selves of interactants, and the "emotional energies" that motivate them to construct social events, routine or otherwise, take the form of *affective deflection* built up by recent events. Deflection gives rise to the experience of emotions signaling the confirmation or disconfirmation of salient identities; and the expression of emotions in event sequences that confirm the identities of participants generates the "common emotional tone" that is, in Collins' terms, an essential ingredient of successful interactional rituals.

Affect control theory measures the "emotional energies" latent in social identities in terms of the evaluation, potency, and activity dimensions of affective meaning. Collins (1990, 50) suggests that evaluation and potency correspond to the status and power implied in property and authority relationships; and activity, to the general underlying dimension (the "ups and downs" or intensity) of emotional energy.

Both theories establish social structure on the foundation of microinteractional events. For Collins, interactional routine is produced by the property and authority reputations of people established by past interactional rituals. For affect control theory, interactional routine occurs as people enact the action implications of their situated identities. The connection between reputation and identity is contained in Collins' statement that

> for the micro-translation of macrostructures, the most important kind of reputations that circulate are simply the parts of talk which identify someone by a particular title ('the chairman,' 'his wife') or organizational membership ('he is with G.E.'), or which tacitly give someone a reputation for certain property or authority ('I went into his office,' 'she sent out a memo directing him to . . . ') (1981, 1004).

For affect control theory, the "parts of talk" that establish the validity of members' property and authority claims are those that define their identity-situated selves. Identities are reputation-based. They are the cumulative product of microsituational events and must be continually validated in social interaction in order to serve as "particularized conversational resources" supporting actors' claims to property and authority. In fact, as discussed in Chapter 8, it is precisely when a person's current identity is no longer sustained by microinteractions that reidentification processes occur.

The affinity between the two theories continues in Collins' (1990) interactional ritual chain theory of emotions. Here, he distinguishes between the "short-term," "transient," often "dramatic" emotions produced by current interactional rituals and those "long-term emotional tones . . . that are so calm and smooth as not to be noticed." The latter include "solidarity feelings, moral sentiments, the enthusiasm of pitching oneself into a situation, or being carried along with it; and at the other end, depression, alienation, embarrassment" (1990, 30–31). Collins identifies these more enduring affective states with the "emotional energies" that mobilize interactional ritual chains, and he proposes that the short-term emotions are built up situationally in interactional ritual chains against the "backdrop of an ongoing flow of emotional energy" (1990, 42).

Like Collins, affect control theory distinguishes between long-term and short-term affective experiences. The former consist of the affective associations that pervade all our cognitions, including the affective meaning of our identity-situated selves and those of others. The latter (emotions) signal the extent to which events confirm or disconfirm the situated identities of self or other. The "emotional energy" latent in social identities becomes activated in the form of event-generated *deflection*. When minimal, as in identity–confirming events, the "emotional energy" of deflection, "so calm and smooth as not to be noticed" (Collins 1990, 31), gives rise to the "characteristic" emotions of socially-identified people. When large, as in identity-disconfirming events, it precipitates the "consequent" emotions, the more "dramatic" and possibly "disruptive" emotions discussed by Collins. (See Chapter 7 for the distinction between *characteristic* and *consequent* emotions and their relation to deflection.)

Affect Control Theory as Sociological Explanation

Because its basic premises and key propositions invoke processes that occur in the minds of individual actors, it might seem that affect control theory does not constitute a sociological explanation. Indeed, the theory might be dismissed by some sociological readers as another instance of psychological reductionism, albeit one that stands Homans, so to speak, on his head.

In this regard, Brodbeck (1968, 286–8) has distinguished between two types of methodological individualism, the philosophical tradition with which psychological reductionism has been generally associated: as a denial of *descriptive* emergence—the view that there are no group concepts which cannot, in principle, be defined in terms of individual behavior; and as the denial of *explanatory* emergence—the view that there are no laws about group behavior that cannot be reduced to laws about individual behavior. According to Brodbeck, the denial of one type of emergence does not necessarily imply the denial of the other.

The first kind of methodological individualism is exemplified in Collins' statement that "strictly speaking, there is no such thing as a 'state,' an 'economy,' a 'culture,' a 'social class.' There are only collections of individual people acting in particular kinds of micro-situations" (1981, 987–988).[5] The second kind of methodological individualism can be found in his assertion "that the ultimate empirical validation of sociological statements depends upon their microtranslation . . . the test of whether the macro statement is a good approximation or a misleading reification" (1981, 988).

Affect control theory does not embrace methodological individualism in the sense of denial of *descriptive* emergence, because its units of analysis and empirical referents of group processes are interpersonal social events. Moreover, because cultural sentiments employed in the impression formation equations and mathematically derived models of the theory are obtained by *aggregating* semantic differential ratings of social stimuli across respondents, the individual becomes a theoretical abstraction, an *homme moyen*, so to speak.

According to Wallace, the reduction of macrosociological phenomena to interpersonal events is not just valid, it is necessary "if their empirical referents are to qualify as social phenomena" (1983, 167). And, he argues that this view does not constitute a denial of descriptive emergence because it maintains that the ultimate constitutents and empirical referents of macrosociologial phenomena "consists in interpersonal behavior regularities and not in the behaviors or experiences of individual people" (1983, 168).

In this regard, while Simmel proposed that only individuals have existential reality, he maintained that society is not thereby reducible to individuals, but rather to individuals who are "bearers of relationships." This is essentially what Mead means when he equates the development of mind with "the importation of the social process." By generating socially structured interaction from (presumably internalized) cultural sentiments, affect control theory operationalizes the conceptual solution to the problem of methodological individualism proposed by Simmel and Mead while avoiding its mystical overtones.

Now, while affect control theory does not subscribe to methodological individualism in the denial of *descriptive* emergence sense, it accepts the position in the denial of *explanatory* emergence sense. That is, the theory deduces macrosociological propositions about social phenomena from psychological propositions pertaining to the covert and overt behavior of individual actors. These deductions are also *reductions* because their premises refer to a more micro level of analysis than that of the deduced propositions (Brodbeck 1968, 286–287).

Consider the proposition from structural-functionalism that socialization and social control mechanisms of social systems operate to ensure their maintenance and equilibrium (Parsons 1951). This can be deduced from affect control theory's proposition that internalized cultural sentiments organize the routine actions of people, generating protective responses (sanctions) to disruptive events:

> affect control theory . . . suggests that the sanctioned deviant must develop a new likelihood for his deviant identity [i.e., by failing to confirm it by additional deviant acts] which implies a change in sentiments about some event element—actor, behavior, object. The folk wisdom is that this change will be of a kind that maintains the cultural system, so everyday sanctioning ends up functional (Heise 1988, 18).

Propositions from macrosociological conflict theory also can be deduced from affect control theory, just as they can from Collins' theory of interactional ritual chains. As argued in the preceding section, property and authority are embodied in social identities (e.g., "capitalist," "manager," "worker"), and the evaluation and potency dimensions of identity-meaning are the subjective counterparts of the status and power dimensions of social stratification. While affect control theory cannot directly account for the *material* basis of socially structured inequality, it can simulate the negotiations and struggles over status and power in microsituational events whose repetitive patterns get summarized in macrosociological propositions about stratification systems and social conflict.

However, affect control theory does provide a direct microtranslation of the kind of social conflict generated by differences in sentiments between cultures or subcultures. Armed with data on sentiments from two or more cultures or subcultures, the theory can simulate the conflicting behavioral intentions and expectations that produce mutually disruptive events. Its application to conflict situations like this may reveal downward spirals of worsening disintegration and conflict, rather than the movement towards equilibrium characterizing relatively stable and consensual social systems.

Despite their explanatory reductionism, however, microsociologies like affect control theory and Collins' theory of interactional ritual chains do not forfeit their claim to sociological status. This is because, as discussed above, their conception of social phenomena as well as their units of analysis are *inter*personal in nature. And, as Wallace argues, while the description of social phenomena cannot be reduced below the level of interpersonal behavior, "the explanation of all social phenomena reduces to the explanation of individual behavior" (1983, 192). By this account, variables of any kind or level—physiological, psychological—may be employed in sociological explanation "insofar as they all seek to explain social phenomena by explaining the behavior of each participating individual" (1983, 191).

At the same time, as Wallace observes, this "does not mean that . . . we may not generalize across . . . individuals, their behaviors, and across their explanations in order to construct descriptions and explanations of more macro levels of social phenomena" (1983, 192). And, despite the vigor with which Collins has seemingly denied both descriptive and explanatory emergence, he acknowledges that "it is strategically impossible for sociology to do without this kind of macro summary," and a macro sociological statement of micro situational events "does not mean that it may not be a useful approximation" (1981, 988). This is also what Kaplan means when he concludes that

> Methodologial individualism is defensible only as the insistence that sooner or later we are committed to observations on individuals if we are to give our statements empirical anchorage. Beyond that, it does not set limits on admissible modes of conceptualizations (1964, 82).

Given their empirical orientation, microsociologies should feel comfortable in adopting the position of methodological individualism in the explanatory sense because the validity and utility of such reductionism is "a matter for empirical determination" (Brodbeck 1968, 286). Empirical evidence becomes the final arbiter in deciding whether or not the microsociological propositions of affect control theory and Collins' theory of interactional ritual chains explain and predict social phenomena better than the macro sociological propositions deduced from them.

Having laid to rest the spectre of methodological individualism, I now consider more fully the kinds of variables employed by affect control theory in explaining social phenomena. Since the theory explains individual behavior, both covert and overt, in terms of internalized cultural sentiments, it constitutes what Wallace (1983) has called an "enculturistic"[6] explanation of social phenomena. Indeed, it is due to the theory's reliance on such variables that I have addressed the issue of methodological individualism in the first place.

However, because affect control theory views individual conduct as taking place in the presence of other people, it also invokes explanatory variables of a social psychological nature, those referring to the *covert* or *psychical* behavior of other people.[7] In addition, the theory employs as explanatory variables the *overt* or *phys-*

ical behavior of other people in an actor's social environment, what Wallace (1983) has labeled "social structural" variables.[8] Finally, because affect control theory views the actor's past, current, and anticipated actions as objects of consciousness directing the process of self-adjusted, cybernetically controlled response, the theory invokes the actor's own physical behavior as an explanatory variable.

Affect Control Theory as Integrative Social Psychology

In the conclusion to Chapter 1, I stated that the production of a social psychology in the spirit of Jackson's (1988) "integrative orientation" is a major aspiration of this book. In this section, I flesh out the outline of Jackson's integrative orientation provided in Chapter 1 and assess the extent to which affect control measures up to it.

In the spirit of Mead, Jackson's integrative orientation views human conduct as a joint construction and coordination of action "within meaningful, bounded social contexts, or social acts" (1988, 119). As a constructed social reality, a social act is predicated upon a *shared symbolic system* of meaning pertaining to the situation, the social objects in the situation, and the behavior of participants. An abstraction from the continuous flow of interaction, a social act is bounded by space, as well as by time. It may consist of a momentary encounter in a single physical location or more extended scenarios comprising many acts across multiple settings.

Like Jackson's integrative orientation, affect control theory views social acts, and the interpersonal events that make them up, as jointly constructed and negotiated realities based on the shared symbolic system of meaning embodied in language. Interpersonal events are the units of analysis in its empirical equations and mathematically derived models; and the shared symbolic system of meaning is accessed through the affective associations evoked by social concepts. With respect to the temporal dimension of social acts, affect control theory can generate a social act consisting of a single interpersonal event, or one comprising an entire sequence of events. As for the spatial dimension of social acts, physical settings are incorporated in the impression formation equations as explicitly measured components of events.

The integrative orientation described by Jackson views social acts as fragile affairs held together by *normative, identity,* and *reference* processes.

Normative Processes

According to Jackson, "the social process is normative to the extent that participants in a social act attempt to coordinate action by taking each other's meanings into account in constructing their behavior" (1988, 125). Jackson argues that this definition of normative processes makes it possible for the integrative orientation to encompass both the *structure* and *process* schools of role theory.

By focusing on the affective level of social meaning, affect control theory gives this conceptualization of normative processes a different spin. As discussed in Chapter 5, the theory supposes that cultural sentiments can regenerate the standard events from which they have evolved, so that the affective system provides the means for storing a society's heritage of socially structured interaction. In addition, cultural sentiments enable interactants to construct interpersonal events in less socially structured circumstances, as in encounters between people maintaining different definitions of the situation. Because affect control theory handles with equal facility both the routine of standard events and the interactional exigencies of novel ones, it integrates the structure and process schools of role analysis.

Identity Processes

The integrative orientation views the construction and confirmation of situated identities as a joint accomplishment of participants and as a prerequisite for the coordination of activity that is the essential ingredient of a social act. From this perspective, the *self-process* consists of establishing and validating situated identities through role-appropriate action and mutually supportive self-presentation and management activity. While social structure limits the choice of social identities that can be claimed in any situation, and cultural structure constrains the construction of those available, there is generally considerable leeway for identity negotiation and for adaptation to novel situations.

Affect control views identity processes in precisely these terms. The theory supposes that "people behave within the framework of their situated identities and the implied social structure; and experiences that confirm fundamental sentiments about these identities are attained by engaging in role appropriate acts" (Heise 1988, 15). The extensive discussions of identity processes in Chapters 3 and 5 obviate further discussion here.

Because the integrative orientation views identity processes as intrinsic to the social act, it supposes that situated identities change in response to changes in the social act:

> When the social act changes, it is not possible to maintain the same conduct and meanings, because these emerge from interaction with a new set of participants in a redefined situation with different shared purposes. A change of social act leads to a transformation of a person's identity (Jackson 1988, 129).

Similarly, affect control theory supposes that when restorative action is either impossible or ineffective in sustaining an act and the current definition of the situation, people reidentify one another through attribution and labeling processes (see Chapter 8).

Reference Processes

The assumption that individual behavior (both covert and overt) is influenced by the thoughts, feelings, and behavior of other participants has become a truism in social psychology; and, indeed, is the basis for a genuinely *social* psychology (Jackson 1988, 129). According to Jackson, the evolution of the integrative orientation in social psychology has witnessed a movement from a cognitive to a symbolic view of what has become widely known, under one or another rubric, as *reference processes.* In the cognitive tradition of Cooley and much of contemporary psychologial social psychology, information derives its meaning from its relationship with other information in the minds of individual actors. In the symbolic tradition of Mead and symbolic interactionism, meaning is a social construction that emerges from the reciprocal exchange and adaptation of individual meanings in social interaction. By the latter account, meaning is neither an external state more or less accurately perceived by individuals, nor part of their private phenomenal worlds, but rather inherently social or significant (Jackson 1988, 130–131).

According to the integrative orientation, reference processes are not only interactive (reciprocal) but *reflexive* and *situated* as well. That is, people utilize internal as well as external significant others; and reference processes are situationally specific to social acts (Jackson 1988, 110).

Finally, the integrative orientation views reference processes as inherent in both normative and identity processes and, hence, as only analytically distinguishable from them. Since social interaction is normative only to the extent that people consider each other's meanings in coordinating their activity in social acts, normative processes are, by definition, reference processes as well. And, because the mutual construction and validation of situated identities by participants necessitates role-taking, so too are identity processes.

The consistency of affect control theory with Mead's emphasis on the social symbolic, reflexive, and situated nature of social interaction has been discussed extensively throughout this book (see especially Chapters 3, 4, and 5). Like the integrative orientation, affect control theory conceptualizes events as occurring within a framework of social symbolic meaning embodied in language. And, while the empirical referent of affect control models is the cognitive-affective processes of individual minds, what gets processed, and the field in which the processing occurs, are conceptualized and treated as profoundly social.

Summary Observations

Clearly, the integrative orientation delineated by Jackson captures the essential features of the generalized framework of symbolic interactionism (Stryker 1968, 1981) discussed in Chapter 5: the conceptualization of an active, reflexive, and socially engendered person whose self is constructed and confirmed through identity processes, and whose conduct is constructed within the context of social acts and a social symbolic system of meaning. At the same time, by proposing a psychological modality of the person that explicitly includes affect and motivation, it makes possible a social psychology of emotion within the cognitive–behavioral framework of symbolic interactionism. What is singularly important about the coincidence of Jackson's integrative orientation with the generalized framework of symbolic interactionism is that it has been derived primarily from a review of the literature in psychological, rather than sociological, social psychology.

The integrative power of affect control theory stems from its embodiment of the integrative orientation described by Jackson. This is exemplified by the theory's capacity to span the same conceptual territory as symbolic interactionism and other theories in sociological and psychological social psychology discussed in this chapter and throughout this book.

Directions for Future Research and Refinement

The decade following the first major program statement of affect control theory (Heise 1979) witnessed a flurry of activity centering on theoretical refinement and extension, model reestimation, and the development of new databases in the U.S. and elsewhere. Like the development of any vibrant theory, this period of activity also raised about as many questions as it answered. These accomplishments and issues are nicely summarized by Smith-Lovin (1988c). I conclude this chapter with an update and reassessment of affect control theory along four fronts: research refinements, theoretical extensions, theory testing, and practical applications.

Research Refinements

At the time of Smith-Lovin's (1988c) assessment of affect control theory, MacKinnon (1985, 1988) had just wrapped up a major Canadian replication and extension of the U.S. study reported in Smith-Lovin and Heise (1988). Since then, Smith-Lovin has analyzed a smaller study of high school students in Northern Ireland, and studies have been conducted in Germany and Japan as well. While the general structure of affect control equations from the U.S. study appears to have been replicated by the Canadian study, an explicit cross-national comparison of the two models has yet to be undertaken. Additionally, comparative analysis of models based on English-speaking and non-English-speaking subjects is necessary to determine whether indigenous equations are required for particular cultures. Cross-cultural analysis of cultural sentiments also should be pursued along the lines of the comparison of emotion-structure between U.S. and Canada subjects reported by MacKinnon and Keating (1989).

Thus far, affect control research has employed convenience samples of university students. While highly literate subjects and relatively homogeneous samples are desirable in the early development of a theory's equations and models, their generalizability requires representative samples of regional and national populations. At the same time, specialized cultural databases must be developed to take account of the diversity of cultural sentiments within a given society. Without subcultural data sets, INTERACT analysis assumes that the cultural sentiments of all interactants—a businessman and a laborer, a cop and a criminal—coincide with those of university students who have contributed to its overall database.

Besides extending and diversifying its database, affect control theory must continue to pursue other methodological refinements. As observed by Smith-Lovin (1988c), for example, the cognitive filters currently employed to frame behaviors (see Chapter 6) and identities (see Chapter 8) must be refined to eliminate institutionally anomalous predictions.

The linguistic framework of interpersonal events also must be expanded. The basic ABO structure of social events has been extended in the last decade or so to include settings (Smith-Lovin 1988b) and identity modifiers (Averett and Heise 1988). As discussed in Chapter 2 and in Smith-Lovin (1988c), we foresee further expansion of the linguistic framework of affect control theory. This includes the incorporation of possessives (the doctor's patient); adverbs (a man roughly hugging a woman); intransitive acts (the man cried); and more complex verb structures (to ask someone about something).

The expansion to adverbs in the form of frequency modifiers has been explored (MacKinnon 1985; Keating 1985)—e.g., a husband ("never" to "always") ignoring his wife—but has yet to be systematically analyzed. A study of frequency modifiers in conjunction with intransitive verbs would coincide with the linguistic frame of Jackson's work on "return potential curves" in classic role analysis (Jackson 1966, 1975; MacKinnon 1974; MacKinnon and Summers 1976), and would extend Jackson's model from evaluation to the potency and activity dimensions of meaning.

Finally, recent work by Britt and Heise (1993) on self-directed action, interpersonal events in which a single individual is both actor and object-person (e.g., "a man praising himself"), represents both an extension of linguistic form and a major theoretical advancement. Self-directed action captures the reflexive nature of the self emphasized by Mead and symbolic interactionists and applies affect control theory to a large part of social interaction it has previously ignored.

Theoretical Extensions

As implied in the preceding discussion of cognitive frames, future work must continue to articulate the interface between affect control theory and cognitive theories. At present, affect control theory cannot predict an initial definition of the situation. And, although it generates possible definitions of the situation in the wake of each implemented event, it does not predict which of these a person will select. For instance, when does a person create a definition of the situation through the attribution of explanatory traits or moods, as opposed to the imputation of new identities? When do circumstances favor a definition of the situation based upon a redefinition of self, as opposed to other (Smith-Lovin 1988c)?

Consider an event from Table 8.1: "A man flees a woman." Engaging in role-taking based on male sentiments, she might think he has fled her because he's "homosexual" or feels "persecuted"; or because he's a "lout" or a "cynic"; or because he has judged her to be a "cruel," "bitchy," or "abusive" woman, or an "adulteress," "scoundrel," or "cad." Her invocation of female sentiments leads to an additional set of possible reidentifications. In addition, she might entertain construals on the response side of reidentification, testing in imagination the implications of accepting one or another reidentification of self or other. The possibilities are simply manifold.

Contemplating the problem of multiple definitions of the situation, Smith-Lovin (1988c, 183) suggests a model elaboration to accommodate the parallel processing of events employing plausible alternatives. However, mind-boggling to envisage, the complexity of such analyses would defy easy implementation (see Smith-Lovin 1988c, n.4). Moreover, because each predicted definition of the situation would have about the same deflection-minimizing capacity, a solution to the problem of selection would have to be sought in cognitive theories.[9]

Closely related to the multiple definitions of the situation problem, we have the issue of multiple identities: predicting which identity a person will invoke and try to confirm in a given situation. On the basis of the extensive discussion of identity and motivation in Chapter 3, one would predict that, all other things being equal, people will generally try to confirm higher rather than lower status identities. However, as also discussed in Chapter 3, people frequently get caught up in the process of confirming negatively evaluated identities. (See also my discussion of Robinson and Smith-Lovin's research below.)

The problem of multiple identities raises an additional consideration. While particular identities shift between foreground and background according to situational opportunities and demands, "latent" identities may impinge upon those currently being claimed and enacted in a situation. Equally problematic, a person may be trying to maintain or confirm more than one identity in a situation—for instance, a gender-related identity like "woman" in conjunction with an occupational one like "executive." Future model elaborations could accommodate these various instances of multiple identities by allowing for more complex definitions of the situation in the set-up for INTERACT analysis.

The importance of combining affect control theory with cognitive theory also becomes apparent when we move from *identity* to *behavioral* predictions. Because the behavioral predictions of affect control theory in any analysis are about equally effective in reducing deflection, we have to appeal to cognitive factors to predict exactly which one will be implemented. Consider an example from Table 6.4, where the behavioral predictions for a *prime minister* vis à vis a *back-*

bencher include "convince," "persuade," "reprimand," "urge," "enrapture," "appoint," "laud," "correct," and "awe." Which of these gets implemented may depend upon, among other things, whether logical preconditions have been satisfied. Perhaps "enrapturing" and "awing" are preconditions for "persuading," just as "persuading" might be a precondition for "convincing," suggesting an orderly sequence of productions as the implementation of one behavior satisfies the preconditions for the next.

Productions systems theory (Newell and Simon 1972; Fararo and Skvoretz 1984) deal with such orderly productions of rational action. Thus, a closer affiliation between productions systems theory and affect control theory, as Smith-Lovin argues, would be mutually advantageous.

> Affect control supplies the creation of the behavioral goal, the impetus to achieve it and the commitment to carry it out; production systems supply the technical knowledge, reasoning and planning necessary for implementation (1988c, 186).

On the one hand, Fararo and Skvoretz (1984) acknowledge that affect control theory may help to explain the stability of institutional action systems; on the other, Heise (1988) suggests that deflections may help to set priorities among behaviors whose preconditions have been equally met, those offering the greatest potential for reducing deflection being produced first.

Additionally, Smith-Lovin (1988c) suggests that affect control explains and models the expressive, ritualistic behavior that accompanies instrumental action. For example, a simulation reported in Chapter 6 predicts that a doctor will initially engage in socioemotional work like "complimenting," "considering," "encouraging," and "talking to" a patient. Instrumental acts like "cure" and "rehabilitate" show up only in a subsequent round of interaction when, following an initial round of socioemotional interaction, a patient "consults" a doctor. Results like these suggest that, in real-life scenarios, circumventing the socioemotional accompaniments and/or prerequisites of instrumental action might derail or sabotage its production.

Since Smith-Lovin's (1988c) exhortations, Heise (1989b) applied the production systems approach to the underlying logic of event sequences, developing an action grammar and a user–friendly micro-computer program, ETHNO (Heise and Lewis 1988b). Unlike affect control models programmed in INTERACT, event sequence models do not predict subsequent events. Instead, they provide developmental accounts of the logical antecedents of given events. The data for ETHNO analysis consist of narratives of events and event prerequisites provided by expert observers. Corsaro and Heise (1990) applied the method to ethnographic data; Heise, to careers (1990) and the development of social theory (MacKinnon and Heise 1993). Despite its merits and accomplishments, however, this work constitutes a parallel development in cognitive theory, rather than a synthesis of production systems and affect control theories.

An attempt to integrate the two has recently been made by Heise and Durig (forthcoming). On the cognitive side of this synthesis, they utilize a case-frame approach and an action grammar to analyze how productive microinteractional events develop into collaborative productions or "macroactions":[10]

> Productive events enable or disable other events by generating products that can fit into the case slots of other events, and thereby productive events become prerequisites and consequences of one another, with sequences of events unfolding developmentally (Heise and Durig forthcoming).

The dual presence of agent and object mobilizes the first event, triggering a process of cascading action that results in collaborative productions. Because action implies the other components of causal sequences, these "improvised" developmental sequences are transformed into "dependable" social productions.

This cognitive account of collaborative productions begs the question of what mobilizes agents of later events to initiate the actions necessary for dependable social productions. This motivational problem creates an opening for combining affect control theory and production systems theory. An important way to ensure that actions become mobilized, other than the imposition of power relations and the maintenance of incentive systems based on reward and reinforcement, is to make events *fulfilling* for an agent. According to affect control theory, this occurs when events generate transient impressions that converge with an agent's fundamental sentiments, particularly for those pertaining to his or her identity-situated self. This brings us back to the identity theory of motivation presented in Chapter 3. The central importance of the actor-in-role in mobilizing actions in collaborative productions requires that social organizations control the induction of self-identities and reinforce commitment to organizationally appropriate ones (Heise and Durig forthcoming).

Testing Affect Control Theory

Until recently, there have been two major tests of affect control theory— Heise and MacKinnon (1988) and Wiggins and Heise (1988)—both of which are discussed in Smith-Lovin (1988c). The MacKinnon and Heise study supported the notion that since conventional social interaction should minimize deflection, the perceived likelihood of events should be a function of affective deflection. The questionnaire part of the Wiggins and Heise study found that behavioral expectations and intentions correlated well with affect control predictions. The experimental part of their study confirmed the affect control prediction that people act in accordance with a principle of behavior-object consistency; specifically, that an embarrassed person will attempt to recover self-esteem and ameliorate status loss by acting nicely with valued others and less positively with delinquent others.

Additional tests of affect control theory have been conducted since Smith-Lovin's (1988c) assessment of the theory. In the first of two experimental studies, Robinson and Smith–Lovin (1992) found that people felt good when they received positive feedback on identity-relevant performance, felt bad when they received negative feedback, and that this pattern prevailed regardless of the self-esteem level of subjects. However, they found that subjects with low self-esteem judged the criticism as more accurate and liked the critic more than the subjects with high self-esteem. Examining the implications of these patterns for social interaction, their second study revealed that subjects with low self-esteem preferred to interact with a critic rather than with someone providing positive feedback on performance. Robinson and Smith-Lovin interpreted this finding as supporting the affect control theory prediction that people will act in order to confirm salient identities, rather than to simply enhance self-esteem.

While continuing to test affect control theory experimentally, future work should extend this effort to non–experimental settings. Smith-Lovin and her graduate students at the University of Arizona currently are comparing affect control predictions about the production of emotions in social interaction against self-reported responses to personal vignettes. Given the affinity of affect control theory and symbolic interactionism, future work should also test affect control predictions with observations in natural settings. One approach, suggested by Heise and O'Brien (forthcoming), would capitalize on advances in sound-image recording technology to code nonverbal emotional expressions (Scherer and Ekman 1982), employing Ekman and Friesen's (1978) classification of facial expressions. This could be used in conjunction with self–reported accounts to determine which definitions of the situation and appraisals of events were operative during the emotion–instigating events being studied.

Practical Applications

The potential applications of affect control theory are both obvious and manifold. Applied to interaction between incumbents of different power and authority positions in social organizations, INTERACT analysis should provide insights into problems of conflict and morale, sensitizing organizational elites and workers to each other's phenomenological perspectives and emotional responses to events. In view of the growing sensitivity to sexual harrassment in the work place, analysis of interaction between men and women would be a timely application. Other obvious applications include staff and inmates in total institutions (Goffman 1961b), teachers and students, and medical staff and patients. INTERACT analysis in organizational settings would be especially powerful if simulations were based on cultural data from different kinds or strata of organizational members.

INTERACT analysis of ethnic and race relations should prove both analytically insightful and educationally fruitful. National or regional samples of black and white respondents in the U.S., or Anglo- and Franco-Canadians, for example, would provide the necessary cultural data for conducting genuine cross–cultural simulations of interracial and interethnic interaction.

The applicability of INTERACT analysis to individual psychotherapy begs to be explored. Individual-specific data on cultural sentiments collected with the software program ATTITUDE (Heise and Lewis 1988a) could be employed in INTERACT analysis during psychotherapeutic sessions. Identifying the affective and cognitive responses of patients to everyday interpersonal events is a major step in establishing healthful patterns of coping responses.

By extension, INTERACT analysis might prove a useful tool in marriage and family therapy. Community-based cultural data would refine INTERACT analysis, and family-based data would refine analysis further still. An objectively presented computer analysis of family dynamics might prove more convincing than the purportedly objective opinion of a therapist taken alone.

Summary

After relating affect control theory to social psychological theories that lie outside the tradition of symbolic interactionism, this chapter assessed the status of affect control theory as sociological explanation and integrative social psychology, and concluded with suggestions for future research and refinement.

Affect control theory is a theoretically integrative, mathematically powerful social psychological theory whose predictions span the cognitive, affective, and behavioral life of the person. The last decade has witnessed a concerted effort and considerable success at theoretical expansion, methodological refinement, and theory testing. There is no reason to doubt that the next decade should witness more of the same.

ENDNOTES

Foreword

1. Citations are expanded in the References at the end of this book.

Chapter 1

1. I make the distinction throughout this book between *affect* (or emotion), a pervasive component of human consciousness that permeates all cognition in varying levels of intensity, and *emotions*, those episodic, situationally specific, and ephemeral affective experiences. For this reason, I refer to the sociology, psychology, or social psychology of *emotion*, a more inclusive term then *emotions*. The theory of affect control, to which this book is devoted, is based on the centrality of affect in human consciousness and social life. At the same time, it provides a theory of emotions (see Chapter 7).

2. Symbolic interactionists have attended seriously to emotion since the late 1970s. In addition to those authors discussed below, Stryker deserves to be acknowledged. Extending his earlier recognition (1968) of the role cathectic and conative modalities of self-response play in identity salience, Stryker (1981) forecast the greater attention symbolic interactionists would pay to affect in the 1980s; and in a more recent paper (1987), he mapped out explicit theoretical avenues through which affect may be admitted to identity theory.

3. One of the best and earliest accounts of Mead's anti–solipsism is provided in Charles W. Morris's Introduction to Mead's *Mind, Self, and Society* (1934). One of the reasons Mead has become increasingly appealing to psychological social psychologists in recent years is his anti-solipsistic position (Jackson 1988, 118).

4. Mead was particularly critical of the psychological theory of parallelism. Because it relegates the sensually experienced world to a separate field of consciousness accessible by introspection, Mead argues, parallelism falls into the trap of solipsism (Mead 1910a/1964).

5. The recent work of Clark McPhail (1991), which incorporates Powers' perceptual control systems theory (1973), is a recent exception to this global assertion, but follows the initial work of Heise by well over a decade. Burke (1980) provides another exception that proves the rule.

6. I am indebted to John O'Brien for suggesting that I address this general issue and for supplying me with several of the references employed. Additional references and dis-

cussion can be found in O'Brien (1992), an unpublished doctoral dissertation that was unavailable to me at the time this book was being written.

7. Following Mead, Jackson (1988, 120) defines a social act as "an organization of multiindividual overt and covert meanings and bounded, directed activity." See Mead (1934, 7n.) for his definition and Chapter 4 for discussion of Mead's concept of the social act.

Chapter 2

1. The propositional account of affect control theory presented in this chapter was drafted by the author in 1987 and re-drafted in 1989. In preparing a chapter for Berger and Zelditch's (1993) book, MacKinnon and Heise expanded this propositional statement considerably to take account of recent developments, particularly those pertaining to emotions. Chapter 2 of this book was revised further in 1990 to be consistent with the number and wording of the propositions in the MacKinnon and Heise chapter. The theoretical discussion of each proposition has generally been expanded here as well.

2. Given three components of an event (ABO) each measured on evaluation, potency, and activity (EPA), deflection consists of the sum of nine squared differences between fundamental sentiments (unprimed) and transient impressions (primed).

$$(A_e - A_e')^2 \qquad (A_p - A_p')^2 \qquad (A_a - A_a')^2$$
$$(B_e - B_e')^2 \qquad (B_p - B_p')^2 \qquad (B_a - B_a')^2$$
$$(O_e - O_e')^2 \qquad (O_p - O_p')^2 \qquad (O_a - O_a')^2$$

While the concept of deflection and its operationalization is unique to affect control theory, the general notion of discrepancy itself is not. Kelley (1984, 97) observes that "some emotion theorists have made disconfirmed expectations the central, or even exclusive, focus of their analysis." For example, Abelson (1983, 47) suggests that the discrepancy between a person's anticipation and construal of what has in fact occurred instigates "an affective process . . . which is both a signal and a symptom of the activity of reconstrual" (as quoted in Kelley 1984). McClelland et al. (1953, 28) propose that the condition necessary for the arousal of affect is a discrepancy between expectation and perception. Similarly, Hochschild (1983) proposes that emotions arise out of a discrepancy between what is culturally expected and actually perceived.

In addition to a difference in cognitions on the stimulus or input side of emotional response, discrepancy also has been employed to refer to an interruption in actions or intentions on the response or output side (Mook 1987, 433–441). For example, Mandler (1984) proposes that interruptions in the mindless, cognitively unattended routine activities of everyday life snaps our attention to what is going on around us, induces autonomic arousal, and causes emotion. Mandler's theory is reminiscent of Peirce's observation, discussed in Chapter 3, that emotions occur when events disrupt the flow of consciousness.

Theories like these apply the idea of discrepancy to the instigation of emotions, and only indirectly to motivation. However, as discussed in Chapter 3, affect control theory applies the notion of discrepancy to *motivation*. In affect control theory, discrepancy does not only contribute to the instigation of emotions, it is a dynamic, motivational principle underlying the production and interpretation of social action itself.

3. In presenting this formal statement, I do not claim that this is the only propositional analysis of the theory possible. Indeed, another theorist could provide a different formal account of the theory, although I expect it would overlap considerably with the one I offer here. In addition, I disclaim any motivation to cast the theory in stone through this attempt at theoretical codification. Affect control theory is still developing and, as it does, additional propositions may be added and existing propositions refined.

Chapter 3

1. According to Parsons and Shils (1951, 5), "the orientation of action to objects entails . . . cognitive discriminations, the location and characterization of the objects." Cognitive orientations include "all existential beliefs—all beliefs about the way the world was, is, and/or will be" (Wallace 1983, 90). For Parsons and Shils, the objects in the actor's situation "are simultaneously or successively experienced as having positive or negative value to the actor . . . Cathexis, the attachment to objects which are gratifying and rejection of those which are noxious, lies at the root of the selective nature of action" (1951, 5). The cathectic (affective) mode of orientation involves "the various processes by which an actor invests an object with affective significance" (1951, 59), and includes "all desires, aversions, . . . and emotions—in short, feeling" (Wallace 1983, 90). According to Parsons and Shils (1951, 59), the evaluative (conative) mode "involves the various processes by which an actor allocates his energy among the various actions with respect to various cathected objects in an attempt to optimize gratification." These "behavior–readying" or "predispositional orientations" include balancing our cognitive and affective orientations because our cognitive appraisals influence our wants, and vice versa; and selecting specific behaviors for implementation to attain cathected ends (Wallace 1983, 91).

2. While independently conceived, this analysis of the primacy issue roughly coincides with Denzin's (1985) application of Peirce's categories to the phenomenological analysis of emotions as "lived experiences." Denzin (1985) identifies his first mode of "sensible feelings" with Peirce's Firstness, those feelings that "are located in a part of the body, but not in the symbolic self process" (1985, 229). The individual "makes this recognition at the symbolic levels of secondness and thirdness" (1985, 229). While Denzin (1985) does not explicitly do so, he had earlier indicated that his second mode, "feelings of the lived body" should be identified with Peirce's Secondness (Denzin 1984). For Denzin, these are feelings that are symbolically recognized and expressed through emotion terms which, through communication, "move emotionality out of the private, inner world of pure sensations into the public realm of interaction and emotional intersubjectivity" (1985, 230). (For Peirce, *externality* is an important characteristic of Secondness.) Denzin identifies his third mode of lived emotions, "intentional value-feelings," with Peirce's Thirdness. These are "feelings about feelings, . . . metafeelings, or interpreted emotions . . . felt reflections, cognitive and emotional, about feelings . . . symbolic objectifications of emotional experiences" (1985, 230). Denzin specifies a fourth mode of lived emotions, "feelings of the self

and the moral person." Since these are "internalizations" of the "broader interpretive schemes" represented by his third category, intentional value–feelings, I would include these under Peirce's Thirdness as well.

3. When Kemper (1978, 47–8) asserts that "cognitive awareness and labeling of the emotions are not necessary, although they are frequent components of the emotions," or Thoits (1984, 223) that "I do not mean that cognitive mediation is necessary for one to experience emotion," they are referring to this highly symbolic level of cognitive awareness.

4. It must be pointed out, however, that what I have presented here as more or less a virtue, Duffy judged to be a conceptual shortcoming. Psychological categories like cognition and affect, she argues, are "literary" and "loose" descriptive terms "uncritically taken over by the psychologist from the layman's vocabulary" (1934, 193). In their stead, Duffy (1941) proposes that all behavior be described in terms of two basic dimensional categories—direction and intensity. Nonetheless, I maintain that the distinction between emotion and cognition is analytically useful. Because cognition and affect shade into one another along the continuum of consciousness is not a sufficient reason to reject their distinction as heuristic, analytical categories. Moreover, the rediscovery of affect and its popularity in recent years belies Duffy's recommendation that we drop the emotion concept, or Meyer's (1933) prediction that the term eventually will be abandoned by psychologists.

5. Stephenson's two papers, especially the latter one (1986b), extend well beyond the issue at hand: the relation between cognition and affect. His major objective is to establish an epistemological foundation for Q-type as opposed to R-type factor analysis. Advocating a quantum theoretic approach in psychology, Stephenson interprets Q factors as indicative of "gaps" or "jumps" in the mind, an "indication of the way the mind works inside" (1986b, 536). Complementarity, according to Stephenson, reveals itself "fundamentally, as gaps in transitive thought, with factors marking them" (1986b, 538). Transitive thought involves self–referentiality. Because the Q-technique is inherently self-referential, the observer being the person observed, it is particularly tailored to study the quantum-like nature of transitive thought. In a nutshell, Stephenson's mission is to establish that "the complementarity of cognition versus feeling," which James identified in human thought and its linguistic expression, "is transformable to operant [Q-type] factors" (1986b, 541). I am indebted to John O'Brien for bringing these two papers to my attention.

6. Heise (1979, 104–106) proposed an argument along these lines, in the context of role learning. I discuss this in Chapter 5.

7. This overview of incentive theories of motivation, including the discussion of McClelland, is based upon Cofer (1972). The following criticism of incentive theories is my own, albeit undoubtedly made by one theorist or another in the literature.

8. Summarized by Cofer (1972, 97), their starting point was that "the unique function of the motivation construct is to energize response through states of [affective] arousal, leaving to other factors the guidance of behavior, i.e., its direction." Once the invigoration of behavior takes place, other factors—like individual abilitites and habits established through reinforcement—exert considerable control over what behavior is implemented. Like McClelland, Cofer and Appley maintain that arousal is induced by either internal or

external cues. However, unlike McClelland, who argues that all motives are learned, they propose that two mechanisms are required for the induction of arousal—one requiring a history of learning, the other depending upon the innate sensitivities of the organism.

9. Cognitive processing is involved on both the input and output side of human motivation. On the input side, preceding the release of energy for mobilizing response, cognition is implicated in the definition of one's identity–situated self and those of others, and in identification of the situation's relevance to one's incentives. On the output side, cognitive processing underlies the determination of response options in terms of their instrumental value for attaining one's ends-in-view, their normative appropriateness, and their consequences for maintaining or asserting the situated identities of self and other in the situation. The conative mode of consciousness subsumes the evaluative and selective processes that precede behavioral response. While analytically distinct, cognition, affect, and conation are inextricably interrelated in consciousness. As argued in the first section of this chapter, all cognitions evoke affective associations, and cognition is implicated in both affective experience and the evaluative and selective processes preceding behavioral response.

10. Paralleling my discussion of cognition and affect in the first section of this chapter, the cognitive processing involved in motivated behavior can range from preconscious or habitual responses stemming from a person's preconceptual system established in early socialization, to highly conscious, symbolically mediated assessments of situations and response options in terms of their implications for an actor's incentives. At this level, motivational impulses become *motives*—an actor's verbalized accounts, to self or others, of what allegedly motivated his or her actions (Hewitt 1990). And, just as culture provides us with a "vocabulary of emotions" for designating our emotional experiences (Gordon 1981), it provides us as well with a "vocabulary of motives" (Mills 1940) for articulating our inferred motivations and justifying our actions.

In the case of both emotions and motivation, the veracity of an actor's verbalized accounts remains a separate and difficult issue. Some authors have adopted a skeptical position. For example, Wilson (1985) distinguishes between two systems: a partly or mostly unconscious system of cognitive and motivational processes that influences an actor's behavior; and a conscious, verbal explanatory system which an actor draws upon to identify the emotions and motives that presumably instigated his or her actions. Wilson contends that since the causes of an actor's emotions and motives are not directly observable, they are unavailable to consciousness and cannot be accessed through the verbal explanatory system of the actor.

11. Foote's outline of a theory of motivation based on language and identification contains all the essential ingredients of what has become known as identity theory in contemporary symbolic interactionism (Stryker 1968, 1977, 1980, 1981; McCall and Simmons 1966/1978; Burke 1980). It is strange, then, that aside from passing reference by a few authors (Stryker 1968; Stryker and Statham 1985; Hewitt 1990), symbolic interactionists have failed to fully appreciate the significance of Foote's analysis. His wonderful articulation of a truly adequate and researchable theory of human motivation based upon language, identification, and commitment has been effectively ignored. For example, Foote is not cited by McCall and Simmons (1966/1978), nor in Turner's 1987 formal statement of the interactionist model of motivation.

12. Bindra (1967) proposes that motivation is generated by the interaction of physiological and incentive stimulation, employing the term "central motive state" to refer to the neural processes underlying this interaction. Bindra also proposes that motivation and reinforcement refer to identical processes, and that the major effect of reinforcement is not the strengthening of a response but the creation of motivational states which influence a wide variety of an organism's behavior, including non-reinforced responses. And, in contrast to Cofer and Appley (1964), Bindra views motivation as accounting for both the invigoration and selection of response. See Cofer (1972) for a discussion of Bindra's ideas.

13. The proliferation of motives in the literature has been widely criticized. As discussed above, Foote (1951), influenced by Burke (1945), rejects the search for predispositional motives that lie behind the self. Recasting such putative motives into identity-confirmation terms avoids the inherent tautology of predispositional theories.

The extensive list of supposed human motives has been criticized on another front—the problem of identifying an underlying state of affective arousal. Cofer (1972, 152–3) queries whether we can find in human motives like aggression and achievement something resembling Bindra's (1967) notion of a "central motive state" corresponding to the interaction of physiological and incentive stimulation. While acknowledging that the incentive stimuli side of this interaction is apparent in many such supposed motives, he concludes that the existence of an underlying physiological state is more problematic. Although there is evidence for its presence in motives like anxiety and aggression that are clearly emotional in nature, he argues, there is no clear evidence for its existence in other putative human motives like achievement. If a physiological state of arousal is found to be associated with such motives, Cofer suggests that it will likely turn out to be of a general, unspecific nature, depending upon the person's interpretation of the situation for its being labeled as one or another motive, like Schachter's cognitive theory of emotions (Schachter and Singer 1962). In short, Cofer (1972, 152–3) concludes that "we should speak of human motives only when the arousal side of the interaction [between physiological and incentive stimulation] can be demonstrated to be present or can be plausibly inferred." This, he argues, "would limit the promiscuous use of the word motive in discussions of human behavior." If, as argued above, identities have affective meaning, then identity-confirmation, conceptualized as incentive, meets the criterion of affective arousal imposed by Cofer. This points to a second major advantage of translating the litany of putative motives identified in the psychological literature into identity-confirmation terms.

14. Thoits cites Stryker's (1987) unpublished paper as an attempt to integrate the affective and motivational implications of self into identity theory. This paper came to my attention after I initially drafted many of the ideas that form the basis of my discussions of motivation, identity-confirmation, and self.

15. Consistent with the idea that maintaining a knowable and meaningful existence is itself a cathected object, and hence an incentive, maintaining a consistent and stable self-image also has motivational impact on the actor (Schwartz and Stryker 1970; Rosenberg 1979; Elliot 1986). However, self–esteem appears to be a more powerful motive than self–consistency, although the issue of their relative motivational impact continues to be a contentious one (Swann et al. 1987). For a recent discussion, see Robinson and Smith-Lovin (1992).

16. This suggests the need for a future study employing cultural data from affect control research, wherein the EPA profiles of subjects' self-reported salient identities are employed in a regression model predicting global self-esteem measured by the individual's EPA response to global self-image stimuli. This semantic differential measure of self-esteem could be cross-validated with measures of self-esteem derived from different measurement models (e.g., the Rosenberg index of self-esteem).

17. The assumption here, of course, is that the person has embraced the cultural sentiments defining high status, power, and liveliness as his or her own. A person would be motivated to validate identities that are not highly evaluated or even stigmatized by the culture at large if these identities are highly evaluated by a particular subculture with which the person identifies or, idiosyncratically, by the person himself or herself.

Chapter 4

1. Mead, in fact, points to two ways in which significant symbols are universal. Besides connoting shared meaning (social concepts), significant symbols designate or name objects. "Signification has . . . two references, one to the thing indicated, and the other to the response, to the instance and to the meaning or idea. It denotes and connotes. When the symbol is used for one, it is a name. When it is used for the other, it is a concept" (1922/1964, 246). As gestures, significant symbols are a phase of the social act and partake of whatever universality acts possess. An act is universal in that it can be stimulated by a variety of objects. Therefore, as a name, a significant symbol is universal because it denotes a large class of objects that can fulfill the requirement of a particular act. For example, any object that one can sit down on can be designated a "seat" and can serve as a stimulus for the act of sitting down; any object with which one can hammer can be designated a "hammer" and can stimulate the act of hammering (Mead 1934, 125–6; 146–7; Morris 1934, xxvii–xxviii).

2. The meaning of objects, like the significant symbols that designate them, is defined behavioristically as well: "[A]n organization of attitudes with reference to . . . objects is what constitutes . . . the meaning of things" (1934, 15).

3. Baldwin (1985, 275–6) suggests two reasons why words may elicit different emotions in self and other: when people have been conditioned differently to words as conditioned stimuli; when people have different positions in the social structure of interaction (e.g., actor and object-persons).

4. Mead refers to "the difference between the purely intellectual character of the symbol and its emotional character," and points out that "a poet depends upon the latter; for him language is rich and full of values which we, perhaps, utterly ignore. In trying to express a message in something less than ten words, we merely want to convey a certain meaning, while the poet is dealing with what is really living tissue, the emotional throb in the expression itself" (1934, 75). While Mead acknowledges that "there is a great range in our use of language," he asserts that whatever part of this range we use to communicate is social; "it is always that part by means of which we affect ourselves as we affect others"

(1934, 75). Otherwise, it is not language: "[W]hat is essential to communication is that the symbol should arouse in one's self what it arouses in the other individual. It must have that same sort of universality" (Mead 1934, 149).

5. Wallace (1983, 14–15, 26–27) defines social phenomena as behavioral (psychic or physical) regularities between two or more individual organisms. Emotions, as conceptualized by Mead, would not constitute social phenomena according to Wallace's definition, and hence could not enter into sociological theories as dependent variable. However, as *independent* variable, emotions could qualify as explanatory variables in sociological theories of other social phenomena. (See Wallace 1983, cpt. 7, especially 193–196).

6. Baldwin (1985, 275–6) also addresses Mead's position on the "natural function of language" and the asymmetry of response that often characterizes words as conditioned stimuli eliciting emotions. However, Baldwin came to a different conclusion than I have as to the role of emotion in Mead's social psychology. He argues that Mead "was aware of the dynamic interaction between emotions and the other components of the social act, i.e., thoughts, words and behaviors: Emotions often arouse thoughts, words, and behaviors; and these . . . often elicit further emotional responses" (1985, 276). I agree with the "dynamic cycle" proposed by Baldwin. Indeed, it describes the reciprocal relation between cognition and affect discussed in Chapter 3 of this book. However, this "dynamic cycle" model relating emotional responses and thoughts, words, and behavior is principally Baldwin's creation, not Mead's. Baldwin concludes correctly that, for Mead, emotional gestures, like all gestures, are "part of the organization of the social act" (1934, 44); but Mead is not at all explicit about the dynamic relation between affect and other components of the social act proposed by Baldwin. Mead was ambivalent at best. He devoted more attention to showing why emotions are not social because of their inherent asymmetry of response, and to why on this account a social psychology must be based on social cognitions rather than on affective experience, which he considered individual in nature.

7. Mead's position on the asymmetrical nature of affective communication obviously runs counter to much of contemporary social psychology. As the dramaturgical metaphor of Goffman (1959) would have it, we *are* actors most of the time, the success of our performance being measured not merely in terms of managing outer impressions to evoke affective reactions in others, but more fundamentally, as Hochschild (1979) observes, in the "deep acting" that produces emotional feelings in the actor himself or herself. On the other hand, Shott's (1979) theory of "empathic role–taking" is foreshadowed by Mead's treatment of sympathy: "[I]n an attitude which is sympathetic we imply that our attitude calls out in ourselves the attitude of the other person we are assisting. We feel with him and we are able so to feel ourselves into the other because we have, by our own attitude, aroused in ourselves the attitude of the person we are assisting" (1934, 299). However, like other scattered instances of Mead's treatment of affective experiences, this exception is eclipsed by his overriding concern with establishing a social psychology on the basis of the social cognitions communicated by language.

8. In Mead's words, "it is absurd to look at the mind simply from the standpoint of the individual human organism; for although it has its locus there, it is essentially a so-

cial phenomenon . . . We must regard mind . . . as arising and developing within the social process, within the empirical matrix of social interactions" (1934, 133).

9. Mead is very explicit here: "Mind . . . lies in a field of conduct between a specific individual and the environment, in which the individual is able . . . to make use of symbolic gestures, i.e., terms, which are significant to all including himself (1922/1964, 247)."

10. Mead states this point emphatically: "I know of no way in which intelligence or mind could arise or could have arisen, other than through the internalization by the individual . . . of the conversation of significant gestures . . . and if mind or thought has arisen in this way, then there neither can be nor could have been any mind or thought without language . . . (1934, 191–2)."

11. "It is in the form of the generalized other," Mead writes, "that the social process or community enters as a determining factor into the individual's thinking . . . only by taking the attitude of the generalized other toward himself, can he think at all; for only thus can thinking—or the internalized conversation of gestures which constitutes thinking—occur (1934, 155–6)."

12. Mead sometimes uses the metaphor of an audience to express the idea of the generalized other as perspective: "[T]hinking is . . . an inner conversation . . . which in its completion implies the expression of that which one thinks to an audience" (1934, 141–2), the internal audience of the generalized other.

13. The meaning of an object does not disappear when any individual ceases to be consciously aware of it in this latter, physiological sense of consciousness because it continues to exist in reflective consciousness, which is social in nature. Reflective consciousness is objectively grounded in the process of social behavior, wherein meaning is defined in terms of the triadic relation between the symbol user, the object denoted by the symbol, and the target person to whom the symbol is directed.

14. In an early paper (1910a/1964, 105–113) Mead attacks the psychological theory of parallelism which, by default, relegates the world as sensually experienced to a separate field of consciousness open to introspection (See also 1934, especially 27–33). According to the doctrine of introspection, Mead argues, the self has no existence outside the field of introspection and one becomes uncertain about the existence of other selves. "Each self is an island, and each self is sure only of its own island, for who knows what mirages may arise above this analogical sea" (1910a/1964, 107). In Mead's social behavioristic theory of consciousness, however, "other selves in a social environment logically antedate the consciousness of self which introspection analyzes" (1910a/1964, 111).

15. This second kind of consciousness can be identified with that mode of "lived emotion" which Denzin (1985, 229) calls "sensible feelings"—those that "are located in a part of the body, but not in the symbolic self process." Unless communicable by language, emotions remain "in the private, inner world of pure sensations" (Denzin 1985, 230).

16. Despite the non-social nature of imagery and sensations emanating from within, Mead attributes a certain objectivity to these phenomena (1924–5/1964, 273–4). My point is that this objectivity is not *social*, within Mead's framework, as in the case of reflective consciousness.

17. In his discussion of imagery, for example, Mead notes that while "it is apt to be of the nature of the vocal gesture" (1934, 246), "the content of this imagery is varied. It may be of vision and contact or of the other senses" (1934, 346, 337–346).

18. Like mind, reflexiveness is an essential characteristic of self: "[T]he characteristic of the self as an object to itself . . . is represented by the word 'self' which is a reflexive, and indicates that which can be both subject and object" (Mead 1934, 136–7). This inherent characteristic of self enables the individual to treat himself or herself as an *object* of reflective or conscious thought. However, the individual does not experience self as an object directly. "The individual experiences himself . . . only indirectly, from the particular standpoints of other individual members of the same social group, or from the generalized standpoint of the social group as a whole to which he belongs (1934, 138)."

19. The solution of Mead and the symbolic interactionists to the problem of social integration "is just another way of saying what has become a truism in sociology and social-psychology: Human society rests upon a consensus, i.e., the sharing of meanings in the form of common understandings and expectations" (Meltzer 1972, 7). As such, it is similar to the solution offered by structural-functionalists: that the basis of social integration lies in value-consensus (e.g., Parsons, 1951).

20. Compare to Collins' (1986) discussion of Peirce's recognition of these two structural features of language.

21. The fully cybernetic nature of Mead's model of mind (and self) was discussed over two decades ago by Walter Buckley. Commenting on Mead's reflexive self, Buckley (1967, 100) states that "self-consciousness is a mechanism of internal feedback of the system's own states which may be mapped or compared with other information from the situation or from memory, permitting a selection from a repertoire of actions in a goal-directed manner that takes one's own self and behavior explicitly into account."

22. There is a strong hint at the function of emotion in the teleology of the act in Mead's (1895, 163) early statement that "the teleology of . . . [emotional] states is that of giving the organism an evaluation of the act before the coordination that leads to the particular reaction has been completed." However, the role played by affect in the cybernetic process of the act appears to have gotten buried in Mead's subsequent work by his one-sided emphasis on cognition. For Mead, the cybernetic process comes down to the playing back of cognitions of future states upon present cognitions and actions. Nonetheless, given Mead's frequent references to the "emotional overtones" of gestures and significant symbols, there is the implication that affect trickles through the act from impulse to consummation. However, once again, we are confronted with Mead's position that the natural function of gestures and language is to communicate cognitive information about the adjustments of each organism to the acts of the other in the construction of the social act. This indicates that affect is of negligible importance to the teleology of the act.

Chapter 5

1. The definition of role as expected, rather than actual, behavior has become generally accepted—either explicitly (e.g., Heiss 1981), or by distinguishing between role "expectations" and "performances" (e.g., Wallace 1983, 73–4). As Wallace (1983, 73) puts it forcibly, "it behooves us stringently to divide the concept 'role' into two logically independent components, namely, role performance and role expectation . . . to speak merely of 'role' would perpetuate a crucial and insidious aspect of the already serious confusion between social structure and cultural structure, and it would unjustifiably take for granted that for every role-performance there is a role–expectation (and vice versa)."

2. As Heiss (1981, 95) observes, "the ultimate dependent variable in social-psychological theory is social behavior, and if roles refer to actual behavior there would be little for roles to explain."

3. This usage has become generally accepted. For instance, Jackson (1988, 125) defines role as "a structure of related and compatible norms," and Heiss (1981, 95) uses the term "role-norm" to refer to "specific behavioral prescriptions."

4. For example, the "sociological" and "symbolic interactionist" (Hewitt 1990), the "structural" and "interactionist" (Heiss 1981), the "structural" and "process" (Jackson 1988), or "role theory" and "symbolic interaction theory" (Stryker and Statham 1985). While an "oversimplification" or "fiction" (Stryker and Statham 1985, 341), the distinction captures conflicting images of the relation between person and society among those who employ the construct of role.

5. Drawing upon the work of Merton (1957) and Goode (1960), among others, Heiss points out that even structuralists of the late 1950s and early 1960s acknowledged the realities and exigencies of social interaction—dissensus among role players, large gaps in institutionalized scripts, role conflict, strain, and overload—that require flexibility, innovation, and ingenuity on the part of interactants. Citing Maines (1977), Strauss (1978), Handel (1979), Stryker (1980), and others, Heiss illustrates the growing tolerance of structural concepts by interactionists, as evidenced by their recognition of structural limitations to "role-making," the transference of roles from one situation to another (Turner 1978), and the predominance in interaction of what Shibutani (1961) has called "conventional roles."

6. Stryker's concept of commitment has always troubled me because it is defined independently of the individual's personal, affective meaning of and attachment to identities and associated roles. Having defined the construct in this way, Stryker (1968, 560–561) views commitment as analytically independent of the affective response to self. Thus, without danger of tautologizing, he can hypothesize that "the greater the commitment premised on an identity, the more that identity will be invested with a positive cathectic response" (1968, 562–563). For me, the affective attachment to identities and corresponding roles is the essence of commitment, as the term is commonly understood.

The definition of commitment proposed by Burke and Reitzes follows in the conceptual footsteps of Stryker. Their definition of commitment as "the sum of the forces, pressures, or drives that influence people to maintain congruity between their identity setting and the input of reflected appraisals from the social setting" (1991, 243) makes no reference to the personal, affective meaning and attachment to identities as a basis for commitment. Instead, they identify two bases of commitment: cognitive (personally perceived costs and rewards); and socioemotional (emotional and identity-sustaining social ties). The first excludes the emotional basis of commitment; the second, its personal experience. Moreover, admittedly "lacking direct measures of the forces favoring commitment," they employ "measures of these two bases of commitment as proxies for direct measures of commitment" (247). Hence, the affective attachment to identities that constitutes commitment is excluded both conceptually and operationally.

7. Burke employed multiple discriminant analysis to define the dimensions that maximally discriminate identities from counter-identities (Burke 1980; Burke and Tully 1977).

8. At the same time, affect control theory measures implicitly the relational property of identities. By projecting identities in EPA space, it measures their commonalities and differences in terms of *affective* meaning. By employing dimensions that discriminate maximally between identities and counteridentities, Burke's procedure measures the commonalities and differences of identities and counteridentities in terms of their *cognitive* meaning. In a nutshell, the difference between Burke's procedure and affect control theory is one of the "I am" versus the "I feel" modalities of self-response.

9. Callero (1988) independently criticized Burke's procedure along these lines. He emphasizes the importance of the generalized other in addition to the specific others corresponding to Burke's counteridentities. This would appear to support the use of culturally general dimensions of meaning as compared to Burke's procedure of deriving specific dimensions that distinguish maximally between identities and counteridentities.

10. In order to incorporate reflexivity into the measurement process, Burke (1980, 26–28) proposed successive rounds of measuring subjects' performances, allowing them to assess the original measures of their identities and to make corrections, or having subjects respond to completed semantic differential forms in terms of the desirability of image conveyed and the manner in which subjects would change that image. This proposal is ad hoc and procedurally messy and, despite the summary measures recommended by Burke, the analyst would become quickly buried in a "mass of data about reflexiveness and the corrective responses of respondents" (1980, 28). In this regard, Stryker (1981, 25) observes that Burke's proposals for measuring reflexivity—as well as the indirect nature of identities and identities as motives—are "more programmatic than actualized at this time."

11. According to Burke (1980), their location would vary according to whether "typical," "stereotypical," "ideal," or "normative" identities and acts are at issue.

Chapter 6

1. More recent inventorial approaches (e.g., Schank and Abelson 1977) avoid this problem by recognizing that social events are often so highly socially structured and situated that most of the possible actor-behavior-object combinations are rendered meaning-

less or irrelevant. For example, it would be socially and culturally anomalous for "waitress" to be found in a school setting, or for "waiting upon customers" to be a relevant behavior in that setting. Heise (1979, 137–9) concludes that such work on routinized social inter-action is complementary to affect control theory, whose unique strength lies in modeling less structured interactions requiring some role creativity on the part of participants. How-ever, because affect control theory is applicable to both standard and non-standard events, it constitutes a more general model. In addition to comparing affect control theory to in-ventorial models, Heise discusses its relation to dimensional, functionalist, and structural-ist perspectives applied to role analysis (1979, 132–151).

2. The simulations reported in this book were conducted before INTERACT 2 (Heise 1991) became available and, therefore, can be replicated exactly only with the orig-inal version of INTERACT.

3. The first act in the initial set of behavioral retrievals for an identity was imple-mented, and additional ones, if any, were added to the end of this set, deleting duplications. The additional retrievals often included one or more sensible expectations.

4. Because the Canadian study lacks data on settings, the U.S. data were used as estimates.

5. In addition to differences in fundamental sentiments between studies, differ-ences between the two models may contribute to the observed differences in behavioral pre-dictions. In the impression formation equations, behavior evaluation (B_e) has a notably larger effect in the Canadian equation for predicting the outcome impression of a behav-ior's goodness (B_e')—.727 compared to .571 for the U.S. equation. This should result in behavioral retrievals that are more sensitive to the inherent goodness or badness of acts and relatively less sensitive to the identities of participants. In addition, actor evaluation (A_e) has a slightly larger impact on the prediction of behavior evaluation (B_e') in the Canadian study (.105 as compared to .071); and object activity (O_a), a larger positive coefficient (.087 as compared to –.003). These somewhat larger, positive coefficients amplify the effect that the more positive and lively nature of police and criminal roles has on behavioral retrievals in simulations with the Canadian data. However, the situation becomes complicated by other subtle differences in coefficients that should counteract somewhat the differences noted.

6. Assuming the theory is correct, retrievals may seem anomalous for any of the fol-lowing reasons (Heise 1989, 15).
(1) Cultural variations in EPA ratings: Verbal retrievals are based on EPA ratings of identities, behaviors, and other components of events. If different from the reader's, results may appear strange. (2) Errors in ratings: While EPA ratings in the Canadian study are av-eraged over 25–35 subjects, for each gender, inaccuracies owing to sampling or measure-ment errors should occasionally occur. (3) Errors in equations: i.e., in parameter estimation. (4) Lexical errors: Those arising from the fact that semantic rules governing word usage are not employed fully in matching words to profiles, or from defining inadequately the con-text of events. For example, the prediction that a wife might *marry* a husband fits the opti-mal EPA behavioral profile generated by the model, but appears strange because projection rules governing the behavioral implications of identities are not fully employed by the model. (5) Misconceptions: What at first blush appears anomalous may, upon reflection, suggest an idea worth serious consideration.

7. The idea that roles are learned at a more elementary level than intact norms is supported in the literature (Heise 1979, 105–106). For example, Goodenough (1969) proposes that the cultural content of social relationships contains various vocabularies and a syntax for their combination into social events. Berger et al. (1977) suggest that we view what people learn in socialization not as internalized norms, but rather as cognitive and evaluative information about social structure ("status structures") that gets translated under the right circumstances into observable behavior. Imershein (1976) proposes that the patterning of activity in social interaction results from a small number of exemplary beliefs or statements from the common social experience of participants. Fishbein and Ajzen (1975) propose a model explaining the origin of attitudes from salient beliefs about states.

8. According to Bandura (1977), a number of factors affect attentiveness. People tend to be attentive when they expect others to be rewarded, when others are similar, when the responses of stress appear to have functional value, when they need the rewards associated with others' behavior, and when they expect to be rewarded for their attentiveness. In addition to these factors, Heiss (1981) points out that the study of interaction by sociologists suggests that attentiveness is greater when one is a participant rather than simply an observer.

9. Heiss (1981) proceeds to show how social learning theory provides a theoretical framework for analyzing the sociological literature on roles, but this part of his analysis is too complex to summarize here, nor is it all that relevant for the comparison I want to make between his theory of role learning and playing and affect control theory.

Chapter 7

1. Solomon (1984, 249) distinguishes between strong and weak versions of the cognitive theory of emotions: "The strong version . . . is that an understanding of the conceptual and learned appetitive functions of emotions is all that there is in identifying and distinguishing them from each other and from non-emotions; the weaker version . . . is that an understanding of the conceptual and learned appetitive structures of emotions is sufficient for identifying them and distinguishing them from each other and from non-emotions." Both versions can be detected in constructionist theories of emotion advanced by sociological social psychologists.

2. Denzin's point of departure is his assumption that while the individual experiencing emotions is located in the world, "people act in the world so as to make that world a part of themselves and a part of their emotionality" (1984, 7). Thus, it is reasoned, emotion has to be studied from within—as a phenomenon in itself. The alliance of Denzin's approach with interactionist-inspired constructionist theories of emotion stems from its emphasis on emotion as process ("emotionality"), the reflective self as the center of emotional experience, and the situation of social interaction, which extends emotionality outward into the world of intersubjectivity. However, his radical subjective orientation sets Denzin apart from other constructionists who draw upon culture, a factor external to phenomena in themselves, to define and interpret emotional experience.

3. Because of his reliance on a Darwinian organismic theory of emotions, along with an emphasis on social structure that approaches Kemper's, Collins (1981) might also be described as a positivist. In collaboration with Kemper (1990), Collins extends power and status from relational dimensions of microinteraction to aggregation at the level of social structure. To cite another instance of the positivist position, Scheff (1983, 343) concludes that the evidence for biological ("culture-universal") theories of emotions is as strong and maybe stronger than that for cultural ("culture-specific") theories. In addition, he has advocated objective methods for measuring emotions (1983). Scheff's work in the social psychology of emotions (1983, 1984a, 1984b, 1985a, 1985b) is eclectic, however, a reflection of his expressed desire to contribute to an integrated social psychology of emotions.

4. It might appear that this criticism is applicable as well to theories that include cognition in their definitions of emotion while maintaining that cognitive appraisal of the situation is a necessary antecedent of emotional experience (as in the primacy of cognition position discussed in Chapter 3). To the extent that cognitive awareness of emotions is analytically distinct from the cognitive appraisal of emotion-instigating situations, definitions of emotion that include cognition can be justified. Radical constructionists go further, however, by incorporating into their definition of emotion not only a cognitive component, but also the supposed social and cultural antecedents of cognition and emotion itself.

5. "Interpretations from outside the lived experience of emotion, or the phenomenon in question, are not sought. They are actively rejected. A social phenomenological interpretation always stays within the phenomenon, seeking understanding from the lived experience. Understanding, explanation, or prediction is not sought in terms of factors external to the phenomenon . . . "(1984, 8–9). While I do not share Denzin's enthusiasm for restricting the study of emotions to descriptive research, I find his social phenomenological analysis both stimulating and insightful.

6. Specifically, according to Kemper, it is the *power* and *status* implications of what people do to one another that are responsible for what they feel. He defines power and status in terms of the motivational orientation of a person to compliance relationships. Power is "a mode of social relationship in which compliance, broadly speaking, is obtained from others who do not give it willingly" (1978, 29). Status is a mode of social interaction in which an individual complies with the will of another "not because of coercion but because he wants to do it, that is, voluntary compliance" (1978, 29–30). Power relationships comprise situations of force, coercion, threat, and the like; status relations, situations of respect, love, and other voluntary acts. Kemper's major proposition is that involuntary compliance by one person to another's wishes bestows power on the other, while voluntary compliance enhances the other's status.

7. Wallace defines *cultural structuralism* as an emphasis on "socially influenced psychical behavior relations among . . . people" that constrain an actor's thoughts, feelings, or behavior (1983, 280). He defines *social structuralism* as an emphasis on "socially generated physical behavior relations between the participants" that constrains a person's thoughts, feelings, or behavior (1983, 248). Gordon (1990, 146) makes the same distinction between social and cultural effects, but narrows his focus on cultural structure to "emotional culture"—emotion vocabularies, norms governing feeling and its expression, and beliefs about emotions.

8. An additional implication or property of the emotions model concerns interaction between emotion evaluation and identity evaluation in the prediction of the transient impression of a person created by events (Heise and Thomas 1989). When incorporated into the emotions equations, this interaction term has the effect of amplifying the negativity of emotions predicted for stigmatized identities; that is, for the same degree of disconfirmation by events, people with stigmatized identities will experience more extreme negative emotions than people with positive identities. And people with extremely stigmatized identities may experience emotions that are chaotic or labile (Heise 1989a, 1992).

9. Kemper (1978) identifies three broad classes of emotion: *anticipatory, structural,* and *consequent.* Arising out of the relatively stable structure of a social relationship, structural emotions reflect each person's level of satisfaction with his or her current status and power in that relationship. Anticipatory emotions result from an actor's forecasting the effects of future interaction episodes for personal status and power. Consequent emotions register the actual outcomes of events for each person's status and power. Kemper connects these three classes of emotions in the ongoing process of social interaction that gives rise to them, asserting that consequent emotions "are the culmination of the chain that links the structural and anticipatory emotions to the actual results of interaction" (Kemper 1978, 49).

10. The structure of this presentation parallels Heise and Lewis (1988a), and is indebted to it.

11. While Thoits (1984) extends the constructionist position on the role of language in emotional experience, she disclaims any allegiance to a radical constructionist position. Instead, as discussed in Chapter 3 of this book, she subscribes to an "associational network theory" of emotions in which any of the four components of emotional experience (situational cues, physiological sensations, behavioral expression, and emotion labels) can evoke a full-blown emotional experience. While Thoits exempts the physiological component of emotion from social construction, Gordon (1981) proposes an "open" system of emotions in which the entire configuration of components, including physiological sensation, is socially constructed.

12. In Kemper's own words, if his interactional "approach . . . has a home, perhaps it is most nearly that of reinforcement theory, broadly conceived" (1978, viii). Yet, one has to be careful here. By his own account, he distances his theory from a behaviorism based exclusively upon the individual as the unit of analysis. Instead, as *relational* concepts, his concepts of power and status draw attention to rewards as voluntarily or involuntarily given in social relationships. Furthermore, Kemper asserts that his power–status model provides a conceptual framework that integrates cognitive theories, like symbolic interactionism, with social exchange and reinforcement theories.

Chapter 8

1. While labeling theorists traditionally have been concerned with the imputation of negative identities in the wake of deviant behavior (Becker 1963; Schur 1971; Scheff 1966), affect control theory also covers the positive reidentifications that result from positive

events. (For criticisms of the labeling perspective, see Gibbs 1966; Gove 1970; Killiam 1981). Hawkins and Tiedeman (1975) provide a systematic and comprehensive discussion of the labeling perspective.

2. Other important contributions to the early development of attribution theory include Jones and Davis's (1965) "correspondent inferences" model, which focuses primarily on the internal dispositions of actors, and Kelley's (1967) "covariation" or "cube" model, which incorporates attributions from both internal and external sources, providing a comprehensive theory of how people apply Heider's principle of invariance. Good textbook discussions of attribution theory accessible to the general sociological reader can be found in Albrecht, Thomas, and Chadwick (1980); Perlman and Cozby (1983); and Smith (1987).

3. In this regard, Stryker and Gottlieb make it clear that they are not comparing attribution theory with the version of symbolic interactionism identified with Blumer (1969). Blumer actively rejected the hypothetical-deductive method, an epistemological position that is quite gratuitous to Mead's thought (McPhail and Rexroat 1979). Instead, Stryker and Gottlieb have in mind the version of symbolic interactionism identified with Kuhn (1964b), Rose (1962), and Stryker (1968) himself. This school of interactionism recognizes no internal contradiction between Meadian social psychology and the scientific method as conventionally understood.

4. Stryker and Gottlieb identify the following differences between the two theories, deriving from their different conceptualization of cognitive meaning: (1) While both interactionism and attribution theory suppose that people are problem-solving, "quiescence-seeking" organisms, the two theories disagree about the nature of the *problem* stimulating symbolic-cognitive activity. For attribution theory, the problem is a logical one deriving from such purported cognitive-based individual needs as consistency and parsimony. For symbolic interactionism, the problem is defined as a social prerequisite—the achievement of a sufficient level of consensus on social meaning to initiate and sustain social interaction. (2) Attribution theory has been preoccupied with assessing the accuracy of a person's perceptions against objectively defined models. Specifically, the theory has concerned itself with the cognitive and motivational biases revealed by "misattribution studies," and with their impact on person and self-perception. In contrast, symbolic interactionism has concerned itself with the extent to which meaning is shared by participants in social interaction. Specifically, the theory has focused on the negotiation of mutually compatible definitions of *self* and *other* in social interaction, which is accomplished when sufficient consensus emerges among interactants on their respective identities and social roles. (3) Finally, symbolic interactionists acknowledge the constraints, largely ignored by attribution theorists, that the sociocultural context imposes upon the meaning of self and other in social interaction. Of particular importance are the identities and roles made available by institutionalized settings and the extent to which these are open to negotiation in social interaction.

5. The impression formation equations reveal other subtle effects for the object-person in social events. For example, object-person evaluation has a small negative impact on the outcome impression of object-activity. A number of two-way and three-way interaction terms between the fundamental sentiments for behavior and object-identities—too complex to discuss here—also affect the impressions of object-person. While the dynamics of the impression formation process discussed here are based on the Canadian equations,

these are structurally similar to the U.S. equations. (See Smith-Lovin [1988a] for a detailed analysis of the U.S. equations.)

6. As a derivative of the event construction model described in Chapter 6, the established model minimizes the deflection of the transient feelings produced by an actor's conduct from the fundamental sentiments for the actor's conduct and the object-person. In order to accommodate an actor's expressed emotion, the expanded model re-specifies deflection as the discrepancy between the transient feelings produced by an actor's conduct from optimal outcome transients rather than fundamental sentiments, where optimal outcome transients are defined by the *observed* emotion and the actor's *unknown* identity. *(Mutatis mutandis,* the solution for object-person reidentifications parallels that for actor reidentifications.)

Heise (1989a) identifies two properties of the expanded reidentification model, implied by the mathematical solution: reidentification outcomes tend to be more extreme when emotions are considered; and when interactants express negative emotions. A more systematic analysis of the model (Heise 1992) identifies situations that lead to ill-defined results owing to the singularity or near–singularity of a matrix in the solution for optimal reidentification profiles. For example, the configurations of behavior, object-person, and actor's displayed emotion that render actor reidentifications problematic include the following: (1) when the actor is directing lively behavior (e.g., thrill, seize) to a quiet object-person (e.g., old maid, scrooge) *or* quiet behavior (e.g., console, beg) to a lively object-person (e.g., coed, mugger); and (2) when the actor's emotion is hedonically bad (e.g., afraid, angry) *and* the actor's conduct involves a bad, strong, lively act (e.g., seize, terrorize) directed toward a strong, quiet object-person (e.g., grandfather, disciplinarian, professor).

Chapter 9

1. I do not mean to imply that Kemper's criticism prompted cognitive psychologists to attend to the objective dimensions of the situation, only that his groundbreaking work predated their efforts.

2. Kelley (1984) identifies four abstract features common to situational theories of emotions in psychological social psychology: (1) the positive or negative outcome of events in terms of a person's affective experience (pleasant–unpleasant, desired-unwanted); (2) the assumption that people respond to general classes of situations, defined by the intersection of event outcomes (positive or negative) and agency (self or other); (3) the assumption that each general class of situations instigates a specific, qualitatively unique affective experience; and (4) the assumption that each affective experience generates a general orientation for subsequent behavior.

3. Kelley does not deny the dysfunctional consequences of affect, acknowledging that "adaptive responses succeed only on the average" (1984, 96).

4. While not denying that people often invoke social norms to explain and justify the behavior of self and other, affect control theory approaches norms at the more elementary level of affective meaning (see Chapter 5). Collins goes one step further, suggesting that

"the terminology of norms ought to be dropped from sociological theory" (1981, 991n). Perhaps a bit more extreme than affect control theory, Collins does not attribute any motivational significance to norms:

> People follow routines because they feel natural or appropriate ... without consciously invoking any general formulations of rules ... and invoke conscious social concepts at particular times [only] because the emotional dynamics of their lives motivates them to do so (1981, 997).

Hence, property and authority are upheld, Collins argues, not by conscious reference to formal rules and anticipated sanctions, but by the routine behavior established by past interactional ritual chains.

5. By implication, according to Collins, "the active agents in any sociological explanation must be microsociological" (1981, 989). Macrosociological concepts are only summaries and abstractions of the repetitive microbehaviors of concrete individuals, "and if the 'structures' change, it is because the individuals who enact them change their microbehaviors."

6. According to Wallace, "enculturism" emphasizes the socially influenced aspects of an individual's mind—"learned norms and values, language and other gestures, tastes, beliefs, hopes, fears, self, and conscience" (1983, 194).

7. These include two types of social psychological variables delineated by Wallace (1983), "psychical contagionism" and "cultural structuralism." Psychical contagionism emphasizes the influence of the "existentially given" (innate) aspects of the minds of other people in an individual's environment "such as fear and dread, love and hope, excitement, attention, awe" (1983, 195). These covert phenomena influence an individual's behavior, of course, only when they become visibly expressed by others (1983, 273–274). Cultural structuralism emphasizes the "socially influenced aspects of the psychical behavior of people" in an interactant's environment, especially their role expectations, but also other aspects of mind included under enculturism, such as language and emotions (1983, 195).

It is obvious that affect control theory employs social psychological variables like those included under "cultural structuralism," albeit it deals with "role expectations" or "norms" at a more elementary level than other cultural structural theories like symbolic interactionism. However, affect control theory's invocation of variables of the "psychical contagionism" type is not as obvious. Because this category subsumes "emotional contagionism" (Wallace 1983, 273), it includes the "emotional energy" that is the dynamic basis of Collins' theory of interactional rituals. And, as discussed in the preceding section, the emotional energy of interactional rituals can be viewed as built up from the affective deflection produced by interpersonal events.

8. Wallace classifies the socially influenced physical behavior of people in an individual's environment, especially role–performances, as "social structural," rather than social psychological, variables. While he considers only the covert behavior of other people as social psychological, I would consider their overt behavior in microsituational events as constituting social psychological variables as well.

9. A related problem concerns which person's definition of the situation prevails and becomes actualized in subsequent events. Smith-Lovin (1988c, 184) suggests that people with high–potency identities will generally command the institutional resources and legal authority to impose their definitions of the situation on others; and "while parallel processing may produce different emotions in high- and low-power actors, the behavioral display will conform to the high-power version of events." However, recalling my discussion of Collins earlier in this chapter, because the power and status dimensions of social structure correspond to the potency and evaluation dimensions of identity-meaning, this explanation does not invoke a cognitive theory external to affect control theory.

10. Besides merging affect control theory and production systems theory, Heise and Durig's work represents a microsociological translation of macrosociological processes, dispelling the "micro-macro mystery" embodied in constructs like "corporate actor." This brings us back to my earlier discussion of methodological individualism in the explanatory sense. Combined with a production systems approach, affect control theory provides a powerful inductive approach to the analysis of macroactions in social organizations.

REFERENCES

Abelson, R.P. 1983. "Whatever Became of Consistency Theory?" *Personality and Social Psychology Bulletin* 9:37–54.

Albrecht, Stan L., Darwin L. Thomas, and Bruce A. Chadwick. 1980. *Social Psychology.* Englewood Cliffs, NJ:Prentice-Hall.

Alexander, C. Norman, Jr., and Mary Glenn Wiley. 1981. "Situated Activity and Identity Formation." In *Social Psychology: Sociological Perspectives*, edited by Morris Rosenberg and Ralph H. Turner, 269–289. New York: Basic.

Allport, Gordon W. 1968. "The Historical Background of Modern Social Psychology." In *The Handbook of Social Psychology*, edited by Gardner Lindzey and Elliot Aronson, 1–80. Reading, MA: Addison-Wesley.

Almeder, Robert. 1980. *The Philosophy of Charles S. Peirce: A Critical Introduction.* Totowa, NJ: Rowman and Littlefield.

Arnold, Magda B. 1960. *Emotion and Personality.* New York: Columbia University Press.

Averett, Christine. 1981. *Attribution of Interpersonal Qualities: An Affect Control Theory Approach.* Unpublished doctoral dissertation, Department of Sociology, University of North Carolina, Chapel Hill, NC.

Averett, Christine, and David R. Heise. 1988. "Modified Social Identifies: Amalgamations, Attributions, and Emotions." In *Analyzing Social Interaction: Advances in Affect Control Theory*, edited by Lynn Smith-Lovin and David R. Heise, 103–132. New York: Gordon and Breach. (Reprint from a special issue of the *Journal of Mathematical Sociology* 13.)

Averill, James R. 1980. "A Constructionist View of Emotion." In *Emotion: Theory, Research, and Experience*, edited by R. Plutchik and H. Kellerman, 305–339. New York: Academic Press.

Baldwin, John D. 1985. "Social Behaviorism on Emotions: Mead and Modern Behaviorism Compared." *Symbolic Interaction* 8: 263–289.

Bandura, Albert. 1977. *Social Learning Theory.* Englewood Cliffs, NJ: Prentice-Hall.

———. 1982. "The Self and Mechanisms of Agency." In *Psychological Perspectives on the Self*, Vol.1., edited by J. Suls, 3–39. Hillsdale, NJ: Lawrence Erlbaum Associates.

Barchas, Patricia. 1976. "Physiological Sociology: Interface of Sociological and Biological Processes." In *Annual Review of Sociology*, Vol. 2, 229–333. Palo Alto, CA: Annual Reviews.

Bateson, Gregory. 1972. *Steps to an Ecology of Mind.* New York: Ballantine.

Becker, Howard. 1963. *Outsiders.* New York: Free Press.

Berger, Joseph, M.H. Fisek, R.Z. Norman, and M. Zelditch, Jr. 1977. *Status Characteristics and Social Interaction: An Expectations-States Approach.* New York: Elsevier.

Biddle, Bruce J., and Edwin J. Thomas, eds. 1966. *Role Theory: Concepts and Research.* New York: Wiley.

Bindra, D. 1969. "The Interrelated Mechanisms of Reinforcement and Motivation, and the Nature of their Influence on Response." In *Nebraska Symposium on Motivation, 1969,* vol. 17, edited by W.J. Arnold and D. Levine, 1–33. Lincoln, NE: University of Nebraska Press.

Blumer, Herbert. 1969. *Symbolic Interactionism.* Englewood Cliffs, NJ: Prentice-Hall.

Bohannan, Paul. 1963. *Social Anthropology.* New York: Holt, Rinehart and Winston.

Bolles, R.C. 1967. *Theory of Motivation.* New York: Harper and Row.

Britt, Lory, and David R. Heise. 1993. "Impressions of Self-Directed Action." *Social Psychology Quarterly* 55:335–350.

Brodbeck, May. 1968. "Methodological Individualisms: Definition and Reduction." In *Readings in the Philosophy of the Social Sciences,* edited by May Brodbeck, 280–303. London: Macmillan.

Buckley, Walter. 1967. *Sociology and Modern Systems Theory.* Englewood Cliffs, NJ: Prentice-Hall.

Buckley, Walter, ed. 1968. *Modern Systems Research for the Behavioral Scientist: A Sourcebook.* Chicago: Aldine.

Burgess, R.L., and D. Bushell. 1969. *Behavioral Sociology.* New York: Columbia University Press.

Burke, Kenneth. 1945. *A Grammar of Motives.* New York: Prentice–Hall.

Burke, Peter. 1980. "The Self: Measurement Requirements from an Interactionist Perspective." *Social Psychology Quarterly* 43:18–30.

Burke, Peter J., and Donald C. Reitzes. 1981. "The Link Between Identity and Role Performance." *Social Psychology Quarterly* 44:83–92.

Burke, Peter J., and Donald C. Reitzes. 1991. "An Identity Theory Approach to Commitment." *Social Psychology Quarterly* 54:239–251.

Burke, Peter, and Judy Tully. 1977. "The Measurement of Role/Identity." *Social Forces* 55:881–897.

Callero, Peter L. 1988. "Measuring the Self." Paper presented at the American Sociological Association Meetings, Atlanta, Georgia.

Cancian, Francesca M. 1975. *What are Norms? A Study of Beliefs and Action in a Maya Community.* Cambridge, UK: Cambridge University Press.

Candland, D.K. et al. 1977. "The Emotion Construct in Psychology." In *Emotion,* edited by D.K. Candland. Monterey, CA: Brooks-Cole.

Cannon, Walter. 1929. *Bodily Changes in Pain, Hunger, Fear, and Rage.* 2d ed. New York: Ronald.

Clark, Candace. 1990. "Emotions and Micropolitics in Everyday Life: Some Patterns and Paradoxes of 'Place.'" In *Research Agendas in the Sociology of Emotions,* edited by Theodore D. Kemper, 305–333. Albany, NY: State University of New York Press.

Clore, Gerald L., Andrew Ortony, and Mark A. Foss. 1987. "The Psychological Foundations of the Affective Lexicon." *Journal of Personality and Social Psychology* 53:751–766.

Cofer, Charles N. 1972. *Motivation and Emotion.* Glenview, IL: Scott, Foresman.

Cofer, Charles N., and M.H. Appley. 1964. *Motivation: Theory and Research.* New York: Wiley.

Collins, Randall. 1975. *Conflict Sociology: Toward an Explanatory Science.* New York: Academic Press.

———. 1981. "On the Microfoundations of Macrosociology." *American Journal of Sociology* 86: 984–1014.

———. 1985. *Three Sociological Traditions.* New York: Oxford.

———. 1986. "Is 1980s Sociology in the Doldrums?" *American Journal of Sociology* 91:1336–1355.

———. 1989. "Toward a Neo-Meadian Sociology of Mind." *Symbolic Interaction* 12:1–32.

———. 1990. "Stratification, Emotional Energy, and the Transient Emotions." In *Research Agendas in the Sociology of Emotions,* edited by Theodore D. Kemper, 27–57. Albany, NY: State University of New York Press.

Cooley, Charles H. 1902/1956. *Social Organization and Human Nature and the Social Order.* New York: Free Press.

Corsaro, William, and David R. Heise. 1990. "Event Structure Models from Ethnographic Data." In *Sociological Methodology: 1990,* edited by C. Clogg, 1–57. Cambridge, MA: Basil Blackwell.

Dahrendorf, Ralf. 1958. "Out of Utopia: Toward a Reorientation of Sociological Analysis." *American Journal of Sociology* 64:115–127.

Darwin, Charles. 1872/1955. *The Expression of the Emotions in Man and Animals.* New York: Philisophical Library.

Denzin, Norman K. 1972. "The Genesis of Self in Early Childhood." *The Sociological Quarterly* 13:291–314.

———. 1980. "A Phenomenology of Emotion and Deviance." *Zeitschrift Fur Soziologie* 9:251–261.

———. 1984. *On Understanding Emotion.* San Francisco: Jossey-Bass.

———. 1985. "Emotion as Lived Experience." *Symbolic Interaction* 8:223–240.

———. 1987. "On Semiotics and Symbolic Interactionism." *Symbolic Interaction* 10:1–19.

de Rivera, Joseph. 1984. "The Structure of Emotional Relationships." In *Review of Personality and Social Psychology,* vol. 5, edited by Philip Shaver, 116–145. Beverley Hills, CA: Sage.

Dewey, John. 1894. "The Theory of Emotion: Emotional Attitudes." *Psychological Review* 1:553–569.

———. 1895. "The Theory of Emotion II. The Significance of Emotions." *Psychological Review* 2:13–32.

———. 1896. "The Reflex Arc Concept in Psychology." *Psychological Review* 3:357–370.

Diederich, G.W., S.J. Messick, and L.R. Tucker. 1957. "A General Least Squares Solution for Successive Intervals." *Psychometrika* 22:159–173.

Duffy, Elizabeth. 1934. "Emotion: An Example of the Need for Reorientation in Psychology." *Psychological Review* 41: 184–198.

———. 1941. "The Conceptual Categories of Psychology: A Suggestion for Revision." *Psychological Review* 48:177–203.

———. 1948. "Leeper's 'Motivational Theory of Emotion.'" *Psychological Review* 55:324–328.

Durkheim, Emile. 1912/1954. *The Elementary Forms of the Religious Life.* New York: Free Press.

Ekman, Paul, and Wallace V. Friesen. 1978. *Manual for the Facial Coding System.* Palo Alto, CA: Consulting Psychologists Press.

Ekman, Paul, Wallace V. Friesen, and Phoebe Ellsworth. 1982. "What are the Similarities and Differences in Facial Behavior Across Cultures?" In *Emotion in the Human Face.* 2d ed., edited by Paul Ekman, 128–143. Cambridge, UK: Cambridge University Press.

Elliott, Gregory C. 1986. "Self-Esteem and Self-Consistency: A Theoretical and Empirical Link Between Two Primary Motivations." *Social Psychology Quarterly* 49:207–218.

Epstein, Seymour. 1984. "Controversial Issues in Emotion Theory." In *Review of Personality and Social Psychology,* vol. 5, edited by Philip Shaver, 64–88. Beverly Hills, CA: Sage.

Etzioni, Amitai. 1988. "Normative-Affective Factors: Towards a New Decision-Making Model." *Journal of Economic Psychology* 9:125–150.

Fararo, Thomas J., and J. Skvoretz. 1984. "Institutions as Production Systems." *Journal of Mathematical Sociology* 10:117–182.

Festinger, Leon. 1957. *A Theory of Cognitive Dissonance.* Evanston, IL: Row, Peterson.

———. 1958. "The Motivating Effect of Cognitive Dissonance." In *Assessment of Human Motives,* edited by G. Lindzey, 65–86. New York: Holt, Rinehart and Winston.

Fishbein, Martin, and Icek Ajzen. 1975. *Belief, Attitude, Intention and Behavior: An Introduction to Theory and Research.* Reading, MA: Addison-Wesley.

Foote, Nelson N. 1951. "Identification as the Basis for a Theory of Motivation." *American Sociological Review* 16:14–21.

Franks, David D. 1985. "Introduction to the Special Issue on the Sociology of Emotions." *Symbolic Interaction* 8:161–170.

———. 1989. "Alternatives to Collins' Use of Emotion in the Theory of Ritualistic Chains." *Symbolic Interaction* 12:97–101.

Friedricks, Robert. 1970. *A Sociology of Sociology.* New York: Free Press.

———. 1974. "The Potential Impact of B.F. Skinner Upon American Sociology." *American Sociologist* 9:3–8.

Gerth, Hans, and C. Wright Mills. 1964. *Character and Social Structure: The Psychology of Social Institutions.* New York: Harcourt, Brace and World.

Gibbs, Jack. 1966. "Conceptions of Deviant Behavior: The Old and the New." *Pacific Sociological Review* 9:9–14.

Goffman, Erving. 1959. *The Presentation of Self in Everyday Life.* Garden City, NY: Doubleday Anchor.

———. 1961a. *Encounters*. Indianapolis: Bobbs–Merrill.

———. 1961b. *Asylums: Essays on the Social Situation of Mental Patients and Other Inmates.* Garden City, NY: Doubleday.

Goode, W.J. 1960. "A Theory of Role Strain." *American Sociological Review* 25:483–496.

Goodenough, Ward H. 1969. "Rethinking 'Status' and 'Role': Toward a General Model of the Cultural Organization of Social Relationships." In *Cognitive Anthropology,* edited by Stephen A. Tyler, 311–330. New York: Holt, Rinehart, and Winston.

Gordon, Steven L. 1981. "The Sociology of Sentiments and Emotions." In *Social Psychology: Sociological Perspectives,* edited by M. Rosenberg and R.H. Turner, 562–592. New York: Basic.

———. 1990. "Social Structural Effects on Emotions." In *Research Agendas in the Sociology of Emotions,* edited by Theodore D. Kemper, 145–179. Albany, NY: State University of New York Press.

Gove, Walter. 1970. "Societal Reaction as an Explanation of Mental Illness: An Evaluation." *American Sociological Review* 35:873–884.

Gregory, Stanford W. 1985. "Auto Traffic as Verdant Grammar." *Social Psychological Quarterly* 48:337–348.

Gross, Neal, Ward S. Mason, and A. W. McEachern. 1958. *Explorations in Role Analysis: Studies of the School Superintendency Role.* New York: Wiley.

Hall, E.T. 1966. *The Hidden Dimension.* Garden City, NY: Anchor.

Handel, W. 1979. "Normative Expectations and the Emergence of Meaning as Solutions to Problems: Convergence of Structural and Interactionist Views." *American Journal of Sociology* 84:855–881.

Harré, Rom, ed. 1986. *The Social Construction of Emotion.* New York: Basil Blackwell.

———. 1986. "An Outline of the Social Constructionist Viewpoint." In *The Social Construction of Emotions,* edited by Rom Harré, 2–14. New York: Basil Blackwell.

Hawkins, Richard, and Gary Tiedeman. 1975. *The Creation of Deviance: Interpersonal and Organizational Determinants.* Columbus, OH: Charles E. Merrill.

Heider, Fritz. 1958. *The Psychology of Interpersonal Relations.* New York: Wiley.

Heise, David R. 1969. "Affective Dynamics in Simple Sentences." *Journal of Personality and Social Psychology* 11:204–213.

———. 1970. "Potency Dynamics in Simple Sentences." *Journal of Personality and Social Psychology* 16:48–54.

———. 1977. "Social Action as the Control of Affect." *Behavioral Science* 22:163–177.

———. 1978. *Computer-Assisted Analysis of Social Action: Use of Program INTERACT and Survey UNC75.* Chapel Hill, NC: Institute for Research in Social Science, University of North Carolina.

———. 1979. *Understanding Events: Affect and the Construction of Social Action.* New York: Cambridge University Press.

———. 1985. "Affect Control Theory: Respecification, Estimation, and Tests of the Formal Model." *Journal of Mathematical Sociology* 1:191–222.

———. 1988. "Affect Control Theory: Concepts and Model." In *Analyzing Social Interaction: Advances in Affect Control Theory,* edited by Lynn Smith-Lovin and David R. Heise, 1–33. New York: Gordon and Breach. (Reprint of a special issue of the *Journal of Mathematical Sociology,* vol.13.)

————. 1989a. "Effects of Emotion Displays on Social Identification." *Social Psychology Quarterly* 52:10–21.

————. 1989b. "Modeling Event Structures." *Journal of Mathematical Sociology* 13:138–168.

————. 1990. "Careers, Career Trajectories, and the Self." In *Self-Directedness: Cause and Effects Throughout the Life Course*, edited by J. Rodin, C. Schooler, and K.W. Schaie, 59–84. New York: Lawrence Erlbaum.

————. 1991. *INTERACT 2: A Computer Program for Studying Cultural Meanings and Social Interactions*. Department of Sociology, Indiana University, Bloomington.

————. 1992. "Affect Control Theory's Mathematical Model, With a List of Testable Hypotheses: A Working Paper for ACT Researchers." Bloomington, IN: Department of Sociology, Indiana University.

Heise, David R., and Alex Durig. Forthcoming. "Macroaction."

Heise, David R., and Elsa Lewis. 1988a. *INTERACT and ATTITUDE Program and Documentation*. Durham, NC: National Collegiate Software of Duke University Press.

————. 1988b. *ETHNO Program and Documentation*. Durham, NC: National Collegiate Software of Duke University Press.

Heise, David R., and Neil J. MacKinnon. 1988. "Affective Bases of Likelihood Judgments." In *Analyzing Social Interaction: Advances in Affect Control Theory*, edited by Lynn Smith-Lovin and David R. Heise, 133–151. New York: Gordon and Breach. (Reprint from a special issue of the *Journal of Mathematical Sociology* 13.)

Heise, David R., and John O'Brien. Forthcoming. "Emotion Expression in Groups." In *Handbook of Emotions*, edited by Michael Lewis. New York: Guilford.

Heise, David R., and Lisa Thomas. 1989. "Predicting Impressions Created by Combinations of Emotion and Social Identity." *Social Psychology Quarterly* 52:141–148.

Heiss, Jerold. 1981. "Social Roles." In *Social Psychology: Sociological Perspectives*, edited by Morris Rosenberg and Ralph H. Turner, 94–129. New York: Basic.

Hewitt, John P. 1990. *Self and Society: A Symbolic Interactionist Social Psychology*. 4th ed. Boston: Allyn and Bacon.

Hochschild, Arlie R. 1975. "The Sociology of Feeling and Emotion: Selected Possibilities." In *Another Voice*, edited by Maria Millman and Rosabeth Moss Kanter, 280–307. New York: Anchor.

————. 1979. "Emotion Work, Feeling Rules, and Social Structure." *American Journal of Sociology* 85:551–575.

————. 1983. *The Managed Heart: Commercialization of Human Feeling*. Los Angeles: University of California Press.

Homans, George C. 1958. "Social Behavior as Exchange." *American Journal of Sociology* 63:597–606.

———. 1961. *Social Behavior: Its Elementary Forms*. New York: Harcourt Brace and World.

———. 1964. "Bringing Men Back In." *American Sociological Review* 29:809–818.

House, James S. 1977. "The Three Faces of Social Psychology." *Sociometry* 40:161–177.

Immershein, Allen W. 1976. "The Epistemological Bases of Social Order: Toward Ethnoparadigm Analysis." In *Sociological Methodology: 1977*, 1–51. San Francisco: Jossey–Bass.

Jackson, Jay M. 1966. "Structural Characteristics of Norms." In *Role Theory: Concepts and Research*, edited by Bruce J. Biddle and Edwin J. Thomas, 113–126. New York: Wiley.

———. 1988. *Social Psychology, Past and Present: An Integrative Orientation*. Hillsdale, NJ: Lawrence Erlbaum.

James, William. 1884/1922/1967. "What is an Emotion." In *The Emotions*, Carl Georg Lange and William James, 11–30. New York: Hafner.

———. 1890. *The Principles of Psychology*. New York: Holt.

Jones, E.E., and E. Davis. 1965. "From Acts to Dispositions: The Attribution Process in Personal Perception." In *Advances in Experimental Social Psychology*, vol. 2, edited by L. Berkowitz. New York: Academic Press.

Jones, E.E., and V.A. Harris. 1967. "The Attribution of Attitudes." *Journal of Experimental Social Psychology* 3:1–24.

Jones, E.E., and R.E. Nisbett. 1971. *The Actor and the Observer: Divergent Perceptions of the Causes of Behavior*. Morristown, NJ: General Learning Press.

Kaplan, Abraham. 1964. *The Conduct of Inquiry: Methodology for Behavioral Science*. San Francisco: Chandler.

Katz, Jerold J. 1972. *Semantic Theory*. New York: Harper and Row.

Keating, Leo J. 1985. *The Effect of Frequency Modifiers on Impression Formation Processes and the Perceived Likelihood of Events*. Unpublished master's thesis, Department of Sociology and Anthropology, University of Guelph, Canada.

Keesing, Roger M. 1976. *Cultural Anthropology: A Contemporary Perspective*. New York: Holt, Rinehart and Winston.

Kelley, Harold H. 1967. "Attribution Theory in Social Psychology." In *Nebraska Symposium on Motivation, 1967*, vol. 15, edited by D. Levine, 192–240. Lincoln: University of Nebraska Press.

——. 1984. "Affect in Interpersonal Relations." In *Review of Personality and Social Psychology*, vol. 5, edited by Philip Shaver, 89–115. Beverly Hills, CA: Sage.

Kemper, Theodore D. 1978. *A Social Interactional Theory of Emotions*. New York: Wiley.

——. 1981. "Social Constructionist and Positivist Approaches to the Sociology of Emotions." *American Journal of Sociology* 87:336–362.

——. 1987. "How Many Emotions are There? Wedding the Social and Autonomic Components." *American Journal of Sociology* 93:263–289.

Kemper, Theodore D., and Randall Collins. 1990. "Dimensions of Microinteraction." *American Journal of Sociology* 96: 32–68.

Killiam, Lewis. 1981. "The Sociologists Look at the Cuckoo's Nest: The Misuse of Ideal Types." *The American Sociologist* 16:230–239.

Kolb, William L. 1944/1972. "A Critical Evaluation of Mead's 'I' and 'me' Concepts." In *Symbolic Interactionism: A Reader in Social Psychology*. 2d ed., edited by Jerome G. Manis and Bernard N. Meltzer, 251–261. Boston: Allyn and Bacon.

Kuhn, Manford. 1964a/1972. "The Reference Group Reconsidered." In *Symbolic Interactionism: A Reader in Social Psychology*. 2d ed., edited by Jerome G. Manis and Bernard N. Meltzer, 171–184. Boston: Allyn and Bacon.

——. 1964b/1972. "Major Trends in Symbolic Interaction Theory in the Past Twenty-Five Years." In *Symbolic Interactionism: A Reader in Social Psychology*. 2d ed., edited by Jerome G. Manis and Bernard N. Meltzer, 57–76. Boston: Allyn and Bacon.

Lange, Carl G. 1885/1922/1967. "The Emotions." In *The Emotions*, Carl G. Lange and William James, 33–90. New York: Hafner.

Lange, Carl G., and William James. 1922/1967. *The Emotions*. New York: Hafner.

Lazarus, R.S. 1982. "Thoughts on the Relations Between Emotion and Cognition." *American Psychologist* 37:1019–1024.

——. 1984. "On the Primacy of Cognition." *American Psychologist* 39:124–9.

Leeper, R.W. 1948. "A Motivational Theory of Emotion to Replace 'Emotion as Disorganized Response'." *Psychological Review* 55:5–21.

Leventhal, H. 1980. "Towards a Comprehensive Theory of Emotion." In *Advances in Experimental Social Psychology*, vol. 13, edited by L. Berkowitz, 139–207. New York: Academic Press.

Lewin, Kurt. 1951. *Field Theory in Social Science: Selected Theoretical Papers*, edited by D. Cartwright. New York: Harper and Row.

Lewis, M., and L. Rosenblum. 1978. "Introduction: Issues in Affect Development." In *The Development of Affect*, edited by M. Lewis and L. Rosenblum, 1–10. New York: Plenum.

Lipset, Seymour M. 1986. "Historical Traditions and National Characteristics: A Comparative Analysis of Canada and the United States." *Canadian Journal of Sociology* 11:113–155.

Lockwood, David. 1956. "Some Remarks on 'The Social System'." *British Journal of Sociology* 7:134–146.

Lutz, Catherine, and Geoffrey M. White. 1986. "The Anthropology of Emotions." In *Annual Review of Anthropology*, vol. 15, 405–436. Palo Alto, CA: Annual Reviews.

MacKinnon, Neil J. 1974. "Profile Analysis in the Search for Structure Underlying Role Expectations: A Multivariate Technique for Role Analysis." *Sociological Methods and Research* 3:62–81.

———. 1985. *Affective Dynamics and Role Analysis.* Final Report, Social Sciences and Humanities Research Council of Canada Project 410-81-0089. Guelph, Ontario: Department of Sociology and Anthropology, University of Guelph.

———. 1988. *The Attribution of Traits, Status Characteristics and Emotions in Social Interaction.* Final Report, Social Sciences and Humanities Research Council of Canada Project 410-86-0794. Guelph, Ontario: Department of Sociology and Anthropology, University of Guelph.

MacKinnon, Neil J., and David R. Heise. 1993. "Affect Control Theory: Delineation and History." In *Theoretical Research Programs: Studies in the Growth of Theory*, edited by Joseph Berger and Morris Zelditch, Jr., 64–103. Stanford, CA: Stanford University Press.

MacKinnon, Neil J., and Leo Keating. 1989. "The Structure of Emotions: Canada-United States Comparisons." *Social Psychology Quarterly* 52:70–83.

MacKinnon, Neil J., and Gene F. Summers. 1976. "Homogeneity and Role Consensus: A Multivariate Exploration in Role Analysis." *Canadian Journal of Sociology* 4:439–462.

Maines, David R. 1977. "Social Organization and Social Structure in Symbolic Interactionist Thought." In *Annual Review of Sociology*, vol. 3, 235–259. Palo Alto, CA: Annual Reviews.

Mandler. G. 1984. *Mind and Body: Psychology of Emotion and Stress.* New York: Norton.

Markus, Hazel. 1977. "Self-Schemata and Processing Information about the Self." *Journal of Personality and Social Psychology* 35:63–78.

Maslow, A.H. 1954. *Motivation and Personality.* New York: Harper and Row.

Mazur Allan. 1985. "A Biosocial Model of Status in Face-to-Face Primate Groups." *Social Forces* 64:377–402.

McCall, George J., and Jerry L. Simmons. 1966. *Identities and Interactions*. New York: Free Press.

————. 1978. *Identities and Interaction.* 2d ed. New York: Free Press.

McClelland, D.C., J. Atkinson, R.A. Clark, and E.L. Lowell. 1953. *The Achievement Motive.* New York: Appleton–Century-Crofts.

McDougall, W. 1908. *An Introduction to Social Psychology.* London: Methuen.

McPhail, Clark. 1991. *The Myth of the Maddening Crowd.* New York: Aldine de Gruyter.

McPhail, Clark, and Cynthia Rexroat. 1979. "Mead vs. Blumer." *American Sociological Review* 44:449–467.

Mead, George Herbert. 1895. "A Theory of Emotions from the Physiological Viewpoint." *Psychological Review* 2:162–164.

————. 1903/1964. "The Definition of the Psychical." In *Selected Writings: George Herbert Mead,* edited by Andrew J. Reck, 25–59. Indianapolis: Bobbs-Merrill.

————. 1910a/1964. "What Social Objects Must Psychology Presuppose?" In *Selected Writings: George Herbert Mead,* edited by Andrew J. Reck. Indianapolis: Bobbs-Merrill.

————. 1910b/1964. "Social Consciousness and the Consciousness of Meaning." In *Selected Writings: George Herbert Mead,* edited by Andrew J. Reck, 123–133. Indianapolis: Bobbs-Merrill.

————. 1912/1964. "The Mechanism of Social Consciousness." In *Selected Writings: George Herbert Mead,* edited by Andrew J. Reck, 134–141. Indianapolis: Bobbs-Merrill.

————. 1922/1964. "A Behavioristic Account of the Significant Symbol." In *Selected Writings: George Herbert Mead,* edited by Andrew J. Reck, 240–247. Indianapolis: Bobbs-Merrill.

————. 1924–5/1964. "The Genesis of the Self and Social Control." In *Selected Writings: George Herbert Mead,* edited by Andrew J. Reck, 267–293. Indianapolis: Bobbs-Merrill.

————. 1934. *Mind, Self, and Society,* edited by Charles W. Morris. Chicago: University of Chicago Press.

Meltzer, Bernard N. 1972. "Mead's Social Psychology." In *Symbolic Interactionism: A Reader in Social Psychology.* 2d ed., edited by Jerome G. Manis and Bernard N. Meltzer, 4–22. Boston: Allyn and Bacon.

Meltzer, Bernard N., and John W. Petras. 1972. "The Chicago and Iowa Schools of Symbolic Interactionism." In *Symbolic Interactionism: A Reader in Social Psychology.* 2d. ed., edited by Jerome G. Manis and Bernard N. Meltzer, 43–57. Boston: Allyn and Bacon.

Merton, Robert K. 1957. *Social Theory and Social Structure.* Glencoe, IL: Free Press.

Meyer, M.F. 1933. "The Whale Among the Fishes—The Theory of Emotions." *Psychological Review* 40:292–300.

Mills, C. Wright. 1940. "Situated Actions and Vocabularies of Motives." *American Sociological Review* 5:904–913.

Monson, T.C., and M. Snyder. 1977. "Actors, Observers, and the Attribution Process: Toward a Reconceptualization." *Journal of Experimental Social Psychology* 13:89–111.

Mook, Douglas G. 1987. *Motivation: The Organization of Action.* New York: W.W. Norton.

Morgan, Rick, and David R. Heise. 1988. "Structure of Emotions." *Social Psychology Quarterly* 51:19–31.

Morris, Charles W. 1934. "Introduction: George H. Mead as Social Psychologist and Social Philosopher." In George H. Mead, *Mind, Self, and Society*, edited by Charles W. Morris, ix–xxxv. Chicago: University of Chicago Press.

Moscovici, S. 1972. "Society and Theory in Social Psychology." In *The Context of Social Psychology: A Critical Assessment*, edited by J. Israel and H. Tajfel, 17–68. London: Academic Press.

Nadel, Siegfried F. 1964. *The Theory of Social Structure.* New York: Free Press.

Newell, A., and H. Simon. 1972. *Human Problem Solving.* Englewood Cliffs, NJ: Prentice-Hall.

Nisbett, R.E., G.C. Caputo, P. Legant, and J. Maracek. 1973. "Behavior as Seen by the Actor and as Seen by the Observer." *Journal of Personality and Social Psychology* 27:154–164.

Nisbett, R.E., and L. Ross. 1980. *Human Inferences, Strategies and Shortcomings of Social Judgment.* Englewood Cliffs, NJ: Prentice-Hall.

O'Brien, John D. *The Problem of Order: Empirical Tests of a Holographic Minimum Unit Model Linking Culture, Cognition–Emotion and Social Action in Substance Abuse Decisions.* Unpublished doctoral dissertation. Department of Sociology, Kent State University. Kent, OH.

Ortony, Andrew, Gerald L. Clore, and Mark A. Foss. 1987. "The Referential Structure of the Affective Lexicon." *Cognitive Science* 11:341–364.

Osgood, Charles E. 1969. "On the Whys and Wherefores of E, P, and A." *Journal of Personality and Social Psychology* 12:194–199.

Osgood, Charles E., W.H. May, and M.S. Miron. 1975. *Cross–Cultural Universals of Affective Meaning.* Urbana, IL: University of Illinois Press.

Osgood, Charles E., George C. Suci, and Perry H. Tannenbaum. 1957. *The Measurement of Meaning.* Urbana, IL: University of Illinois Press.

Parsons, Talcott. 1937. *The Structure of Social Action*. Glencoe, IL: Free Press.

———. 1951. *The Social System*. Glencoe, IL: Free Press.

Parsons, Talcott, and Edward A. Shils. 1951. *Toward a General Theory of Action*. Cambridge, MA: Harvard University Press.

Peirce, Charles S. 1931, 1935, 1958. *The Collected Papers of Charles Sanders Peirce*, edited by C. Hartshorne and P. Weiss (vols. 1–6) and A.W. Burks (vols. 7–8). Cambridge, MA: Harvard University Press.

———. 1956. *The Philosophy of Peirce: Selected Writings*, edited by Justus Buchler. London: Routledge and Kegan Paul.

Perlman, Daniel, and P. Chris Cozby. 1983. *Social Psychology*. New York: Holt, Rinehart and Winston.

Pieters, Rik G.M., and W. Fred Van Raaij. 1987. "The Role of Affect in Economic Behavior." In *Handbook of Economic Psychology*, edited by W. Fred Van Raaij, Gery M. van Veldhoven, and Karl-Erik Warneryd. Amsterdam: North–Holland.

Powers, C. 1980. "Role-Imposition or Role-Improvisation: Some Theoretical Principles." Paper presented at the Pacific Sociological Association annual meetings.

Powers, William T. 1973. *Behavior: The Control of Perception*. Chicago: Aldine.

Raynolds, Peter A., Shiori Sakamoto, and Gennie H. Raynolds. 1988. "Consistent Projective Differential Responses by American and Japanese College Students." *Perceptual and Motor Skills* 66:395–402.

Reck, Andrew J. 1964. "Introduction." In *Selected Writings: George Herbert Mead*, edited by Andrew J. Reck, xiii–lxii. Indianapolis: Bobbs-Merrill.

Robinson, Dawn T., and Lynn Smith-Lovin. 1992. "Selective Interaction as a Strategy for Identity Maintenance: An Affect Control Model." *Social Psychology Quarterly* 55:12–28.

Rogers, Carl. 1951. *Client-Centered Therapy*. Boston: Houghton–Mifflin.

Rose, Arnold M. 1962. "A Systematic Summary of Symbolic Interaction Theory." In *Human Behavior and Social Process*, edited by Arnold Rose, 3–19. Boston: Houghton-Mifflin.

Roseman, Ira J. 1984. "Cognitive Determinants of Emotion: A Structural Theory." In *Review of Personality and Social Psychology*, vol. 5, edited by Philip Shaver, 11–36. Beverly Hills, CA: Sage.

Rosenberg, Morris. 1979. *Conceiving the Self*. New York: Basic Books.

Rosenberg, Morris, and Ralph H. Turner. 1981. "Preface." In *Social Psychology: Sociological Perspectives*, edited by Morris Rosenberg and Ralph H. Turner, xv–xxiv. New York: Basic.

Rosenberg, Seymour. 1977. "New Approaches to the Analysis of Personal Constructs in Person Perception." In *Nebraska Symposium on Motivation, 1976*, vol. 24, edited by A.W. Landfield, 179–242. Lincoln: University of Nebraska Press.

Ross, L. 1977. "The Intuitive Psychologist and His Shortcomings: Distortions in the Attribution Process." In *Advances in Experimental Social Psychology*, vol. 10, edited by L. Berkowitz, 174–221. New York: Academic Press.

Russell, J.A., and A. Mehrabian. 1977. "Evidence for a Three–Factor Theory of Emotions." *Journal of Research in Personality* 11:273–294.

Sacks, Harvey. 1972. "An Initial Investigation of the Usability of Conversational Data for Doing Sociology." In *Studies in Social Interaction*, edited by D. Sudnow, 31–74. New York: Free Press.

Schachter, Stanley. 1964. "The Interactions of Cognitive and Physiological Determinants of Emotional State." In *Advances in Experimental Social Psychology*, vol. 1, edited by L. Berkowitz, 44–90. New York: Academic Press.

Schachter, Stanley, and J. Singer. 1962. "Cognitive, Social, and Physiological Determinants of Emotional State." *Psychological Review* 69:379–399.

Schank, Roger C., and Robert P. Abelson. 1977. *Scripts, Plans, Goals and Understanding: An Inquiry into Human Knowledge Structures*. Hillsdale, NJ: Lawrence Erlbaum Associates.

Scheff, Thomas. 1966. *Being Mentally Ill: A Sociological Theory*. Chicago: Aldine.

———. 1979. *Catharsis in Healing, Ritual and Drama*. Berkeley: University of California Press.

———. 1983. "Toward Integration in the Social-Psychology of Emotions." In *Annual Review of Sociology*, vol. 9, 333–354. Palo Alto, CA: Annual Reviews.

———. 1984a. "The Taboo on Course Emotions." In *Review of Personality and Social Psychology*, vol. 5, edited by Philip Shaver, 146–169. Beverly Hills, CA: Sage.

———. 1984b. "A Theory of Catharsis." *Journal of Research in Personality* 18:238–264.

———. 1985a. "The Primacy of Affect." *American Psychologist* 40:849–850.

———. 1985b. "Universal Expressive Needs: A Critique and a Theory." *Symbolic Interaction* 8:241–262.

Scherer, Klaus R., and Paul Ekman. 1982. *Handbook of Methods in Nonverbal Behavior Research*. New York: Cambridge University Press.

Schur, Edwin M. 1971. *Labeling Deviant Behavior: Its Sociological Implications*. New York: Harper and Row.

Schwartz, Michael, and Sheldon Stryker. 1970. *Deviance, Selves, and Others*. Washington DC: American Sociological Association.

Shaver, Philip. 1984. "Editor's Introduction." In *Review of Personality and Social Psychology*, vol. 5, edited by Philip Shaver, 7–10. Beverly Hills, CA: Sage.

Shibutani, Tamotsu. 1961. *Social Psychology*. Englewood Cliffs, NJ: Prentice-Hall.

———. 1968. "A Cybernetic Approach to Motivation." In *Modern Systems Research for the Behavioral Scientist: A Sourcebook*, edited by Walter Buckley, 330–336. Chicago: Aldine.

Shott, Susan. 1979. "Emotion and Social Life: A Symbolic Interactionist Perspective." *American Journal of Sociology* 84:1317–1334.

Smith, Herman W. 1987. *Introduction to Social Psychology*. Englewood Cliffs, NJ:Prentice-Hall.

Smith-Lovin, Lynn. 1988a. "Impression From Events." In *Analyzing Social Interaction: Advances in Affect Control Theory*, edited by Lynn Smith-Lovin and David R. Heise, 35–70. New York: Gordon and Breach. (Reprint from a special issue of the *Journal of Mathematical Sociology* 13.)

———. 1988b. "The Affective Control of Events Within Settings." In *Analyzing Social Interaction: Advances in Affect Control Theory*, edited by Lynn Smith-Lovin and David R. Heise, 71–101. New York: Gordon and Breach. (Reprint from a special issue of the *Journal of Mathematical Sociology* 13.)

———. 1988c. "Affect Control Theory: An Assessment." In *Analyzing Social Interaction: Advances in Affect Control Theory*, edited by Lynn Smith-Lovin and David R. Heise, 171–192. New York: Gordon and Breach. (Reprint from a special issue of the *Journal of Mathematical Sociology* 13.)

———. 1990. "Emotion as the Confirmation and Disconfirmation of Identity: An Affect Control Model." In *Research Agendas in the Sociology of Emotions*, edited by Theodore D. Kemper, 238–270. Albany, NY: State University of New York Press.

Smith-Lovin, Lynn, and David R. Heise, eds. 1988. *Analyzing Social Interaction: Advances in Affect Control Theory*. New York: Gordon and Breach. (Reprint of a special issue of the *Journal of Mathematical Sociology* 13.)

Snider, James G., and Charles E. Osgood, eds. 1969. *Semantic Differential Technique: A Sourcebook*. Chicago: Aldine.

Solomon, Robert C. 1984. "Getting Angry: The Jamesian Theory of Emotion in Anthropology." In *Culture Theory: Essays on Mind, Self and Emotion*, edited by R. Schweder and R.A. Levine, 238–254. Cambridge, MA: Cambridge University Press.

Sowa, J.F. 1984. *Conceptual Structures: Information Processing in Mind and Machine*. Reading, MA: Addison-Wesley.

Stephenson, William. 1986a. "William James, Niels Bohr, and Complementarity: I—Concepts." *The Psychological Record* 36:519–527.

———. 1986b. "William James, Niels Bohr, and Complementarity: II—Pragmatics of a Thought." *The Psychological Record* 36:529–543.

Stone, Gregory P. 1962. "Appearances and the Self." In *Human Behavior and Social Processes*, edited by Arnold M. Rose, 86–118. Boston: Houghton Mifflin.

Strauss, Anselm. 1978. *Negotiations: Varieties, Contexts, Processes, and Social Order.* San Francisco: Jossey–Bass.

Stryker, Sheldon. 1968. "Identity Salience and Role Performance: The Relevance of Symbolic Interaction Theory for Family Research." *Journal of Marriage and the Family* 30:558–564.

———. 1977. "Developments in 'Two Social Psychologies': Toward an Appreciation of Mutual Relevance." *Sociometry* 40:145–160.

———. 1980. *Symbolic Interactionism: A Social Structural Version.* Menlo Park, CA: Benjamin/Cummings.

———. 1981. "Symbolic Interactionism: Themes and Variations." In *Social Psychology: Sociological Perspectives*, edited by Morris Rosenberg and Ralph H. Turner, 4–29. New York: Basic.

———. 1987. "The Interplay of Affect and Identity: Exploring the Relationships of Social Structure, Social Interaction, Self and Emotion." Paper presented at the American Sociological Association Meetings, Chicago, IL.

Stryker, Sheldon, and A. Gottlieb. 1981. "Attribution Theory and Symbolic Interactionism: A Comparison." In *New Directions in Attribution Research*, vol.3, edited by J.H. Harvey, W. Ickes, and R. Kidd, 425–458. Hillsdale, NJ: Erlbaum.

Stryker, Sheldon, and Anne Statham. 1985. "Symbolic Interaction and Role Theory." In *The Handbook of Social Psychology.* 3rd ed., vol. 1, edited by Gardner Lindzey and Elliot Aronson, 311–378. New York: Random House.

Swann, William B. Jr., John J. Griffen Jr., Steven C. Predmore, and Bebe Gaines. 1987. "The Cognitive-Affective Crossfire: When Self-Consistency Confronts Self–Enhancement." *Journal of Personality and Social Psychology* 52:881–889.

Thoits, Peggy. 1984. "Stress, Coping, Social Support, and Psychological Outcomes: Emotional Process." In *Review of Personality and Social Psychology*, vol.5, edited by Philip Shaver, 219–238. Beverly Hills, CA: Sage.

———. 1985. "Self-Labeling Processes in Mental Illness: The Role of Emotional Deviance." *American Journal of Sociology* 92:221–249.

———. 1989. "The Sociology of Emotions." In *Annual Review of Sociology*, vol. 15, 317–342. Palo Alto, CA: Annual Reviews.

———. 1990. "Emotional Deviance: Research Agendas." In *Research Agendas in the Sociology of Emotions*, edited by Theodore D. Kemper, 180–203. Albany, NY: State University of New York Press.

Tomkins, S.S. 1962. *Affect, Imagery, Consciousness* (2 vols.). New York: Springer.

—————. 1981. "The Quest for Primary Motives: Biography and Autobiography of an Idea." *Journal of Personality and Social Psychology* 41:306–329.

Turner, Jonathan H. 1987. "Toward a Sociological Theory of Motivation." *American Sociological Review* 52:15–27.

Turner, Ralph H. 1962. "Role-Taking: Process Versus Conformity?" In *Human Behavior and Social Process*, edited by Arnold M. Rose, 20–40. Boston: Houghton Mifflin.

—————. 1978. "The Role and The Person." *American Journal of Sociology* 84:1–23.

Wallace, W. 1983. *Principles of Scientific Sociology*. New York: Aldine.

Webb, Wilse B. 1948. "A Motivational Theory of Emotions. . . ." *Psychological Review* 55:329–335.

Weinstein, Eugene, and Paul Deutschberger. 1963. "Some Dimensions of Altercasting." *Sociometry* 26:454–466.

Wiggins, Beverly, and David R. Heise. 1988. "Expectations, Intentions, and Behavior: Some Tests of Affect Control Theory." In *Analyzing Social Interaction: Advances in Affect Control Theory*, edited by Lynn Smith-Lovin and David R. Heise, 153–169. New York: Gordon and Breach. (Reprint from a special issue of the *Journal of Mathematical Sociology* 13.).

Wilson, Timothy. 1985. "Strangers to Ourselves: The Origins and Accuracy of Beliefs about One's own Mental States." In *Attribution in Contemporary Psychology*, edited by J.H. Harvey and G. Weary, 9–36. New York: Academic Press.

Wrong, Dennis. 1961. "The Oversocialized Conception of Man." *American Sociological Review* 26:183–193.

Zajonc, R.B. 1980. "Feeling and Thinking: Preferences Need No Inferences." *American Psychologist* 35:151–175.

—————. 1984. "On the Primacy of Affect." *American Psychologist* 39:117–123.

AUTHOR INDEX

SUBJECT INDEX

act, 66, 68, 76–7, 198n. 22
See also social act
action
  cognitive, cathectic, and conative orientations towards, 120
  evolution of cultural sentiments for, 116
  expressive vs. instrumental, 185
  inhibition of, 66, 76
  intransitive, 183
  normatively structured, 95–6
  rational, 185
  restorative, 23, 29, 115–6, 138–9, 180
  and role socialization, 117
  self-directed, 183
action grammars, 20, 28, 186
action theory, 10, 43, 52, 191n. 1
activity dimension, 18, 58, 174
aesthetic distance, 46
aesthetics, 69
affect control theory
  affect control principle, 22–3, 25, 28, 91
  affective reaction principle, 20–2, 25, 28
  amalgamation equations, 31, 36, 127–8, 155
  attribution equations, 36, 127–8, 155
  and attribution theory, 159–61
  and Burke's role-identity theory, 88–93
  Canadian research, xi–xii, xv
  and cognitive theories, 16, 183–6
  and Collins' theory of interactional ritual chains, 173–5
  computerization of, xiii
  and conflict theory, 177
  and constructionist theories of emotions, 145–150
  and constructionist vs. positivist debate, 144–8
  and culture, 7
  description of the theory, xi, 4–5
  dispositional inferences, 30, 34–7, 151–2, 155, 180
  emotion principle, 31
  emotions model, 31–2, 127–9, 154, 162, 204n. 8
  empirical basis of, xiii
  empirical referents of, 176
  event assessment (recognition), 24–7
  event construction model, 99–100, 133, 154–5, 206n. 6
  event production, 27–31
  explanatory variables, 178–9, 207n. 7
  as extension of identity theory, xv, 84, 88–96
  as extension of Mead, 5, 15–7, 65, 74–81
  as extension of symbolic interactionism, xv, 5, 15–7, 65, 81, 84, 88, 159–61
  formal propositional statement of, 15–40, 198n. 3
  fundamental sentiments, 18–9, 21–2, 79, 128–31
  and Heiss's theory of role socialization, 119
  historical development, xi–xii, 15
  impression formation equations, 21, 75, 80, 136–7, 157, 179, 201n. 5, 205n. 5
  impression management equations, 23, 30, 34, 80, 91–2, 95

Printed in the United States
18343LVS00004B/272

9 780791 420423